In Honor of Fadime

UNNI WIKAN

In Honor of Fadime

MURDER AND SHAME

Translated by Anna Paterson

THE UNIVERSITY OF CHICAGO PRESS   *Chicago and London*

UNNI WIKAN is professor in the Department of Social Anthropology at the University of Oslo. She is the author of numerous books, including *Behind the Veil in Arabia*; *Managing Turbulent Hearts*; *Tomorrow, God Willing*; and *Generous Betrayal*—all published by the University of Chicago Press. *In Honor of Fadime* is a revised and extended, partly rewritten, version of her book *For ærens skyld*, which was first published in Norwegian in 2003.

The University of Chicago Press, Chicago 60637
The University of Chicago Press, Ltd., London
© 2008 by The University of Chicago
All rights reserved. Published 2008
Printed in the United States of America

17 16 15 14 13 12 11 10 09 08   1 2 3 4 5

ISBN-13: 978-0-226-89686-1   (cloth)
ISBN-10: 0-226-89686-2   (cloth)

Originally published as *For ærens skyld: Fadime til ettertanke*
© Universitetsforlaget 2003.
This translation has been published with the financial support of
NORLA.

Library of Congress Cataloging-in-Publication Data

Wikan, Unni, 1944–
    [For ærens skyld. English.]
    In honor of Fadime : murder and shame / Unni Wikan ;
translated by Anna Paterson. — Revised and extended,
partly rewritten version.
        p. cm.
    Includes bibliographical references.
    ISBN-13: 978-0-226-89686-1 (cloth : alk. paper)
    ISBN-10: 0-226-89686-2 (cloth : alk. paper)
    1. Sahindal, Fadime. 2. Honor killings—Sweden. 3. Family
violence—Sweden. 4. Kurds—Sweden. I. Title.
    HV6197.S8W5513 2003
    306.87—dc22

                                        2007033557

For
Songül and Nebile

CONTENTS

INTRODUCTION

What drives a man to murder his child—for honor's sake?

What makes a mother testify in favor of a man who has murdered their child—for honor's sake?

You will come to understand, if I have managed to do what I endeavored: explain honor and honor killing. My motivating force was the murder of Fadime Sahindal in Uppsala, Sweden, on January 21, 2002. Fadime's fate left me no peace. Of Kurdish origin, she had lived in Sweden from the age of seven until her death at age twenty-five. A luminous example of courage and integrity, she had done more than anyone to warn against the failure of Sweden's integration policies in regard to persons like her parents. She had tried to make the nation understand that "honor"—as practiced in some communities—can be a deadly affair. She had warned that she might be killed for choosing her own love in life, Swedish-Iranian Patrik Lindesjö. But she was defeated when she least expected it—almost four years after the death threats against her had subsided.

Fadime's death was a Swedish tragedy, a Swedish trauma. As I was watching her funeral service in the stately old cathedral in Uppsala, televised live on Swedish TV, I realized I had no choice: I must try to understand; I must do my utmost to comprehend what was at stake. Why was she not saved? What honor was there in murder? And what could be done in the future to avoid such tragedies?

I was no neophyte to the issue. I had worked for years in the Middle East and was accomplished within the field of research on "honor and shame," as it was called. But the fate of Fadime Sahindal (pronounced Fah-'dee-meh Shah-'een-dahl), and the fates of others who had gone before her—like Sara and Pela, both Swedish residents—challenged my powers of comprehension. In all my research in the Middle East I had never come across actual instances of honor killing. Like many other scholars, I believed honor killing to belong to rural backward communities and to be on its way out. When it appeared in my own backyard, in Scandinavia, I was unsettled.

Fadime's case haunted me. I *had to* understand why she was liquidated, and what people meant when they said, as some did, "Her father had no choice; it was the last resort."

How can killing one's own daughter be "the last resort"? "The final solution," the father called it in court. "The problem is over now."

I hope you will come to understand what lies behind such seemingly absurd and horrible statements. And that they do not come from a monster. A human being is speaking: a man in deep despair, who feels betrayed by society and by "this daughter, who is dead." A person for whom Fadime felt real compassion. "Poor Daddy," she said three times on the evening she was killed.

We will meet a man who is incapable of finding any way out of his shame, humiliation, disgrace—except by taking a life. A man who was made a laughing-stock for all the world to see, as he experienced it. "World opinion"—*världsopinionen*—is crucial to the story that follows.

Nowadays, shame and humiliation seem distant notions to men and women in the West. If we ever feel disgraced, we prefer trying to ignore it. Offense and humiliation are familiar enough to most of us, but to let on is to admit defeat. Everything centers on being in control of one's life, or at least to *seem* to be in control.

But in many regions of the world you can find communities where insult, humiliation, and shame are central ideas and common actual experiences. In some places, *shame* is too weak a word. Dishonor is the demon, the ultimate disgrace, the point of no return—except if you act to avenge your honor. Fadime's murder served such a purpose.

Fadime's story can help us to take a step along the road to understanding what shame and dishonor mean in specific communities—without stigmatizing. Fadime stepped into the breach when she tried to create understanding for people like her parents. This book is written in that spirit and with the same goal.

Fadime's story carries my narrative. I want to cast light on her life—and death—and to honor her memory.

But I also have more far-reaching intentions: to contribute to our understanding of honor and honor killing and, among other things, try to clarify why there is no basis for linking honor killing to Islam, as some people did "after Fadime." That she was murdered only four months after 9/11 did little to alleviate a seeming connection between Islam and honor killing.

But honor killing is an act based on a set of ideas that occurs across the whole spectrum of religious belief, as well as among nonbelievers. Honor killings have been reported to take place among Christians as well as Muslims, Hindus, Sikhs, Jews, Buddhists, and Confucians, but only in specific local communities. It is custom and tradition, rather than religion, that is the driving force, although religion can be used, and *is* sometimes being used, to justify honor killings.

Honor killing is also not an easy way out, even in communities where it is deeply rooted. Many try to prevent it. Alternative ways to avert dishonor have been developed to avoid acts of violence or loss of life. I describe some such alternatives and also the grief and despair felt by many who are close to the victim when the "final solution" nonetheless takes place.

Honor killing is contested, even in communities where it is part of time-honored tradition. Many are actively at work, openly or in secret, to save human lives and secure humane values. So too in

Fadime's own community. Her death was tragic for her mother and sisters and many others—yes, even for her mother, who, in the end, chose to support Fadime's father in court. I hope to cast some light on the fate of the mother.

Murdering one's own daughter—or a close family member—for the sake of honor is not a tradition that was ever part of European codes of honor, according to the historical record. But it is so now. Honor killing, by which is meant murder of a family member for the sake of collective honor, has become a part of European reality. Fadime spent much of her life speaking out against such traditions and alerting the liberal-minded Swedes to the danger such codes pose to human rights and social justice. Her stature today in Sweden, and beyond, is testimony to her being ahead of her time. Honor-based violence and honor killings may have come to stay in the new multicultural Europe. But lives can be saved and needless suffering avoided if we come to understand better what "honor" is all about and how it can be given a new meaning and used to further humane values.

Fadime has become an icon in Sweden, a symbol of a liberty-loving person who sacrificed all—even her life—for what she held dear. But Fadime was more than that: she was a full-fledged human being, who felt forced into making an inhuman choice and became weighed down by the path she had chosen. It meant cutting herself off from her family as the price she had to pay for a life with the man she loved. When he died, a year later, she was utterly alone. Her friends became her new family. But they could not replace her mother and her little sister, whom Fadime had looked after like a mother. Fadime returned to be with them, and paid with her life.

Contrary to what became a widely held opinion—that Fadime was killed because she loved Patrik—my analysis suggests that *other* circumstances were decisive. We cannot escape the questions raised by the timing. Why was she allowed to live for almost four years after Patrik's death in a traffic accident (1998)? She did not have a secret identity: she had never gone into hiding, and she lived openly. She was murdered only a week before she was due to leave for Kenya, where she planned to stay for six months. Why was she killed at that point? Why was her murder so long delayed?

Only the murderer, together with any accomplices he may have had, knows the answer. But my analysis—based on a painstaking examination of all the transcripts of the police interviews and records of the proceedings of two trials, my talks with individual family members, and my general ethnographic knowledge of shame and honor—shows that several circumstances played a role. Fadime had defied her family, and not only in her choice of love and her claim to independence. She also violated the ultimatum for life she had been given: exile or death. Exile is a long-established solution in some communities, including Turkish Kurdistan, which was Fadime's family homeland. If your behavior has dishonored your family, you are forced into exile, and that "exempts" other members of the family from the obligation to kill you.

Fadime—Swedish by now—hardly understood the meaning of exile. Besides, she did not accept it, and soon returned to enemy territory. From her place of study, her "exile" in Östersund, she traveled to Uppsala to meet secretly with her mother and two sisters. In this way Fadime managed to have a share of family life during the last year of her life.

But she was playing with fire. Exiles may be shown mercy, but they cannot demand rights. Fadime threatened to split the system apart from inside. She was breaking every rule in the game, not only those concerned with sexual honor and choice of husband. She violated her exile too, and that after exposing the family to scorn and criticism in the media. Fadime had become a multiple offender, from a certain point of view. Fadime's tragedy cannot be understood apart from that. This is not to make less of it, just to make it easier to comprehend.

Simple explanations of human fates make for strong dramatic effects, for easily understandable characters. Here the drama is about the perpetrator and his victim—the beauty and the beast. The media presentation of Fadime's story imposed a dramatic structure on it. This is how we will come to remember her, and it is how we *should* remember her: as a beautiful young woman fighting a heroic battle, putting her own life on the line.

We do not think less of what she did because we realize that, in the heat of the battle, she caused severe pain to people she cared for. Fadime's story is also the story of a family that saw itself as under siege and actually was besieged by the media's use of Fadime, and hers of them.

Fadime went for the limelight because she hoped it would save her life. She also hoped that by speaking out and giving the problem a human face, she could help other girls in her situation. My analysis suggests that her strategy weakened her chances of survival. In many ethnic communities the ultimate disgrace is to see the internal councils of the family exposed. Shame does not damage the family honor until it has become public knowledge. Dishonor is not a fact that has to be dealt with until "everybody knows"—and in Fadime's case, her family felt that their dishonor was even trumpeted in front of Parliament. Fadime gave a talk in the Old Parliament Building on November 20, 2001. Two months later she was dead.

The complex reasons for the murder do not make it more forgivable, only more understandable. The road to insight into why people are driven to take a life for the sake of honor must take into account a worldview in which the privacy and peace of family life are alpha and omega and public exposure is the most extreme kind of shame. Fadime's tragedy forces us to realize that our multicultural society now includes people with ideas about what is "private" which dictate that publicity should be avoided, whatever the cost. Shame can be coped with as long as it stays hidden. Humiliation can be endured, but only in privacy. Family conflicts can be resolved, but only behind closed doors and through mediation. It did not work in Fadime's case; no one stepped forward to take on the responsibility. But afterward many commentators, including members of the Kurdish community, pointed out that the situation could have been handled in this way.

Swedish jurisprudence is very special in one respect: the records of police interviews are available to the public. I had access to all the witness statements in Fadime's case, including those made by individuals who later withdrew from testifying in court or who were not summoned. These documents, some three hundred pages of text, have allowed me to see the case from many different points of view and have proved an invaluable source of insight.

There have been times when I faltered because I came to feel too much sympathy for people I didn't want to sympathize with. I wanted to be fully and wholly on Fadime's side, and never expected to find it difficult. I am still wholeheartedly on Fadime's side—but with much better understanding of the situations of some of her nearest friends and foes. In that sense I have moved a great step forward in my understanding of honor and honor killings.

I had set out convinced that honor killing—when it comes to taking the life of your own child—cannot be understood unless you belong to a community where such a tradition prevails. I believed this despite being an anthropologist with thirty years of experience in cross-cultural understanding and many years of fieldwork in the Middle East and Asia. I thought then, and I still do, that there are limits to understanding when it comes to grasping something emotionally and not just intellectually. However, through my work on this book, I am now able to comprehend honor killing. I hope to share my insights with you, the reader, but must go about the process gradually. To match my own struggles with the material and my slow progress toward understanding, I will take you with me step by step. Sometimes it may seem that we are going round in a circle, sometimes even contradicting ourselves. But there will be a resolution, and, when all is said and done, my hope is that you will agree with me: yes, it was worthwhile to follow this route!

I started to write in the middle of February 2002, and the first draft was finished barely four months later. During that time I had been sitting through two trials of Fadime's father. The first one, at Uppsala District Court, took place between March 12 and 15, and the second, after an appeal, was at the High Court in Stockholm between May 22 and 25. It was all very efficient, but efficiency was of no advantage to the researcher: I had hardly digested the trial in the lower court before the appeal court hearings made much of my understanding collapse. One set of explanations flatly contradicted another. The murderer backtracked, and so did his wife.

I choose to record this as it happened, letting the reader follow the collapse and the turnaround of my ideas. It is part of the story and all about strategy—ways and means of getting the better of the legal system. The code of honor stands against the rule of law.

Some might find my account too crude, too naked. Should I not have explained more, guided the reader throughout? Possibly. But the danger was that reaching the goal would become so easy that valuable insights to be gained by stepwise progress might be lost. If readers draw conclusions different from my own, nothing is lost. On the contrary, it is important that the material should speak for itself, without my didactic voice-over. The facts are still there, held within the shape and structure of the book, and impossible to avoid.

Another possible objection is that I have exploited people who made highly personal, often emotional statements to the police. They may not have given a thought to—or even been aware of—the possibility that the records of what they said would become publicly available and therefore open to the kind of use I have made of them. This objection is definitely important, but all the same, I have chosen to make use of my right to access and work on these documents. Part of my reason is that they are unique: they give insights into the inherent problems of honor and honor killings that cannot be found anywhere in literature on the subject. One example of this is the testimony of Fadime's little sister. It is, in character and content, unlike anything I have seen reported and carries a message about the fate of a child who is hurt when an honor killing breaks a family apart. A child who is desperately trying to grasp that her father is a murderer, her mother swayed by a storm of emotions, her brother a possible accomplice to murder—could he be?—and her much-loved big sister damned for causing Father so much grief that his despair drove him to kill her.

Women must not be present at honor killings, my colleague Veena Das says. Das, a highly regarded Indian anthropologist, expresses amazement at the fact that Fadime was killed in the presence of her mother and sisters. In Das's experience in India and parts of Pakistan, this is unheard of.

Fadime's thirteen-year-old sister is also surprised that her father could act as he did in front of her, but she comforts herself with the belief that he did not know she was there. She grapples with the thought that she could have prevented the killing. Like most children, she takes adults' problems very seriously and feels responsible. And she is overwhelmed by fear of being left all alone. After Fadime is shot and her mother runs out to get help, the girl panics: is Mummy going to kill herself now?

The teenager tells it all to the police, clearly and precisely—a testimony in the crude language of a thirteen-year-old. She is angry about the media exploitation of Fadime and Fadime's exploitation of the media, and she is angry with the police as well. She doesn't believe that they are taking her seriously: "I know it! I know it. It isn't just something I think! I know!" she insists, and protests wildly against the way her family is presented in the media. She wants to know why no one has contacted her. Why has nobody let her speak out?

Fadime has become an idea, an icon. But she is much more than that, precisely because of her humanity and her compassion. Fadime came to understand how much pain she had caused her family by using the media in the way she did in 1998, even though it was out of pure survival instinct. Later she reined herself in. There is evidence that she regretted the way she had been going all out. This is one aspect of "Fadime's case." It claimed many victims, also persons who saw themselves as having been degraded, directly or indirectly, by the way they had been represented in the media.

Inescapably, every statement derives meaning from its context, and so the narratives we tell, about ourselves and others, start with our situation in life. Words Fadime spoke to the media at a time when her entire family, including her mother, had abandoned her, and her father and brother threatened to kill her, later became hard to bear. Her regret came too late. The media are merciless to that extent: what is said is said. Fadime's mother will have to live with the public's knowing that she told her children that all Swedish girls are whores. Fadime's little sister has seen her telephone gossip as an eight- and nine-year-old circulated in the press. The young girl's protests deserve to be heard. That is why she has been given a lot of space in this book.

Fadime is great enough for us to make use of her story to think through and reflect on what it means to see one's family portrayed as "monstrous," how this portrayal hurts the innocent, and what can be done to spotlight oppression of and violence against individuals without branding a whole community. As we do this, we act in Fadime's spirit. She wanted inclusiveness and rejected segregation. She wanted integration, not marginalization. She wished to resist antihumanitarian and totalitarian powers without condemning those who themselves were victims—even when, in their turn, some of them were complicit.

To the last, she longed to be reunited with her family—even her father and brother who had threatened to take her life.

I / *Swedish Lives*

1 Fadime, in Remembrance

On February 2002, Fadime Sahindal was buried after a service held in the ancient cathedral in Uppsala. The ceremony was attended by Crown Princess Victoria, the head of Parliament, the ministers of integration and of justice, the archbishop, and other dignitaries. Fadime's own family, the Sahindals, made up some two hundred and fifty persons among the two thousand that the cathedral could hold. At least another two thousand stood outside on that cold, rainy day to pay Fadime their last respects. The ceremony was broadcast live on Swedish TV.

The canon, Tuulikki Koivunen Bylund, officiated. Fadime's family wanted a dignified ceremony in a sacred place, she said. Fadime loved Uppsala and had wished both to marry in and be buried from the cathedral. Hence this ceremony, even though Fadime was not a member of the Swedish Church.

No wedding though, only her funeral. Fadime's beloved, Patrik Lindesjö, had died in a car crash on June 3, 1998. Four years later, Fadime met her death, murdered by her father because she stood by her love for Patrik and her right to a life of her own. "Fadime was a whore," her father told the police. "The problem is over now."

Was it then an honor killing? Or a so-called honor killing? Bishop Gunnar Stålsett calls it a shame killing. Let us free the concept of honor from the taint of violence and fear, he seems to say. The world needs true honor. Let us respect it and live accordingly.

One man who would agree with the bishop was kept under lock and key in Lørenskog Prison outside Oslo. He murdered his wife and was atoning for it by serving a twelve-year prison sentence. He claims that it was hammered into boys like him, from childhood on, that if a female brought dishonor on the family, she must be killed—whether daughter, sister, cousin, or wife. "We need a new concept of honor," he says.

A concept of honor that recognizes the integral value of the individual exists. It is found in many cultural settings, within the Western sphere of influence and outside it. Part of my intention with this book is to show that honor in the *best* sense of the word is understood and practiced by men and women of very diverse societies, some of which we might categorize as "traditional." In many non-European communities, Fadime's murder and similar horror stories reported in the media—for instance, death threats against young people who refuse to be forced into marriage—would cause as much revulsion and condemnation as they do in the West. This is true of Muslims, Hindus, Buddhists, Christians, and people who do not belong to any of the world religions.

Yet there is no denying that honor killings exist. They are not "so called." They are for real. We might well, in the spirit of Bishop Stålsett, label them shame killings. It would signal our condemnation of such acts, monstrous acts despite the pretense of high moral principle. But it is only by facing up to the facts that we can hope to fight these terrible crimes.

Worldwide, the concept of honor has different meanings and is practiced differently among diverse groups of people. I deliberately avoid using words like *cultures* or *societies*—words that easily create the impression that everyone belonging to this or that culture or society will react in a particular way. This is not the case. Even where honor killings are part of a local tradition, it is probably rare to kill your daughter, sister, or wife in order to cleanse the family of the shame she has brought on it. Compassion, pity, and love deter murder. People find other, less brutal solutions. But the fact that killing for the sake of honor is a time-honored tradition—even part of the law—in some societies is a measure of what Fadime had to contend with.

Fadime's death was not a so-called honor killing. She died at the hands of a murderer—a murderer obsessed with notions of honor and dishonor, who had threatened to kill her several times. Already in 1998, Fadime's father and brother had beaten her and leveled death threats against her. She had reported them to the police, and both men were sentenced. Her brother's second assault got him five months in jail. Fadime had lived in constant fear for her life. And she was aware of the forces she was challenging: not mad jealousy or drunken, heedless violence, but convictions considered rational and sober when seen from a particular perspective. From that perspective, it is possible to wash away shame by taking the life of a daughter, sister, mother, or wife.

An approving audience is a precondition. For shame to be "washed away" and honor to be restored, you need a community of people who will reward you with acclaim—validate the killing and the code of honor that prescribes it. Fadime's father was part of such a group. There is plenty of evidence proving that he felt buoyed up by friends and relatives who told him that he was right and also reinforced his feelings of shame and defeat. Afterward, some individuals still backed him, confirming that he had no choice: he had to kill.

Honor killings are not crimes of passion or motivated by jealousy. In the wake of Fadime's death, there were those who argued that killing for the sake of honor amounts to the same as killing for the sake of jealousy. This is a mistaken conclusion. True, an honor killing can be driven by jealousy, but only as one factor that is neither the most critical nor the most relevant. Honor killings presuppose an approving audience, a group of people who will reward the murder with honor. This is what sets honor killings apart. Honor killings are committed with a view to the public—and they are generally planned and premeditated. You cast off your burden of shame, which is possible only in relation to an audience. True, your feelings of shame may be profound, without "the others" knowing. True, you can hurt in secret from insults and humiliations. But within the traditions we are discussing, you can be "cleansed" only after the shame has become known. Shame, as we construe it here, is a *public* phenomenon. Shame depends on dishonor's becoming a fact to outsiders. This misery befell Fadime's family, and it cost Fadime her life.

She went public. She spoke out. She stood up for her right to a life of her own and for her love of Patrik, even after his death. She reported the bullying and death threats, and her father and brother were charged and convicted. This fanned the flames under the boiling rage of the family. An official charge was the final humiliation—proof that the men had failed to stay in control.

Fadime hoped that the publicity about her problem, about her case—publicity she sought not only for her own sake—would protect her and save her life. But the effect on the men from whom she needed protection was precisely the opposite: their shame was on show in the marketplace. They were pilloried. In that situation, what can you do to recover your "honor"? You do what Fadime dreaded: you kill. To get back in control you must show who holds the reins, who is lord and master.

So it is not about jealousy. It is about power and control. That is why killing for the sake of honor is different from crimes of jealousy. It is not about unrequited love or a couple's relationship. It has to do with the rights of the collective over the individual and the individual's duty to submit. It has to do with structures and systems, social categories of people indoctrinated into the belief that they exist to serve the system.

Fadime's father is a victim too—a victim of a "culture" demanding that he must be in charge, rule, control, punish; that he must accept no challenge to his honor, which is not just his own. He is only a stakeholder, someone who manages a share in the tribal honor—as everyone must, for the sake of the tribe. The group has a stranglehold on the individual.

This is true also of Fadime's mother, who supported her husband and son in the court case brought by Fadime in May 1998—to her daughter's disappointment. Fadime's mother is a victim too, another individual sacrificed on the altar of the collective. Fadime spoke about this when she addressed an audience in the Old Parliament Building two months before her death: her mother had been blamed when Fadime broke with her family, a necessary choice if she was to live on her own terms.

The child's shame will haunt the mother, because it is her duty and responsibility to ensure that the values of the father and his forefathers are passed on to the children. Virtue is crucially important—for girls. Every sexual contact before or outside marriage is extremely shameful—for girls. Here *sexual* has a broad meaning. Socializing, which most Westerners would regard as innocent, counts as sexual in these tradition-bound communities. Being seen in the company of a boy might be enough. A rumor that you have been seen talking to a boy might be enough. Reputation matters more than the truth. Young women have paid with their lives for flimsy tales about their flawed virtue. They were not even given the chance to defend themselves.[1]

But in the case of Fadime there was evidence. Her father had seen her with Patrik in the street. The date was September 3, 1997. This was the point of no return. She must separate either from Patrik or from her family. She chose Patrik.

Fadime still stood by her choice after Patrik's death. He died in a road traffic accident on July 3, 1998, the very day they were going to move in together. She was buried, as she had wished, next to Patrik in the Old Uppsala Cemetery. That it came to be was perhaps in part due to the events of September 11, 2001.

On this fateful day, Fadime had been in New York. She had gone for a week's vacation, but she turned back to Sweden immediately after the terrorist attack on the Twin Towers. Sudden, unexpected death, and how it can hit anyone, became once more an experiential reality for Fadime, who had lived with death threats for so long and had also lost Patrik to sudden, unexpected death. She wanted to be prepared. So just after 9/11, on her return to Sweden, she contacted close friends and told them to make sure that when her time came, she would be buried next to Patrik.

Time was of the essence, as according to Muslim tradition the deceased should be buried before the next sunrise or as soon as possible afterward. Fadime's good friends acted expeditiously. The memorial service for Fadime came to be on a grand scale; it was an exquisitely beautiful and solemn event. But for Fadime, all that mattered was to have her last wish fulfilled: to be laid to rest beside Patrik.

Will we ever understand honor killings? How can mothers ever agree to these murders? They sometimes do (though not in Fadime's case). Over the years I have been asked such questions again and again. I too struggle to answer them. Is honor killing understandable? In what terms? I have arrived at the following conclusion.

No, we cannot ever understand it as a "lived experience." In order to do so, I believe, one would have to be part of a tradition that justifies such acts. And even then it can be difficult. That a much-loved family member should be made to pay with her life is hard for those close to her to understand, even when it is part of tradition and thus "the way things should be." But also in matters of life and death, there are contingent choices to make, depending on the circumstances. Honor killing is never an easy way out.

As I am an outsider, the best I can do is try to explain what honor killings are all about, while knowing full well that there will inevitably be a gap between explanation and true understanding. And that is just as well. It is reassuring that there are limits to empathy in cases such as Fadime's. Nowadays many like to claim that "nothing human is alien to me." But come what may, no one is able to embrace more than a fragment of humanity's variability, its endless diversity.

Still, we can take an important step toward comprehension by trying to grasp the kind of crises that lead to honor killings. "He had no choice," said some who condemned Fadime's murder but sympathized with her father. "It was the only way out." This is what we must attempt to take on board: that killing your own child can become "the only way" and might even be a *solution* to a problem.

At the heart of the matter lies a feeling of shame and degradation, of having been offended and humiliated, laughed at, and made to look ridiculous in full view of the public.

Later we will consider the trial of Fadime's father. On display will be a culture clash so total that her father exclaims: "What she has done to me—I don't know how I can explain it to you!" He appeals to the court as best he can and bursts out, addressing the prosecutor: "This Fadime, the way she behaved . . . if you had a daughter like her, you would've wanted to shoot her too!" Then, the next second: "No, no, I was sick of course. No father would kill his daughter if he wasn't sick!"

This is not wild shadowboxing but a tormented man's despairing attempt to translate from one culture to another. He knows how necessary Swedish sympathy is for him. Swedish people will understand that no man would willingly kill his child. They must surely also understand that he was pushed to extremes and, besides, that he was sick. It is very human.

We all try to tune in to others, find some kind of resonance, by playing on themes of experience and feeling that we believe are held in common. The trouble is, our words tie us down. They may hinder as well as help our project. Fadime's father used words that boomeranged. He had misunderstood his audience. None of "us" could agree that if we had a daughter like Fadime, we too would have wanted to shoot her.

But we respond to the man in front of us when we see his profound despair, because he perceives himself to have been hounded and forced to act in self-defense. To gain insight into what honor killing is all about, we must look "beyond the words"—read between the lines—and try to engage with a very human dilemma.[2] This applies to cultural understanding in general: we mustn't become fixated on words but recognize that rhetoric sometimes obscures the fact that we lead comparable lives. From cradle to grave we struggle with similar existential problems, and we recognize this despite a sea of differences and discrepancies separating our core ideas, lifestyles, personalities, and material circumstances. And this is somehow comforting.

That could also be the reason why some believe that honor killing is the same as, or very similar to, killings driven by jealousy. We need to understand. Categorizing honor killing in this way at least helps us avoid seeing "the Other" as apart. Instead he is "one of us." Someone you recognize. We too have felt jealous—yes, perhaps even been so inflamed by jealousy that murder seemed thinkable.

So far, but no further. The comparison ends here. For it is a matter of murdering, or being prepared to murder, your own child—for honor's sake. Even when wives are victims of honor killings, the deed is often done by relations on her side of the family. She is murdered by her own people.

And she is killed for gain. The outcome is recovered reputation and prestige, which can also be turned into money and other material advantages. The market value of the family increases, as it were.

Without honor the family becomes a laughingstock; everyone looks at them with derision. The girls become worthless in the marriage market. The boys are regarded as wimps—unmanly. Socially and politically, the family is beyond the pale.

"Now we can walk with our heads held high," eighteen-year-old Amal said after her sixteen-year-old brother had killed their sister. The family was Palestinian. "We were seen as the most prominent family, had the highest reputation," their mother said. "And then we were dishonored. Even my brother and his family stopped talking to us. No one came visiting. They only said: 'You must kill her.'"[3]

This story centers on Basma, a woman suspected of adultery. Terrified that she would be killed, she ran away with her alleged lover. Her husband divorced her, and she secretly married the other man. Contempt for her family spread all around their Palestinian village in Jordan. Basma's mother took a rifle with her when she went off in search of her daughter. In the end the fatal shot was fired by Basma's sixteen-year-old brother, who had been only ten when she ran away.

In some traditions that sanction honor killing—they vary—a woman is never free of her own family. Even after she is married off, she can still cast them into the depths of shame. Time is no healer. Unless cauterized, the shame festers and grows more and more deadly. In Fadime's case it took four years. Four years of mortal danger before they finally killed her. This slender young woman exerted a "terrible power" over her family. Because she had chosen Patrik, with whom she never even had the chance to live, and because she insisted on leading her life on her own terms, she had to die. Four years after Patrik's death she paid the price. Can this be understood?

Fadime's family had lived in Sweden for twenty years. They were Kurds from Elbistan near Malatya, a provincial capital in southeast Turkey.[4] Some three hundred members of the clan are in Sweden, but many have settled in other European countries or are still in Turkey. Back home, honor killings are not unusual.[5] Fadime's maternal uncle was the first of the Sahindals to migrate to Sweden, and he arrived at the end of the 1960s. Fadime's father followed him in 1981. The rest of the family joined him in 1984; Fadime was seven years old at the time. In Turkey, the Sahindals are powerful and influential. Fadime's parents are cousins, and her father's sister is married to her mother's brother. Fadime's two older sisters are also married to sons of siblings. Her two younger sisters and her brother are unmarried.

In Sweden, Fadime's father worked for sixteen years, until 1998, and his employers speak well of him. He had learned a bit of Swedish and was a sociable man. He had not been in trouble with the law prior to the conviction for threatening to murder Fadime (May 1998). He admits to murdering Fadime. She lived to be twenty-five years old.

Even Fadime's immediate family struggle to answer the question: how could he? People need to understand. Not just "we," the outsiders, but also, and especially, those who were closest to her. How could Fadime's father bring himself to kill her? Reconciliation seemed imminent. Just a little earlier, their father had hinted as much, according to his eldest daughter, Fidan.

"Hearing that was such a wonderful relief. Daddy said the time for forgiveness might have arrived. He admitted to having made a lot of mistakes and wrong decisions," Fidan says. "I had a vision of the day when the whole family would be united again."[6]

The second daughter, Elmas, backs her up. "We are just an ordinary family. None of us believed that he could ever act like this."[7]

When Fadime died, her mother was present and tried to prevent the killing by stepping between the murderer and his victim. Fadime's two younger sisters, Nebile and Songül, were present too. Afterward they received treatment for shock.

Mother and sisters had come together to say goodbye to Fadime, who was to go off to study in Kenya the following week. They met in secrecy, as they had done three or four times earlier that year. It is not known how the father found out that they were in Songül's flat in Uppsala Old Town. When they didn't open the door the first time he called, he left. The women were scared. As Nebile and Fadime prepared to leave (their mother was staying the night), Nebile checked the landing through the peephole in the door. It looked safe. But her father had returned. As he rushed the door, he shot Fadime in the face and the back of her head at close range. "You filthy whore!" he shouted.

He was sick in the head, Fadime's eldest sister says, and other members of the family agree. Only a sick person would do something like that. He was not accountable. Too desperate, incapable of thinking straight. Some family members cling to this explanation, which is understandable and reasonable—human, in short.

Others disagree. He had to kill, some immigrants told the Swedish media. He had no choice, no alternative. Fadime's death is tragic but cannot be condemned; it was indeed a life-and-death matter. Her father's back was against the wall—and not only his.

"I have ruined the life of my whole family," Fadime said in 1998. "No one will marry the girls now. They are all branded as whores."

At Fadime's memorial service, the tributes included wreaths from the government and Parliament, underlining the importance attached to this small but great human being: she was honored with a ceremony that was as close as possible to a state funeral.

In her memorial address Canon Koivunen Bylund said, "Fadime was a martyr of our time. Let us thank God for Fadime, that with her fearlessness, strength, and love of life, she has given courage and strength to so many." Fadime had been heartbroken after Patrik's death but had not given up; instead she gathered herself together and devoted her life to fighting for the individual's right to choose how to lead her own life. "Why does death undo the bonds of love? Why does death tear apart what life builds?" the canon demanded; she concluded that we have no answers.

Fadime's mother and sisters sobbed before the memorial service began. Weeping spread among many of Fadime's friends and in the rest of the congregation, including Crown Princess Victoria. "The heavens wept too when Fadime was buried," the newspaper *Dagens Nyheter* reported. Rain poured down as she was interred next to her beloved Patrik.

Was Fadime a Muslim? The question has been repeatedly debated in the media. No, she was not a Muslim, the Islamic Council in Norway has pronounced. Many agree. But some of Fadime's relatives told the media differently: Yes, we are Muslims. Songül, one of the sisters, says that the whole family, including her father, are Muslims but, as far as she knows, not practicing.[8] The reporter presenting the funeral broadcast on Swedish TV commented: "The family is Muslim, but not active worshipers." A student told me: "Believe me, the Sahindals are not Muslims—they just say they are. In fact, they are Yazidi, and that's completely different."[9] Another student said, "If they were Muslims, why did they have Fadime's funeral in a church and not a mosque?" A third exclaimed: "They prayed Our Father in church. And she's supposed to be a Muslim?"

The arguments about Fadime's beliefs, if any, are symptomatic of the direction of the public debate in Norway in the wake of her death. In Sweden the response was different. The Norwegians focused on honor killings in the context of Islam. The Swedes took note of the fact that the murderer was Kurdish, in this as well as in the two most talked-about earlier cases. We will look into possible explanations for these attitudes later. Meanwhile, it is worth noting that one recent honor killing (1994) in Sweden took place within a family of Palestinian Christians: a girl who had refused a forced marriage was killed by her father.

On the day of Fadime's funeral, a Swedish Moroccan girl said to me, "It's the Kurds who have a hard time in Sweden now, not the Muslims." Most Kurds are Muslims; however, what she was stressing was that the public's attention would focus on the traditions and the role of women within certain ethnic communities. Many among the Kurds had actually stated their condemnation of the killing of Fadime. Murder is, and remains, an exception.

What would Fadime have said about all this speculation—and all this conflict—about what she was, or was not? Why should a human being be boxed in like that? No one knows what Fadime believed at heart. If she was a Muslim, she kept it to herself. According to Islam, every human being is responsible before God. It is not for others to sit in judgment.

The family respected Fadime's wish to be buried from the cathedral in Uppsala. It may or may not signify that they felt pressured to accept and had no option but to agree once her funeral was under the aegis of the state and would be attended by members of the royal family, the government, and other authorities. However, we do know some things for certain.

Fadime broke through barriers; she wanted to build bridges. She stood for an inclusive view of humankind, universal in its emphasis on the individual's irreducible value. She represented freedom and equality, regardless of gender, religion, and ethnicity. She was against narrowness of vision and wanted to reconcile warring factions among those who believe that they are the only guardians of truth, a truth that is theirs for ever. Fadime embraced all and everyone. This too, characterized the ceremony when she was laid to rest: It brought persons of many religions and ways of life together under one roof. The selection of music and songs was drawn from many times and cultures, tunes, which allowed everyone to feel at home. It was how Fadime had wanted it.

The music at her funeral was secular as well as religious: "Tears in Heaven" by Eric Clapton; "Bridge over Troubled Water" by Simon and Garfunkel, sung in Swedish; the hymn "Härlig är jorden" (Splendid Is the Earth); "Till mine" (In Remembrance), an organ chorale without words by Nils Lindberg; a sung version of the sonnet "Shall I compare thee to a summer's day" by William Shakespeare; "Fatime," a Kurdish folk tune; and Fadime's favorite, U2's "One."

Canon Koivunen Bylund took care to find words that would soothe and comfort, words that would offer inclusion and support, not rejection—of forgiveness and reconciliation. She reminded the congregation of how, in days gone by, they would have left their weapons on the porch before entering the sanctuary of the church. In that spirit, she went on to say, let us now leave our bitter feelings behind and walk forward together. In the declaration of faith she inconspicuously changed the wording so that the Muslims would not feel too much like outsiders. The Holy Trinity—as in "the name of the Father, the Son, and the Holy Ghost"—was taken out of the introduction, because the Trinity conflicts with the teaching of Islam. Everyone prayed to Our Lord; Muslims, Christians, and Jews all believe in one God, and Muslims too call him "Our Lord."

As Fadime's coffin was about to be carried out of the cathedral, six women, bareheaded, all clad in black, stepped forth. They were her cousins and friends, all but one Kurdish by descent. According to Muslim tradition, *men* should carry the coffin, and this was what the canon had been led to expect until a few minutes before the funeral, when the women presented themselves and demanded to be the pallbearers. The canon told them to sort the matter out with the men, which they did. Then she said, "But won't it be too heavy for you?" "God will give us strength," answered the women. In this way they made history.

It was an unforgettable moment. One woman holding a large photo of Fadime led the procession as the coffin, draped in white carnations, Fadime's favorite flower (fifty thousand such carnations graced the cathedral), was carried out into the rain and fog. The spectacle of the black-clothed, black-haired, bare-headed women, Muslim by birth, leading Fadime's way out of the church toward the place where she had wanted to be laid to rest bespoke an uproar, a protest. It was not just an act of solidarity with the victim but a momentous message: "She is ours now. You have betrayed her." The male members of Fadime's clan had not heeded her calls for support during the four years that she had lived with death threats. Her brother had tried but failed to kill her. Others had concurred that she should be killed.

Surrounded by women, sustained by a silent procession of pall-bearers, Fadime's coffin was carried to the car that would take her to her final resting place in the Old Cemetery.

"To me, this is a free country!" Fadime said in protest against being exiled by her family, who had driven her away from Uppsala and threatened her with death if she returned. "I have a right to come back to the place where my beloved is buried."

Fadime did come back home.

2 Sara: "Too Swedish" for a Right to Live

When Sara made Swedish history, Fadime was twenty years old and had fallen in love with her Patrik.

Sara was only fifteen when her sixteen-year-old brother and seventeen-year-old cousin murdered her. They caught her one evening when Sara was on her way home from an "Iraqi night" at a discotheque. She feared for her life and would have liked to go home in a taxi with her friends, but the taxi was packed and she took the bus instead. It is likely that she took a good look around to make sure she was safe. The boys must have hidden well. She was found strangled on a pile of snow near her home. The place was the northern town of Umeå, and the date December 15, 1996.

Sara's mother admitted that her son had threatened to kill Sara two weeks earlier. "Sara's a whore," he said. "She sleeps around with Swedish guys." His mother asked: "What about you then? You sleep with Swedish girls, don't you?" He replied: "Yes, but that's different." He's a man. And besides, he wouldn't dream of doing it with Iraqi girls. Only with Swedish girls, with whores.[1]

Three days after the murder, Sara's mother gathered up all her son's belongings, his clothes, CDs, everything. She carried the bundle to the pile of snow where Sara had breathed her last, laid a fire nearby, and burned what she had brought, waiting until the last fragments had gone. The sound of the sparking flames mingled with her quiet keening. This was her way of saying: to me he is dead now, as dead as my Sara.

A mother had lost two of her children. With less than a year between them, they had been almost like twins, she said. Even their names were similar: Maisam and Maitham.[2]

In Sweden, Maisam had begun to call herself Sara.[3] Her proper name was Maisam Abed Ali.

Sara's mother knew of fear and violence in her bones. She had divorced Sara's father, against time-honored tradition, and had incurred his family's wrath. Their land of origin was Iraqi Kurdistan, but they had lived in Sweden since 1992. Male relatives had apparently been threatening Sara: "Don't figure you'll get away with it just because your mother did." Sara's father had said he would kill her mother if she remarried (she had fallen in love with someone else) or if he was refused custody of the children.

He was given custody. It did not take long before Sara was subjected to frequent, severe beatings. Her father complained that she was turning "Swedish" and shamed her relatives. The social services intervened and found a foster home for Sara on the island of Gotland. She liked it there and wanted to stay, but her own family insisted on getting her back. When the guardianship was given to one of her uncles, Sara feared for her life and fought the decision. She did everything to get away. The child protection agency noted: "To effect the new placement required police assistance."[4]

Yasser, one of Sara's murderers, was the son of her new guardian. It emerged that her father and uncles—five in all—had, about a year earlier, held a meeting to discuss how to handle "the Sara problem." They decided to kill her but did not pick a killer. That choice must have been made later.

In the public debate that followed this act of child murder, Nalin Baksi, a Kurdish-born member of Parliament, stated, "The two lads would not have acted on their own initiative. They wouldn't have dared to. Life or death is a question of the family's collective will and power. The boys were mere tools. Others stood behind."[5]

Sara's murder in 1996 shook the Swedish public—but not because it was the first murder that had the restoration of honor as its main motive. In 1994, a Swedish-Palestinian girl had been killed by her father because she rejected a forced marriage. The family was Christian. In the autumn of 1996 Varna (age twenty-six), a mother of six, was murdered by her husband. Earlier doctors and social workers had noted that she had been badly beaten and reported the husband to the police. Varna did not dare to testify in court. Her husband was convicted all the same and sentenced to six months in prison, but he was granted an early release for good behavior. He went straight home and killed Varna—and then went along to the police station to give himself up, carrying the family's youngest child, a baby, in his arms.

To give yourself up to the police is part of a "good" honor killing tradition. It shows that you stand by your deed and your honor. Maitham and Yasser also reported what they had done, little more than twenty-four hours after killing Sara.

But despite the earlier cases, it was Sara's story that set off alarm bells in Sweden. You could say that her murder started a new era. For the first time Sweden had to confront the consequences—especially affecting girls and young women—of the country's failing integration policy. Sudden daylight fell on hidden facts. It became possible to talk and write and argue about previously taboo subjects.

Politically correct Swedes had to take on board the way in which this young woman's fate became part and parcel of public consciousness in every corner of the country. And in the wake of this came a new awareness of events that until then had gone comparatively unnoticed, like a couple of murders of immigrant women. Among them was Varna, who died just two or three months before Sara.

Another murder and an attempted murder within one month of Sara's death further underlined the seriousness of the situation. A young Lebanese woman was killed by her husband because she had become too Swedish. A Kurdish girl was stabbed twenty-one times by her brother and became partially paralyzed. She had broken with her family after having been forced to marry.

Nalin Baksi told the media, "I'm surprised at your surprise." Other immigrants, both men and women, backed her up. As one of them put it: "These things happen time and again. The Swedes simply don't want to know."[6]

Jesús Alcalá, a journalist with legal training, went to great lengths to inform the world about Sara. The broadsheet *Dagens Nyheter* allocated generous space to his two major articles: "Not a Murder—an Execution" and "The Men in the Family Should Be Charged." The articles helped a great deal to focus attention on the murder of Sara.

On February 8, Alcalá wrote: "Fundamentally, the concept of individual integrity and worth entails that every human being has a right to respect, also beyond her membership in a group, even in the absence of friends who share her views, even in her recalcitrant independence, even in her solitude. . . .

"There are many like Sara. Let us not betray them."[7]

Five years later, the funeral service in Uppsala Cathedral was evidence of yet another betrayal. Shortly before her death, in her speech in Parliament, Fadime argued, "If society had taken its responsibility and helped my parents to feel that they had a greater stake in Swedish society, then perhaps this might have been avoided." By "this" she meant her being forced to break with her family and the pain it had caused them all. In retrospect her words have a prophetic ring. This murder might have been avoided. It should have been avoided.

"We have failed. I have failed," Mona Sahlin, minister for integration, admits now—she is apparently deeply affected by the tragedy.[8] Analyzing the case of Sara is useful if we want to understand how Fadime's murder came about and what can be done to prevent such tragedies. What does it teach us?

Sara's murder raised fundamental questions. Who has a right to "be Swedish"? Who should be allowed to benefit from the values that are fundamental to the welfare state: freedom and equality? What are the limits to cultural tolerance? How can we guard human rights, not in China or on Cuba but in our own country? And are we truly prepared to put in as much effort in our own backyard as we do elsewhere, in a global context?

Questions concerning responsibility also became central: Two boys admitted to having killed Sara, though they claimed it was by mistake: to scare her they had tightened a belt round her neck. Had they acted of their own accord? Were they driven by an honor code? The boys denied this. Can we trust them? Was Sara's murder an honor killing? What would be the significance of saying that it was? Would that not be to stigmatize a whole community and its distinctive culture?

During winter and spring 1997 Sara was at the center of the public debate, but it came to include much more. As Alcalá wrote: "Among Muslim women of faith—also in Sweden—there will be many, maybe a majority, who want to be veiled and think it perfectly proper that men make the decisions in family and wider social matters. So far so good. But here we are talking about the women who do not wish to submit to this order of things. Simply: How do we deal with Sara? What is—was—our responsibility for Sara?"[9]

Which brings us back to the question, who has the right to "be Swedish"? Fadime did not, in her family's view, even though they had lived in Sweden for twenty years and had become Swedish citizens. Fadime's family had fled from Turkey, Sara's from Iraq. "Here, where at last we could feel safe and free, our family split apart," Sara's mother said to the police. The tragedies of these children force us to think; they paid with their lives for the freedom their families sought. For Sara and Fadime, the price of freedom was death.

How are we to handle the fact that in the eyes of certain Swedish citizens to "be Swedish" is a crime punishable by death—if you're a girl? Fadime's brother lived with his Swedish fiancée. His relationship was never questioned, but he beat Fadime and threatened to kill her because she wanted to be with Patrik. Yasser, Sara's killer, had a Swedish girlfriend. At the same time these young men were "guardians" of a culture that regards girls as whores if they choose a normal Swedish lifestyle. They are not alone in this, as Nalin Baksi reminds us: while they are still minors, boys cannot act of their own accord in cases serious enough to involve a sister's or cousin's life or death. There has to be a shared opinion, a consent, that legitimizes what they do. In some cases they can become heroes of their communities. "Defending the family honor makes you a hero," the Swedish-Syrian Farryal Messö Bolos has said.[10] It seems likely that the number of honor killings and attempted killings would be much greater had not most of the girls submitted to community norms.

As one of Sara's friends commented afterward: all Sara did was lead the life of ordinary Swedish girls, but she did it openly and freely.[11] She stood out from the rest, was up front about her right to a life of her own. Her fate is a warning. She was made to pay a price that will strike fear into the hearts of those who want to follow her example.

Bernadita Nunez is the chair of Terrafam, an organization set up to help immigrant girls in Sweden. She believed that still more girls would fall into line after Fadime's death. Terrafam had never before received such a large number of calls for help from frightened girls. They seemed more terrified than ever before of the risks they would run if they broke free. "Everyone who has phoned us—we've had several hundred calls—has been afraid. No one sees any light at the end of the tunnel," Nunez stated.[12]

Fadime said that having Swedish friends was forbidden when she was growing up. It's a familiar theme in the growing number of stories told by girls of immigrant background. Families often fear that the daughters will become too Swedish, Norwegian, Danish, etc. Sons do not escape: they are often kept strictly in line. They are sometimes sent back to the parental homeland for reeducation; they too can be forced to marry. But boys do not risk being killed by their own family. If they sleep with "whores," the honor of the family isn't affected.

Sara never spoke about how she was brought up. She was never a celebrity in her lifetime. Sara did not become part of history until her death. Her story is told by others, people like her mother and foster parents, her uncle's ex-partner, social workers, female friends, researchers, journalists, and politicians. But Sara remains "a case," despite the many who have worked to protect her memory as a whole person. Sara's life and death will stay a case history, because her death remains a source of conflict. What did it mean? What lessons can we draw from it?

In February 1997, the debate in Sweden was raging: Was murdering Sara a culturally conditioned act or simply murder? Do honor killings exist? Was Sara killed for honor's sake? If so, who is guilty—Maitham and Yassar alone?

Alcalá reveals gaps in the police investigation into the behavior of the two boys and hence into nature of the deed. With hindsight we may note that for a murder to be classified as an honor killing, certain conditions must be fulfilled. To save the honor of the immediate or extended family is a collective duty: the family's rights rank above the individual's, and the individual must be ready to submit. There must be a shared understanding that taking a life can "wash away shame." There must be patriarchal power, giving men in the family the right and duty to control female sexuality. There must be a rigid hierarchy of authority that is respected and followed; the young *must* obey their elders. But we are anticipating the unraveling of the case. The gaps in the police investigation, which are mentioned below, came about partly because at the time (winter and spring 1997) honor killing was an unknown concept among most Swedes.

"Ingrid," one of the police witnesses, was once the partner of one of Sara's uncles. She states that all the brothers (five of them) met in 1995 to sort out "the problem with Sara" and decided that she should be killed, though not who would do it. The man who was Ingrid's partner thought he might be picked, because he was a childless bachelor. Ingrid was told that she mustn't blab or they'd "do" her too.

Ingrid feared for her life and said nothing. The men in the family were violent, and some had problems with alcohol. Also, she couldn't believe that they meant what they said about what they would do to Sara.

When Sara told her foster parents about a death threat against her, they too failed to take it seriously. Who would believe a fifteen-year-old saying she'll be killed because she dresses "Swedish style" and goes to discos? In the Nordic countries of the mid-1990s, most people thought that she was fantasizing or exaggerating her fears. Since then we have crossed a watershed—at least some of us have. As Nalin Baksi said: "I am surprised at your surprise." Nowadays such threats tend to be taken at face value. Fadime's tragedy has been an eye-opener.

After Sara's death, Ingrid went to the police to tell them what she knew. The police still didn't interview Sara's father and uncles about their possible connections with the murder. Did the police regard the murder as solved? Or did Ingrid's statement seem incredible? The police didn't question the men until Alcalá's article was published. It was called "The Men in the Family Should Be Charged." Under the subtitle "I Accuse," he wrote:

> When I read the transcript of the interview with Ingrid I was astonished and also felt very disturbed. Ingrid's information is extremely awkward for Sara's father and uncles. Their meeting in the winter of 1995, which led to an agreement to kill Sara, is in itself a crime: conspiracy to murder.
>
> If Sara's father and uncles urged Hassan and Tareq [not their true names] to murder Sara—and there is much to suggest they did—then they committed another crime: incitement to murder.
>
> In fact, only one of Sara's uncles has been interviewed in the course of the police investigation. It was a very brief affair, unlikely to have taken more than a few minutes, and did not deal with the uncles' own threats against Sara. Instead he was asked about Sara's life and personality. She was independent and difficult, her uncle said, and added: "I tried to bring her up properly and set firm limits." These exchanges,

and one question asking if the uncle had heard Hassan and Tareq threaten Sara, make up the entire transcript, about half a page. No follow-up questions, no attempt to investigate whether the uncle had threatened Sara himself. Sara's father was not interviewed at all. And this is how it came about that the five brothers, including Sara's father and her uncle, whom she dreaded, vanished from the police protocols.

It is strange and, in legal terms, impossible to understand.

And it is stranger still that Ingrid's information does not form part of the police investigation report. The crown prosecution service has apparently decided not to use her statement in the trial. Why? What caused the prosecution service to abandon such an important source?

For the sake of justice, for the sake of truth, and, last but not least, for the sake of Sara, it is absolutely critical that the investigation into the crime is completed. The District Court in Umeå has the power to demand that the prosecution service complete the investigation. It should use that power. For my part, I hereby charge Sara's father and uncles with a criminal offense.[13]

His report was effective. At least the men were questioned, though not charged. Swedish law, like Norwegian, looks for perpetrator(s), and in this case they were known: Maitham and Yasser had confessed to the killing, and the forensic evidence backed them. But as Nalin Pekgul (previously Baksi) said in the wake of the trial of Fadime's father: "The police is still looking for one perpetrator, but in the case of honor killings, several people are usually involved in the planning and execution."[14]

It is obvious from what I have written above that I believe Sara's murder to be an honor killing. Some disagree. Sara's case led to a heated public debate about the justification for the term and whether the usage is politically acceptable. The same arguments were repeated after Fadime's death. Strong forces and well-known names were engaged on both sides. The fundamental issue is the role of "culture," if any, in certain types of violence against women. Could it be that the real problem is structural violence—that oppression of women is universal and that this mindset in isolated cases manifests itself as grievous bodily harm and murder? Professor Eva Lundgren and her colleague Åsa Eldén presented the "universal" view in their article "Criminal Violence against Women Is Not Exotic." They argue that violence against women is a general problem in Sweden, pushed out of the limelight by the acceptance of gender equality. The focus stays on the individual every time a Swedish man kills a woman. Why drag culture into the case just because the perpetrator is an immigrant?[15]

They were supported by Charles Westin, head of the Center for Research in International Migration and Ethnic Relations. His point was that most immigrants to Sweden lead law-abiding lives and condemn Sara's murder. The problem is misuse of power over women, regardless of stated motives such as jealousy or honor.[16]

But some members of immigrant communities challenged these views. Swedish-Kurdish Idris Ahmedi insisted, "The academics trick themselves when they ignore culture. They worry about stirring up racism. But the debate is meaningless if we don't speak openly. Culture and traditions matter a great deal and change only slowly."[17]

Jan Hjärpe, a highly regarded professor of comparative religion, was one of the academics who dared to speak up. He wrote: "Swedish men also kill women, but no one applauds them."[18] In his article "Can Culture or Religion Excuse Murder?" Hjärpe points out that honor killings are committed in communities with a distinctive social structure in which the extended family (the clan) demands absolute loyalty. The head of the family (or clan) has "legal" authority over its members, and the honor of the family depends on the chastity and modesty of its women. Hence the applause when the men "cleanse the family of shame." This holds true even when honor killing is the exception rather than the norm within the community in question.[19]

The evidence suggests that Sara's killers had been brought up within a strong tradition of "honor" and "shame." They gave themselves up to the police after the killing but refused to speak to the female desk officer; a male officer had to be called. Both their friends and Sara's mother had heard them threaten to kill Sara because she was a "whore." Previous girlfriends speak of their aggressive attitudes, based on the notion that women are the property of men. The boys themselves deny categorically that the murder had anything at all to do with their cultural background. The killing was an accident. They had been angry with Sara and tightened the belt round her neck just a little too hard.

However, the words *shame* and *honor* turn up everywhere in their talk and actions. Alcalá wrote:

> This is not simply a matter of loose, habitual jargon. It signifies a certain mindset and emotions teetering on the brink of violence. The boys beat her up, threatened her and finally killed her, all in order to rise above their perceived humiliation and defend their own honor and that of the family.
>
> Sara's murder was not "ordinary," as it were. It was an execution. A girl of fifteen had been condemned to death for trying to lead her life in her own way.[20]

Picking minors to carry out the deed is actually quite common in societies with a tradition of honor killings. It ensures that any sentences imposed are mild. This, at least, is true in societies where there are no legal paragraphs that define honor killings as self-defense and hence deserving only a minimal sentence. But even when no such legal sanction exists, regional courts often fall back on precedents that justify killing for the sake of honor. Because the punishment is negligible and the gain is great (i.e., honor is restored), the killers should give themselves up—as Maitham and Yassar duly did.

Maitham allegedly told friends that because he was minor, the authorities wouldn't punish him hard for killing Sara. He was right. His sentence was imprisonment for three and a half years. Yasser got four years, because his role was regarded as the more crucial. The judge stated in his summary that if they had been adults, he would have sentenced both of them to life imprisonment.[21]

People who campaign against honor killings complain that in some countries the law allows for a lenient sentence in cases of honor killing. *Discount* is a word they use. The Nordic countries too have a system of discount, which applies to sentences for murder. In terms of the sentencing of her killers, Sara's life came cheap.

In 1998 Fadime spoke in public about Sara's murder: "All my relatives agreed that what happened was right. Girls mustn't play around. Sara was no stranger to the rules, but broke them all the same. She knew what she was doing.

"In their view [the murder] was admirable and the murderers were like martyrs."[22]

Sara's death did not change policy. The Swedish authorities concluded that violence against women is universal—that culturally determined violence does not exist and consequently honor killings do not exist. The fear of stirring up racism meant that the problems related to culture were swept under the carpet.

Fadime was among those who paid the price. "I hope you will not turn your back on them," she said in her speech in Parliament, five years after Sara's death. By "them" she meant girls like herself. Both Pela and Fadime were to lose their lives before officialdom in Sweden woke up. Apparently Sara had been forgotten.

3 Pela, or History Repeats Itself

When the murder of Pela Atroshi came before a Swedish court in December 2000, no one doubted what kind of crime it was. It was an honor killing. According to the international media, such as the *New York Times*, Pela's murder was the first case of honor killing to be heard in a European court. This may sound strange, but it is actually understandable. The special feature of the Pela case was that it had already been dealt with in an Iraqi court: two alleged perpetrators had been convicted and sentenced to six months each in prison. On a suspended sentence.

In other words, it was definitely an honor killing. In Iraq, ordinary murders are punished much more severely. Iraqi law itself does not recognize honor killings as a special category entailing a lenient sentence due to "honorable motive," but Pela's alleged murderers, her father and an uncle, were convicted in a local court in Dihok, in Iraqi Kurdistan. So the sentence of six months inside was suspended.

But there was one snag. Pela's sister Breen, who had witnessed the murder, managed to contact the Swedish police. She knew that four men were responsible for the killing—her father and his three brothers. The shots were fired by one of her uncles. He and another uncle, both Swedish citizens, had gone back to Sweden soon after the murder. To get them into a Swedish court, Breen had to testify, and the Swedish police helped her to return from Iraq. The uncles were sentenced to life imprisonment—a sentence that was confirmed by the High Court in June 2001.

A suspended sentence of six months in prison in Iraq, a life sentence in Sweden. Two punishments but the same crime. Possibly this was what the *New York Times* journalist had in mind when he wrote that the case brought against Pela's killer was the first honor killing case in a European court. Perhaps this was the first time a "regional" sentence had been tested in a European court and overruled. Anyway, Pela's murder made history. After Breen's testimony, it was no longer possible to state that honor killings did not happen in Sweden.[1] The murder had been planned there; the fact that it was committed in Iraq was a matter of tactics. The perpetrators were Swedish citizens.

The Swedish authorities made every effort to bring the case to court. Not only were policemen sent to Iraq to get Breen out safely—a risky enough mission—but they also had to find legally acceptable grounds for charging the two uncles. National courts are normally bound by sentences passed in other countries, but in cases of violence against a person which would carry a guideline sentence of four years or more in prison, overriding a previous foreign sentence is permitted.

Pela's two uncles felt quite safe in Sweden. The police kept them under observation but stuck to the decision not to arrest them until Breen was back home, when the official reason to make the arrest was that her life was now in danger. The charge against them was based on Breen's testimony.

It nearly went wrong. The day before the start of the hearing, the police received a phone call from a journalist, who wanted to tell them that the relevant legal paragraph no longer existed in law—the basis for the charge had disappeared. A police special investigator has spoken of the despair she felt, especially on behalf of Breen. Was the case to be dismissed now, after all she had been through with such incredible courage? But there was a solution: the rule that if part of a crime is planned and/or committed in Sweden, the entire crime is under Swedish jurisdiction. The case was brought, and the two uncles were sentenced to life.

The family's strategy had been to kill in Iraq in order to have the deed dealt with in a Kurdish court. It had failed. Breen commented: "I came back because I wanted them to be punished."[2]

Pela's "crime" was the same as Sara's and Fadime's: she had become "Swedified." She and her family had arrived in Sweden in 1995. At fifteen, Pela was the oldest of the seven children. Breen, one year younger than her sister, says that at first their new life in Sweden was really terrific, but the joy didn't last long. Their father laid down strict rules for his daughters. They must not "cross borderlines." They were not to start "living the European way" and must "stay away from the society." Their father timed them to the minute, watch in hand, when they came back from school. He was terrified that they might do something to ruin the family's reputation. They were not allowed to go out to cafés or to shops on their own.

Pela did well at school and got high marks. She was sociable and popular but "stood out somehow," according to her friend Sahar. "Pela was playing a role"; she seemed unnaturally easygoing for a girl in her situation. She spoke proudly about her relationship with a Kurdish boy, saying, "It's not wrong, what I'm doing, because my father supports me." In the company of her schoolmates, her dreams of freedom led her to fashion an identity that did not match reality.

In the end she couldn't take it any more and ran away. During the previous six months Pela had had noticeable problems coping at school. She was falling behind but spoke to no one about her struggles. Running away was dangerous. The men in the family had warned, "If one of our daughters sleeps away from home for one single night, she must die."[3] It made no difference that when Pela ran away, the friend she stayed with was a girl.

The family's reputation was now ruined. Even the Kurdish friend Pela had been so proud of would have nothing to do with her. The whole community gossiped about Pela and her family. Breen says, "Pela was trying to break free and build her own future, but they were too powerful." She was an outsider, both in the Kurdish community and in Swedish society generally, and struggled to find her identity. Without her family, who was she? "The family threatens you, but you long for them all the same," Breen said, drawing parallels between Fadime, Pela, and herself.

The family failed in their attempts to trace Pela, but she returned home on her own. Breen tells us: "She said, I love my brothers and sisters. I can't live without my family. Forgive me!" Her father responded, "If you want to make me happy, you must marry." Pela agreed and was glad to travel to the Kurdish region of Dihok for the purpose. "She was so pleased about going back," Breen says. "So pleased," because she had been reunited with her family.

According to Pela's friend Sahar, "Pela loved her family better than she loved herself. She was like, she put herself on a tray and said, I'm all yours, do what you like with me!"

Pela thought that she was to be married to a cousin. Breen explains that Kurds respond to threats to the family's good name by trying to keep the shame within the family. On May 30, 1999, Pela, her mother, and a baby sister traveled to Iraq. Once the school term was over, her father, Breen, and other siblings were to follow, traveling with some uncles. Although these men came all the way from Australia, Breen was not surprised: it was only natural that they would want to attend Pela's wedding. Still, it seemed odd that they traveled via Sweden instead of going directly to Iraq.[4]

On June 24, Breen, her younger siblings, her father, and three uncles left for Iraq, but the paternal grandparents remained in Sweden. On his arrival, the father announced that Pela was not to marry after all.

The men of the family slaughtered her instead, in her bedroom in the family home. She stayed alive for a few minutes after the first shot. "What's happening?" she asked Breen. "What have I done?" She begged to be taken to hospital. One of her uncles fired a second shot, in the presence of Breen and the girls' mother.[5]

The planning of the deed had been kept secret from Pela's mother. It was done on June 24, 1999.

The case was tried in Dihok, and the sentence was pronounced on October 9, 1999. Pela's father and one of his brothers were sentenced to six months in prison. The sentence was suspended, even though it was mild. According to a police officer, the usual jail sentence for an honor killing is one to two years.

The judge commented on Pela's murder as follows: "Because the motive for the killing was honorable and had as its goal to cleanse the family of the dishonor that had befallen it . . . [the judge] had decided to suspend the enforcement of the term of imprisonment."

In a police interview Pela's uncle said:

> We couldn't accept Pela's behavior, because it gave the family a bad reputation. Despite many family meetings, which aimed at dealing with the problem, we weren't successful because the victim insisted on carrying on with her bad behavior.
>
> I am a brother of Pela's father and I believe in my heart and because of the badness I saw in her and the awful things I heard about her in the foreign country, that she deserved worse than death. This I say because she was ruining the reputation of an old, honorable family, highly respected among Kurds.[6]

Later, on Swedish TV, Pela's father denied that the murder had anything to do with honor. By then a "wanted man" notice had circulated internationally, but he regarded himself as the target of a smear campaign. Generally, he came across as a successful businessman whose honor had been completely rehabilitated.

Breen shows goodwill toward her father: "I have always liked my father. But what I don't like about him is that he can't make up his own mind. He doesn't even know how he should behave toward his own children." She goes on to say that her father had been unemployed in Sweden and felt lonely. "He wanted to be just as powerful as he was back in Kurdistan."[7]

Breen believes her father did not have the heart to kill Pela and that was why his brothers did it. She is convinced that her grandfather, the head of the family, had ordered his sons to act. His power was such that they would have to obey.

According to the Swedish police, eleven persons conspired to carry out Pela's murder: two Australians, two Swedes, and seven Iraqis.

Breen goes to sleep thinking about what happened and wakes up with the same thoughts preoccupying her. "They never leave me," she says. She is haunted by the possibility of suicide. "It too would be a kind of murder for honor's sake, but rather that than dying the way Pela did."

Suicide would be one way of dealing with the fear that Breen lives with day and night. Her identity is secret, but she has no answers to the questions raised by her future and the prospect of solitude. Her mother, who divorced her husband after Pela's murder and stayed in Sweden to look after three of her children, thinks that Breen should stand up for the honor of the family and marry a man chosen by them. "Mum thinks that if I marry, I can start living normally again." Her mother wants the best for her daughter and cannot imagine any other solution. And Breen has no better ideas to offer. But she won't give in. In her eyes, a normal life means "that you decide about your own life, like a human being." Rather suicide than a forced marriage.

But she also says, "They want me dead, so I have decided to stay alive.

"Pela lives inside me. We have the same soul. If I die in Iraq, I will be buried with Pela and come closer to her. Not here, among strangers."

"I failed her," Mona Sahlin, the Swedish minister for integration, admitted after Fadime's death. "I failed her because I was afraid of fanning the flames of racism. . . . I had made them and their problems invisible."[8] By "them" she means girls from immigrant families. It was Pela's sister, Sahlin says, who made her feel a traitor. After Breen had delivered her testimony in court, Sahlin thought, "I must meet her!" Their meeting allowed her to understand more: "The thinking behind honor killings is very special. All forms of oppression are not similar." Sahlin goes on to refer to how, in the court case against Fadime's father, no one knew anything and no one remembered anything. Only one witness from inside the family spoke out—Fadime's sister Songül. The similarities between Songül and Breen are striking. Under the headline "Bravest in the World," journalist Britta Svensson writes:

> They are alike; you see it in their eyes and hear it in their voices. But most of all, it is Songül's heroic courage that reminds you of Fadime, her big sister.
> Fadime's younger sister was the only relative who yesterday dared to testify against Rahmi Sahindal.
> "I want him convicted," she said about her own father.
> I have seen it once before. Still I could hardly believe my eyes.
> Couldn't believe that there is another young Kurdish girl who dares to be so courageous, dares to bear witness against her own family, dares to speak up about what honor killing means. . . .
> Until yesterday, Pela Atroshis's sister was the most courageous woman I have ever seen.
> Now there is one more "younger sister," just like her."[9]

For some time a large photograph was set on Fadime's grave, a portrait of a lovely young woman. It was Pela. The picture was placed to the left of the gravestone. To the right stood a photograph of Fadime, the same size but full length. She faced us, characteristically upright, her eyes unafraid. Two icons, Pela and Fadime, side by side. Gifts of flowers were scattered on the grave; many were tied with ribbons bearing the text "Glöm inte Pela och Fadime" (never forget Pela and Fadime). A society formed in memory of Pela— Never Forget Pela—now always mentions Fadime's name as well. They are linked in death, as they never were in life.

Fadime did not want to make a statement about Pela's murder. She was too aware of the dangers. To take sides in public would mean to challenge her family, and that would intensify the death threats against her. She had gone for celebrity status in 1998 in an attempt to protect herself ("Perhaps they won't dare to kill me, now that so many people know who I am"), but later Fadime kept a low profile. To comment on the killing of Pela, or on the court case, was too risky.

Fadime's grave has become a place of pilgrimage also for those who want to honor the memory of Pela. I asked one of Fadime's cousins what he thought about it. He shrugged: "People figure they were on about the same thing." Fadime's two older sisters stared uncomprehendingly at me when I asked them. Perhaps they had not visited the grave. Perhaps they just did not know.

So what does Fadime's mother make of it, I wonder, if *she* has been to the grave? Or little Nebile, who loved her dead sister but distances herself from Fadime's manner of relating to the family and the media? Is it right to annex a grave in this way, even for a good cause?

Some Kurdish women in Sweden complain about the way Fadime has become a cause. Everyone wants a piece of her now.

In Iraq, Pela was laid to rest in a nameless grave in Dihok. The place is marked with a plain stone. The marker was raised by the family on her mother's side in the face of protests from her father and his relatives, who would have preferred to see Pela's memory wiped off the face of the earth.

It makes sense that Pela's friends and supporters borrow a corner of Fadime's grave.

Pela and Fadime—do not ever forget them.

II / *Honor*

4 | *What Is Honor?*

Honor is a word with a very special quality in English as in Swedish
and other European languages. It has an alluring, almost seductive
appeal. I think its spell derives from its archaic and poetic overtones. Honor has a ring of heroism and nobility. It harks back to
a time when men had high moral principles and were chivalrous
and brave.

I say "men" deliberately. In both Western and non-Western history the idea of honor is qualified by gender. The use of set expressions suggests this: "a man of honor" is much more common than
"a woman of honor." Women are more likely to be "chaste" and to
behave "with propriety." To switch such phrases around—"a chaste
man"—doesn't sound quite right, does it? It is fine for men to be
honorable, or worthy of honor; "a woman of honor" somehow does
not trip so easily off the tongue. It used to be that men had honor,
women a sense of shame. Men were in charge of the honor of the
family and represented it to the world at large. Meanwhile women,
as sexual beings, were potential threats.

In Europe, as in the Middle East and several other regions, honor
has had a paradoxical quality: men's honor depended to a large extent
on the sexual behavior of *women*. Men therefore faced a problem.
The male notion of honor made a man extremely vulnerable to how

his womenfolk behaved. Rather than being accorded honor on the basis of his own behavior, he could become a target of scorn and abuse if one of his women—a daughter, sister, niece or wife—departed from the norms of chastity and modesty.

There are no general answers to questions about what these norms of decency were all about and to what degree they are still operational. In some modern cases an entire family is dishonored because a girl in her teens has a boyfriend or goes to a disco, like fifteen-year-old Sara in Sweden. By contrast, in the nineteenth century a woman in northern Italy could give birth out of wedlock without damaging the family honor, provided that the newborn was got out of the way somehow. Orphanages where such babies could be disposed of were set up with the aim of averting dishonor. An alternative was for the father to marry the child's mother, though not necessarily at once. Later the couple might well decide to bring the child home rather than having it brought up in an institution.[1]

Back in those days, marriage saved a woman's reputation and her family's honor, and in many communities it still does. It can even be seen as a valid way of dealing with rape; if the rapist marries his victim, honor is thought to be saved. Until 1995, such legal let-out clauses were in place in fourteen Latin American states.[2] In Egypt, a pioneering Middle Eastern country with regard to women's rights, a similar law was not abolished until 2001. Concern about the honor of the family is still a dominant issue in many places. A law that encourages marrying the victim off to the man who raped her can even be seen as a liberal device. The alternative could be killing her—for the sake of honor.[3]

Throughout European history, stories have been told of the fates befalling men—and women —who broke the norms of sexual propriety. The duel was an institutionalized response. A man must be prepared to face death to defend his honor. If a woman in your family—your wife in particular—was desired by another man or had an irregular sexual relationship, it was a humiliation of the worst kind.

The duel was one way to restore your honor. The rule was "Better die a man of honor than live with shame." Another extreme action was available: kill the woman.

History furnishes examples of the acceptability of both "solutions" in different places and at different times. The duel had a strong following in much of Europe, starting in the sixteenth century, when it spread from northern Italy toward the north and west. It remained an important part of life well into the twentieth century, especially among the upper classes in Germany and the Balkan states. Duels were fought for many reasons other than affairs with women. It goes without saying that it was men who died. In that sense the duel convention was good to women. But women too might be made to pay with their lives for not meeting standards of chastity and decency. In contrast, history provides relatively little information about the fates of the women. In the eighteenth century, killing an unfaithful wife was probably a much more widespread practice in Spain than, for instance, in England. The English contented themselves with expelling such a woman from the social group. Her family would refuse to have anything to do with her, or else they would all become outcasts and be stripped of their honor.[4]

The parallel with Fadime's fate is obvious. Fadime was expelled from her family when she chose Patrik. In the end the ultimate sanction was set in motion. "The final solution," as her father called it in court.

But the relevance of European history is limited.[5] It was never part of any European tradition that you should kill your own child for the sake of honor. Wives possibly, but not daughters.

Issues arising from women's chastity—and especially the threats against men's honor that lapses entail—are familiar, recurring themes in world history. The development has not been in one direction only, that is, toward greater tolerance of and respect for the integrity and autonomy of women. Instead, progress has varied with time and place inside different communities and between them. For instance, the Icelandic sagas tell of some women who behaved like men and therefore had honor in their own right—but such women were spoken of as "a good lad" (*drengr góðr*) as if they had acquired male characteristics.[6] Until well into the twentieth century, this was true of Albania too: some women were in charge of their own honor, wore men's clothes, and fulfilled masculine roles. But they were chaste, above sexuality.[7]

In the Nordic countries, in parts of the Middle East, and elsewhere, recent changes have caused a backlash, and men's attempts to control female sexuality have actually intensified. Advances that had seemed secure after decades of battling for greater gender equality now seem valid only for part of the population—witness the fates of Fadime, Sara, and Pela. In 1993, old legislation against forced marriages was abolished in Norway, because it was believed to be an anachronism. It had to be reinstated two years later, when we learnt what happened to Nasim Karim. She was nearly killed in Pakistan when she protested against being forced to marry, but she managed to escape back to Norway. Her story became known when she wrote *Izzat: For the Sake of Honor* (1996), a book about a fictional character called Noreen. Thanks to Karim's courage and enterprise, and to the political follow-up of her story, forced marriages were once more outlawed in Norway in 1995. When it became clear that the practice was quite common, several further legal measures were introduced. In 2004, Norway criminalized forced marriage; it was the first country in Europe to do so.

Forced marriage is based on a concept of honor that by now is flourishing and spreading throughout Europe. There are academics who claim that the current risk of women's being subjected to violence in the name of honor may be greater in certain ethnic groups living in Europe than in their countries of origin.[8]

Fundamentalist groups in many Middle Eastern and Asian countries have undermined the progressive practices encouraged by secular, moderate governments. Sexual freedom for girls is not the issue—not for the majority who actually value modesty as a precious ideal. The concern is about women's right to honor: their right to be seen as responsible for their own lives and identities.

But we are anticipating the process of analyzing the meaning of honor. Another liberal concept of honor makes it a matter of moral integrity—that is, the individual's responsibility for her own self, including her moral standards. We might think of this as a "sense of honor."

We must take a step or two back in time: this concept of honor developed fairly late in European history. In most countries, honor was not widely seen as synonymous with moral integrity until the eighteenth century. The shift in emphasis started fitfully during the thirteenth century, but it took another five or six hundred years for it to become widely accepted.[9]

Before this, "honor" focused primarily on reputation—recognition by others—as it still does in many non-Westernized communities, in Europe and outside it. For example, a man who failed to take up a challenge to his honor would be shamed, provided the affront was made public. Honor lay in what was in the public eye. Repute is lost only in the eyes of others.

Let us examine this older idea of honor, because it gives us the best chance of insight into the tragedies of Fadime, Pela, and Sara.

In European history until the eighteenth century, honor remained mainly a matter of a person's worth *in the eyes of others*. Social recognition was more important than the individual's sense of self and of being honorable. Now self-worth and social recognition are linked; they are two aspects of the same thing. This is why the technical literature in this area refers to a *dual* theory of honor. The concept is made up of two components, one internal and one external; "honor" is one phenomenon with two distinct aspects.

But the two facets of honor are not necessarily interdependent: I might well have a solid sense of honor, but all the same I realize that I am not as honored—as respected and highly regarded—as I feel I deserve or could demand. Or I may be honored and respected but nonetheless feel inferior because those around do not know me for who I am; people are naive and I have tricked them.

These examples show how a discrepancy can exist between the inner and outer aspects of honor, between the subjective feeling of worth and the views and responses of the outside world. In other words, you can be honorable without being respected, and honored without feeling worthy of it.

Would it clarify matters if we spoke simply of respect and recognition? Do we need *honor* any more? Perhaps it is an old-fashioned notion, ripe for replacement with another, more contemporary word—one that would suit women as well as men?

If we are to understand Fadime's fate and what happened to others like her, the answer must be no. Fadime said, "I am their face to the outside world. Whatever I do, I must consider the men in my family, because everything I do reflects on them. If I smoke a cigarette, it reflects on them." In this context, "face to the outside world" means honor. In some languages, including Kurdish and Arabic, "face" is often used interchangeably with "honor."[10] It implies recognition of the outward-directed quality of honor. Among the Japanese and Chinese too, "face" can stand for "honor."[11] In languages like Norwegian and English it is possible to "lose face," for instance by doing something silly, without being dishonored.[12] In some communities, however, loss of honor inevitably has dramatic consequences. "I have trampled on their honor, I have robbed them of all they have that matters, I have ruined the lives of all my relatives. . . . To kill me is the only way they can regain their honor, their pride," Fadime said.

"It's a question of honor," her father told the court. He explained how he had been exposed before world opinion because of what she had done, "that daughter who is dead now." He added: "The problem is over now."

World opinion is a powerful concept. What is left for you when everyone laughs at you? What are you worth? What is there to hope and strive for? Remember that from this perspective, the laughter is inescapable. Then honor becomes a matter of survival for you and the others whose honor depends on yours.

In order to grasp what "honor" means in this context, we need a clearly defined technical term. *Honor* is ambiguous in most of the

Western European languages because it has such a wide frame of reference. This holds true of *heder* (Swedish), *ære* (Norwegian), *Ehre* (German), *honneur* (French), *honor* (Spanish), *onóre* (Italian), and so forth. True, we have to use the actual word, just like Fadime and her father: "It's a question of honor," he said. "Their honor is the only thing that matters to them," she said. The mechanics of translating between languages and cultures force us to use whatever linguistic tools we have. But at the same time, we should try to rid the word of some of the common meanings associated with it.

There is no general agreement about how to do this: *honor* has different associations for different people. Which is precisely why it is so problematic. Nowadays the whole concept seems faded, washed out. It survives in phrases like "it's an honor," "my word of honor," and "dishonored." But what must you do to be dishonored? Can someone else dishonor you? Most people of Western European origin become vague at this point. It is not even certain what constitutes libel in law, even though the distress it causes can be sensed in every part of your body.

But Fadime knew. Her father, brother, mother, and sisters also knew. Pela knew, and agreed to an arranged marriage. To them, honor was a real and clearly defined entity. Its meaning seemed both precise and easy to understand (even when unacceptable). Our challenge is to grasp *their* concept of honor. We need a delimited concept to help us understand why honor killings are carried out—or not carried out—and what we might do to prevent such atrocities.

We can learn much from the pioneering book *Honor* (1994) by the anthropologist Frank Henderson Stewart. In it he attempts a comparative analysis of honor, based on a wealth of interdisciplinary material drawn from both historical and regional sources In my view, *Honor* greatly facilitates an understanding of what the author calls "this most elusive of social concepts" (cf., however, Patterson 1982).[13]

Keep in mind that the concept of honor as Stewart defines it and that we will use from now on does not necessarily entail violence against women. Drawing on his own field studies, carried out over many years among Arab Bedouin in Sinai, Stewart recounts several incidents when expected reprisals did not happen. He observed three cases of unmarried girls' becoming pregnant without any punishment as a result and also four cases of infidelity in which the woman's family directed its anger toward the seducer—the man was killed while the woman was not even divorced by her husband.[14]

After many years of studying Arab communities in rural Israel, Joseph Ginat, an Israeli anthropologist, also reports that breaches of the norms of female chastity often were tolerated, even when babies were born outside marriage. Ginat's book *Women in Muslim Rural Society* (1982) is one of the few empirical studies showing how honor operates. His book explodes stereotypes and gives insights into the actual options and decisions of people when their honor is at stake. Organized mediation may help people to avoid strife and open confrontations, keep the peace, and promote reconciliation. Honor, in the sense we now use the word, does not entail killing by definition, even though history shows that violence against women is quite common in honor-driven communities.

Men too are sometimes victims of honor killings. Among the examples drawn from studies of Sinai Arabs are cases in which the male seducers were killed while the women went unharmed. In recent years, several young men living in Europe have been victims of murder or attempted murder for the sake of honor, that is, for having courted a girl against the wishes of her family. Blood feuds between tribes or clans, fought in the name of honor, have claimed thousands of lives throughout history and continue to do so. There is an extensive literature about feuding, but it is not part of my subject.

I am primarily interested in a much less well investigated area: the role of women in the history of honor and honor killing. Still, as noted, victims of honor killings are not always female: this is why violence in the name of honor cannot be understood simply as "systemic violence against women" or "globalized oppression of women." To argue this is to ignore the underlying ideology of honor. It is specific and something we must learn to understand.

Not just to condemn it but also to further the work that Fadime began.

In some non-Western societies, as well as in the European past, honor is specified in a *code of honor*. The "code" is a set of rules stating what is and is not part of the honor system. Fundamentally, honor can be lost as well as gained. Stewart regards the fact that honor can be lost, its "losableness," as a defining feature of the concept we are interested in now.[15]

Just like the nose on your face, honor is a thing you have—or not, as the case may be. The world is made up of people with or without honor. The code determines which group you are in.

The rules are clear and specific, leaving no room for doubt. The standards laid down in the code are selected for their overriding importance; they are *minimum* standards. Honor is lost if you fail to meet them.

Honor and respect go together in societies with a code of honor. A man with honor has a claim to respect. It is his right because he lives as his community demands and cares for his honor according to the rules. The community he belongs to could be called an "honor group," i.e., a group that adopts the same code of honor and acknowledges this in each other.

The code ensures a *right to honor*—every man has the right to be treated as a person of worth. Honor confers respect; it empowers you to expect it. The group has a duty to grant a man of honor the status and respect due to him.

Stewart recommends the concept of "personal honor" to express the legal aspect of honor: it implies a right in law to be treated as a full or equal member of the honor group. When Fadime's father tells the court that "it's a question of honor," he speaks as a man among equals. In other words, we are also defining honor as egalitarian.

In many languages, including Kurdish, Arabic, and Persian, there is a special word for this kind of honor. There is another concept of honor that goes with rank—honor within a hierarchy, rather than on the level (Stewart uses the word *vertical* in opposition to *horizontal*). Hierarchical honor—or rank, or status—can change by degrees, grow or diminish. Horizontal (personal) honor cannot be increased, only lost—and, possibly, regained. It is an all-or-none phenomenon.

I have introduced the concept of personal honor and made it clear that it entails a claim right to equality in law. But honor has also a *collective* aspect: it belongs to the family, the clan, or the tribe— sometimes to a nation-state. Members of the collective have a stake in the shared honor: if one of them is dishonored, so are they all.

In such societies, honor is a public matter. What matters is the opinion of others, rather than your own moral standards. Honor is dependent on how things seem to the world around you. Hence, reputation is alpha and omega. Rumors can ruin an entire family's honor and standing in society.[16] A young woman's moving into her own apartment could spell catastrophe for her family, because it "must" mean that she has a lover. "For us, rumor is a grave matter," a Kurdish girl once told me. Rumors are social facts that you have to deal with. It follows that protecting your private life is hugely important. You should *never* give people reason to gossip. "The situation is closed" (*mastur ilhal*) is an Arabic reply to the question "How are you?" It translates as "Fine, thank you—my home and my family are screened from view." Now think about Sara, Pela, and Fadime from this perspective. They flaunted the family shame.

Fadime spoke Swedish in public. In court, her father's statements were translated from Kurdish and Turkish into Swedish. This meant that an important shade of meaning got lost in translation: Swedish has only one word for honor, while Kurdish, like Turkish, Arabic, and Persian, has two with entirely different frames of reference. The Kurdish (and Turkish) word *namus* is used only in the context of the purity and propriety of women, while *shirif* refers to other norms such as hospitality, courage, and so forth. When Fadime's father says, "It's a question of honor," or when Fadime says, "I have trampled on their honor," which honor is meant? Undoubtedly the kind the Danish-Palestinian parliamentarian and author Naser Khader calls "sex honor"—the kind that depends on the chastity and modesty of women.[17]

At this point we need to look more closely at shame. Actually shame is not the counterpart of honor, even though in the West we think of "honor and shame" as if paired—opposite aspects of the same phenomenon. Within the traditions we are trying to understand, the opposite of *honor is without honor* (dishonored). *Shame* is too weak a word. Honor is absolute. It has an either-or quality, while shame can change by degrees: you can be more or less shameful, and you can be more or less shamed.

As a concept, shame is more accessible to mainstream Westerners than honor is. We recognize the feeling; it is a concept we have grown up with. Children, and sometimes adults too, might be told, "You should be ashamed of yourself." Shame is part of everyday experience. In some contexts, to "have shame" is to be worthy of honor (honorable)—it is the equivalent of honor, rather than its opposite. Shame is an ambiguous and diffuse concept. It can refer to anything from minor mistakes to major misdemeanors. But in the traditions that concern us here, the feeling that is the counterpart to shame is pride, not honor. The egalitarian traditions of northern Europe do not encourage pride or showing pride, which makes also this view of honor harder to grasp.

honor ≠ pride

Honor affects the entire person. Honor is a badge, a seal of quality. Honor is affected by only certain kinds of shame. Dishonor is worse than shame.[18]

To understand honor in the same way as members of Fadime's family and the community around them do, we need to take another look at the language of honor. In the West, honor is spoken of mainly in set phrases that have an abstract feel to them: "have the honor" to do something or other, like escorting the bride to the altar, or in expressions like "to honor and obey" or "debts of honor." Contrast this with Fadime's world, in which honor is a personalized property: honor belongs to people—it is spoken of as the father's, brother's, or family's honor. Look again at what Fadime said and observe how clearly she states it: "I have trampled on their honor. . . . To kill me is the only way they can regain their honor, their pride."

Honor belongs to a person or to a collective. It is hard to replace with any other concept. You might think that *respect* is a synonym, but it is not. You show respect toward a person, or you enjoy the respect of your community. But honor is different: you have it or you don't—it is part of yourself, like your nose.

As I have noted, there are instances when both *face* and *pride* can be used to mean honor. Fadime said, "To the outside world, I am their face. Whatever I do, I must consider the men in my family." In other words, to the outside world she is an embodiment of the men's honor. In several Middle Eastern languages, the phrase "a white face" means honor and "a black face" dishonor. To blacken someone's face is to cause him to be dishonored. To be honorable is to have your pride and dignity intact, to walk with your head held high.

Body metaphors, like "face" and "head," are well suited to express exactly what honor is: an integral part of a person, and a part that is on show in public. "Private parts" must be shielded from view; all members of the honor group have an absolute duty to be loyal to each other and to their shared privacy.

Fadime committed sacrilege twice over. She chose her own boyfriend, but it was probably more important that she went public. The resulting media interest blackened her family's face. Their dishonor—their humiliation—was complete.

The time has come to articulate a precise, technical concept of honor that can serve as a useful tool in cross-cultural studies.

Honor entails respect, in the sense of a *right* to respect. Society has a duty to be respectful for as long as the rules of the code of honor are kept. If they are not, the person is dishonored. Because honor is shared, the collective he belongs to will be sucked down with him as he sinks.

The code is clear about how to lose and regain honor. Within the group, everyone knows what is required. The rules are regarded as minimum standards. Any breach means dishonor. The dishonored man and his family are regarded not only as of inferior status but as contemptible.

Honor can be lost; it is a defining feature. The rules state in specific terms what must be done to regain it.

Not only your own acts can dishonor you. There are two other routes to dishonor: you can be affected by the acts of other men of the family or clan and also by the acts of the women under your guardianship—a daughter, sister, wife, cousin, or niece. This is particularly true of acts that are in any way related to sexuality.

A man of honor must navigate along a problematic course, avoiding any risk of dishonor to himself, his women, or his family. He is in charge of a part of the common good. One faltering step and he might be plunged into the abyss.

Women have no honor. [19] Honor is a male prerogative; men have honor, women have a sense of shame. To avoid being shamed, women must know how to behave with propriety, as prescribed in the code of honor. A shameless woman can throw the entire family into dishonor. Her family can decide to turn a blind eye to her shame, though, either because they love her or because they hate the person who molested her and have good reason to put all the blame on him. For those who live in the West, there is another incentive to mercy: the risk of a life sentence for murder.

Islam allows clemency to be shown to disgraced women. It is written and often stated by Muslims that judgment belongs to God and not to humankind. Hence relatives can escape the obligation to use violence in order to "cleanse" themselves of their family member's shame. In certain circumstances, this also applies to men who break the code of honor: the family may treat him with respect and dignity and let God be the judge.

In every case, dishonor is a public phenomenon. Shame becomes real only when it is disclosed. Shame is in the eye of the beholder. As in medieval Europe, so too among many immigrant groups in today's Europe: shame is an external rather than internal phenomenon. Dealing with shame becomes essential only when it is known. Dishonor is the result of your community's evaluation of you.

But "publicity" alone is not sufficient to blacken a family to such an extent that it becomes necessary to act in order to save its

honor. That "everybody knows" is not decisive.[20] You can stonewall
and get away with it. Joseph Ginat describes several cases among
Israeli Arabs of "shamelessness" that did not lead to intervention.
I noted this too during my field studies in Oman, a state on the
southeastern edge of the Arabian Peninsula. "Everyone" knew that
some women acted dishonorably, but they were still treated with
respect. Even men who had sworn never to let their wives socialize
with these women (in case their wives picked up ideas) allowed a
gap between theory and practice: the wives got on with all their
female neighbors, without exceptions. No one raised the situation
with the "dishonored" husbands or the women's families, and so
there was no need for anyone to take offense.

Drawing on his fieldwork among the Sinai Bedouins, Frank
Stewart presents similar examples of men who had broken the code
of honor in various ways but were nonetheless treated with respect
and dignity. Breaches did not have the consequences one would expect theoretically or on the basis of what people say.[21]

Empirical observation in the field is essential if we are to know
what happens in practice. We have too few such datasets. So far,
honor has been more studied in the abstract than as a living reality.[22] But honor is primarily a matter of practice—of deeds rather
than words. We are still novices when it comes to studying honor
in action.

The use of violence against women to "wash away" shame is conditional on factors other than publicity. One such factor is that male
family members must be confronted—openly challenged—with
their failure to exert control. The social setting is crucial. Dishonor
is not part of any action but emerges from the reactions of others.
This means that the community can come to the rescue of their
own, so they do not have to carry out any "final solution."

True, the media can subvert possible peaceful solutions. What
does it serve that no one speaks to my face about my dishonor, if
the story is broadcast worldwide? In that situation, it doesn't help
to lie low or stonewall.

"Everything went to pieces when the media got in on the case.
He felt robbed of his dignity, his pride, his honor," a daughter says
about her father.[23]

There is another angle for us to consider: the never-ending confrontation between honor and the law. Honor is often in conflict with law and order. It was true of late medieval Europe. It is still true today of many societies within and outside Europe.

This conflict can be studied as part of the social history of Germany and Spain, where for centuries "honor" was protected by the legal system. Even in these countries, honor operated mainly outside the law. Honor, not law, had laid down the rules for paying gambling debts and dealing with insults that were of no interest to the courts. For example, in Germany toward the end of the nineteenth century, seducing a girl over sixteen years of age was not regarded as illegal but was a classical cause of dueling.[24] "Men of honor" often chose to trust their own devices, even when the law would actually have backed them. The most striking opposition between law and honor was that honor would insist on violence that was often condemned in law. The anthropologist Julian Pitt-Rivers, who is famous for his research into honor and shame, based on his fieldwork in Spain, observed in 1968, "The conflict between honor and legality is a fundamental one, which persists to this day."[25] Stewart sums it up like this: "Honor is a notion that from a formal point of view fits easily enough into a legal system, but that in modern Europe, above all because of its link with the duel and other forms of violence, has had a generally uneasy relationship with the main body of the law."[26]

Later we will observe how the conflict between honor and law flares up in the trial of Fadime's father: Members of the family, with one exception, refuse to testify. They stand by the murderer. Then, at the last stage of hearing the case, a nephew suddenly insists that he was the one who had killed Fadime but that her father had wanted to carry the guilt. And that is only the beginning: law and honor are set on a collision course. In the future, Europe is likely to face many such confrontations.

It is also worth keeping in mind that one reason people in certain societies are so strongly aware of honor is that honor is a matter of self-interest, a necessary condition for political and social success. The state is in no position to step in and is more likely to be an obstacle or an outright enemy. The group you belong to—your family or clan—must show strength and pride sufficient to defend its honor and look after the interests of its members. The concerns of the individual are secondary to those of the collective. Its good name and reputation is all that matters. So honor is not a luxury, not a sideline, but crucial to welfare, status, and position—things that matter everywhere. In some societies, the welfare state protects (or should protect) the citizens' interests. In others, the family or clan has similar functions. And in some, the citizen amounts to nothing—and can achieve nothing—without honor.

I have defined honor as objective and external, as an indivisible, all-or-nothing phenomenon. This has not been the only way to see it, neither in modern times nor historically. The definition we have arrived at here—a technical, limited concept—is not the only one. As Pitt-Rivers famously put it in 1965: "Honor is the value of a person in his own eyes, but also in the eyes of his society. It is his estimation of his own worth, his *claim* to pride, but it is also the acknowledgement of that claim; his excellence recognized by society—his *right* to pride."[27] This definition differs from the one we have arrived at, since it emphasizes a person's worth in his own eyes as well as in the eyes of others. It is allied to a universal view of humankind: everyone is born with a unique body and mind, including the ability to be aware of the self and the world around it—that is, with a sense of one's own worth, individually and socially. A universal honor concept is useful for resonance: it helps to build bridges between people.

But a universal concept of honor does not help us to grasp what is at stake in the special cases, that is, in societies or groups where honor is above all a matter of how you are seen by others and where women are not allowed honor in their own right. In such societies honor does not come by degrees: it cannot be portioned out (you cannot have more or less honor). Honor is an absolute and not subject to compromise.

It is to get a better grip of *that* kind of society that we, following Stewart, have arrived at our definition. The code of honor and the honor group are central, as is the fact that honor can be lost (its "losableness"). As we have already observed, it must be possible to lose honor—not only diminish it—if we are to be able, by our definition, to speak of an honor-based society.

The justification for discussing just these criteria for honor is that they raise many questions, often in the context of cases that most people in the West find baffling. It is this kind of honor that causes people to ask me, as an anthropologist, "What *is* honor, really?" It is a kind of "honor" that motivates acts we cannot relate to, an incomprehensible notion with archaic overtones. It is not like "our" kind of honor; it is not what I have in mind as I try to cut a fine figure when I am lecturing or talking with people I appreciate. Not at all: these special manifestations of honor are different, and both demand and deserve an explanation.

Stewart's concept of honor has proved useful for describing and analyzing certain non-Western societies. What with the new migrations into Scandinavia and other countries in Western Europe, and the multicultural societies created there as a consequence, this concept is not only helpful but essential if we are to understand the ongoing developments within the setting of our long-established welfare states.

This is how Naser Khader, a Danish Parliament member and author of Syrian-Palestinian origin, puts it:

> For many traditionalist Muslims, honor and shame are at least as important parts of everyday life as is Islam. More than religion, *it is the unwritten rules of honor and shame* which perpetuate cultural differences between men and women, the gender divide, the veiling of women, the significance ascribed to virginity and so on. The entrenchment of honor and shame creates more problems for integration in Denmark than does Islam, which in many ways is a pragmatic religion.[28]

Khader's "unwritten rules" include two concepts of honor: one more general, the other solely concerned with women's virtue. The norms forming part of the general concept include absolute loyalty to the family, the clan, or other groups, such as gangs. Inger-Lise Lien has demonstrated how the honor codes in gangs of youths tend to lead to violence that breeds more violence.[29] Gangs without an immigrant background also use honor codes that can be understood in terms of the concept I have developed along Stewart's lines.[30] Because this kind of honor demands total loyalty to the group, rather than to society at large, and pitches its own laws against the state's, they can, just as Khader points out, hamper integration.

"We need a new concept of honor." This is said by a man, imprisoned for killing his wife in the name of honor. In chapter 6 we will get some insight into a traditional Muslim society in which the code of honor operates hand in hand with a humane philosophy of life. It is worth reminding ourselves that a concept of honor emphasizing moral integrity and personal responsibility for one's actions—that is, one that has an "internal" aspect—is a recent development in Europe. There are indications that this attitude to honor took hold here and there in Western Europe at different times from the late twelfth century onward. However, it seems that these ideas only became widely held by the eighteenth century. By then *honor* had changed to mean primarily a personal sense of integrity and rectitude, as well as an awareness of how important it is not to bargain about one's deeply felt values. "Internalized" honor soon took precedence in all the big European languages: English, German, French, Italian, and Spanish (not that the concepts of honor were all identical—the codes varied).

In line with this transformation of honor into a matter of personal integrity, the general idea also changed, from being a badge handed out on objective grounds to becoming linked to internal truth: "To thine own self be true."[31] Stewart has spoken about the likelihood of a connection between the collapse in Western Europe of some of the old customs connected to honor (e.g., dueling rules) and the stress that increasingly came to be put on a personal sense of honor. If honor cannot be lost because your evaluation of yourself is intact—that is, the punishment for breaking the rules no longer is loss of honor—then there is little point in hanging on to conventions that allow you to regain honor. The codified system has become irrelevant. "The code" offers, as we have seen, a real risk of losing honor, but if I pass the final judgment of whether I am honorable or not—if it is primarily my ideas that matter—the need for external enforcements fades away. By contrast, in societies with a code of honor, your family will close ranks to demand back what they see as theirs: their honor. They insist because they operate within an honor-based system.

This is why Fadime had to be killed. "The problem is over now," her father said in court. Had the setting been their home territory in Turkish Kurdistan, his statement would have carried legal weight. There, as I noted, the local courts often pass minimal sentences for crimes of honor. Honor killings still tend to be regarded as self-defense.

Yet there is no consensus, not even in societies where honor killings are part of a tradition. Honor is a controversial subject, and people disagree about how it should be practiced. Often they are united about the principles but disunited about the practice. Sometimes the basic principles are disputed too. Such controversies are not always made public and transparent. Power and oppression make themselves felt in different ways. The mothers of Fadime, Sara, and Pela wanted their daughters alive, not dead, and did everything they could to avert the murders.

That said, don't go away believing that only women stand by women or that all women back each other. A Danish-Turkish woman tells of how her father backed her in her wish not to be forced into a marriage, but her mother won: she allied herself with his elder brother, who was the more powerful, and forced the marriage. Individuals differ, as do the circumstances under which they act. What we do know is that people disagree about the precise values and that in many cases when "honor" would have prescribed an extreme action, they instead respond humanely. As already mentioned, both Stewart and Ginat tell of specific instances of women living in traditional Muslim communities who have given birth to babies outside marriage and, even so, escaped any punishment.

In terms of "honor," conception out of wedlock is an open-and-shut case of ultimate shame. But who would kill their own flesh and blood? You'd have to be sick, as Fadime's father put it. There are communities in which such "sickness" does not exist. Society averts its eyes from the disgraced women and sympathizes with their plight—something I too have observed during my fieldwork in Oman.[32]

Honor, as we have seen, can mean different things in different groups and settings. The concepts defining what honor entails, and who has a right to it, have varied with time and place. The norms have been very variable too, as well as inconsistent and often ideologically driven. Those in power, including the churches, have waded into the European debate in an attempt to take charge of "honor." In medieval times the church manned the barricades in battles about matters of honor. There were clergymen who insisted that to be honorable you had to be a Protestant, because only Protestants had the insight to live according to honorable norms.

In our century the concept of honor is being revised in certain fundamentalist circles. "Honor" can become linked to nationalism and ethnic resurgence. Within social groups, from families to nations, women are the symbols of its solidarity and continuity.[33] Women are trumpeted as the guardians of cultural identity. It follows that the cultural and/or national identity of the men must express itself in control of the women. As the British-Iraqi Kurd Nazand Begikhani, a researcher and human rights advocate, has said: "It is interesting to observe how in such contexts, honor has nothing to do with virtue and honesty, but is firmly linked to proper behavior by the women."[34] Roonak Faraj, who is the editor of a newspaper in Iraqi Kurdistan, argues that because the Kurds have been an oppressed and stateless people, the consequence has been that, at home and in exile, they cling to old traditions, which include clan mentality and violence against women. When she was interviewed in Sweden, Faraj said, "Those who come here bring their traditions—it matters a lot to them that their culture should not be lost."[35]

The sociologist Masoud Kamali, a Swede of Kurdish origin, confirms this: "Many traditions are strengthened in the diaspora. What Fadime did was perceived as a threat toward the entire ethnic group."[36]

There is much evidence to suggest that immigrants to European countries often revise their concepts of honor in a conservative direction: they can feel surrounded by hostile neighbors, infidels, and uncivilized strangers and react by setting a greater value on traditions of honor. The chastity of their girls becomes more important in exile than, for instance, it is in modern Syria. Similar strengthening and intensification of the honor concept is seen in today's Istanbul, due to the influx of people from the countryside.[37] Within some population groups in the Nordic countries, old ideas of honor have led to serious acts of violence against women.

Fadime fought against these ideas. Many will carry on her struggle. We need to understand the forces they confront. The limited and specific concept of honor that I have developed here should help us to do so, without stigmatizing any one group. People bound by codes of honor are caught and held by wearisome constraints. The perpetrators are often victims too. Fadime realized this. She said, "Poor Daddy."

Let us hope that our narrowly defined concept of honor will help us expand our understanding in ways that will benefit the community as a whole.

5 The Cross-Cultural Context of Honor Killing

Honor killing can be found across religions and faiths. It happens among Christians, Muslims, Hindus, Buddhists, and others, as well as among people who confess to no particular religion or have no religious beliefs. Diki Tsering, the mother of the Dalai Lama, writes in her autobiography that in Amdo, her native region of Tibet, a woman would be killed by her own family if she had been unfaithful. "Such was the penalty."[1]

In other words, honor killing is a matter of tradition rather than religion. The story told by the Dalai Lama's mother dates back several decades. We do not know what happens in Amdo nowadays, and that need not concern us now. The point is that it is mistaken to believe, as many do, in an exclusive link between Islam and honor killing. True, Muslims do commit murder in the name of honor, and some Muslims claim that the teachings of Islam justify such acts. Muslims are far from alone, though. Christians, Hindus, Sikhs, Confucians,[2] and others also have maintained traditions legitimizing honor killings; and some still do.

But because the West is more involved with Muslims than with the other groups, we know more and have better documentary evidence about honor killing among them. I did not know about murder for family honor in rural Tibet until I read the biography by

Diki Tsering. She does not use the words *honor killing*, but the local norms applying to the behavior of young women when she grew up sound interchangeably similar to those we know are operating in strict, conservative Muslim communities.[3]

So honor killing occurs in certain groups, living in certain regions or localities, and even within such communities there can be much disagreement about the justification for carrying out an honor killing in a given situation. As Nicole Pope observes, "In spite of the pressure of tradition, and above all the pressure of the community, some families manage to stand firm and resist the call to do 'the right thing' and cleanse their honor. Others will kill without hesitation, believing it is the easiest way out of a scandal that had a disastrous impact on their lives."[4]

The incidence of honor killings is presumed to be greater in rural settings than in towns and to be more common among poorly educated people than among highly educated people. However, we have too few studies to draw any definite conclusions. With increasing urbanization worldwide, it may well be that the locus of honor killings today is as often an urban site, a town or city, as a village or camp. This is certainly true of the European scene: the majority of honor killings take place in cities and metropolitan areas. Many of the perpetrators are urbanites of long standing; they didn't arrive from a village only yesterday. And though some have close connections with their tribal home region, tribes themselves are mainly settled in urban settings nowadays. So the presumption that honor killing is a rural phenomenon has no solid basis.

Nor do we know enough about the role of education. Honor killing is presumed to be less likely among better educated than among poorly educated people. One study from Lebanon showed one-third of perpetrators to be illiterate or to be working in jobs requiring physical labor.[5] But we also know of well-educated, high-status families that have resorted to honor killings. More studies are needed if we are to draw any firm conclusions regarding the relationship between education and honor killing.

A recent study from Turkey illustrates stereotypes and attitudes that may be prevalent elsewhere as well: "Interviewees in Istanbul, especially Istanbul natives, discussed honor killings as a rural problem. . . . Their position was more like that of a distant observer, analyzing a problem that belongs to 'others.'" Surprisingly, similar evaluations were made by young university students with an urban background living in regions with a high frequency of honor killings: "They stated that honor killings do not occur in urban settlements of their province, are a problem of rural areas and are changing over time."[6]

This is what many of us would like to believe, that it is a problem of "the other." This is what Fadime warned against: averting your eyes from those who seem less developed, more tradition-bound than yourself.

Indeed it is hard to tell how much social standing or class matters. High status can mean that more is at stake, making it especially important to "cleanse yourself of shame." But high status can also mean greater freedom, because well-situated families have more room for maneuver. A Pakistani woman who had been given asylum in Norway because she married the man she loved against her family's protests observes: "The higher your standing in society—the more money you have or the more well known you are—the more honor you have to lose and the more tightly you keep the women in your family caged. I have no real evidence, but I think that at least in Pakistan, which is the country I know personally, honor killings are much more common among the elite than among people lower down in society."[7]

Even though honor is an absolute quality—a matter of either-or, as I have said—real life rarely allows people to be that definite. You have to exercise judgment and be ready to compromise. Status, prestige, reputation, class, or caste might affect the choices that are made by—or are forced on—an individual or a family. At present, we do know that honor killing is particularly widespread in certain communities living in Central and South Asia, the Middle East, North Africa, and Europe. We define an honor killing as a murder carried out in order to restore honor, not just for a single person but for a collective. This presupposes the approval of a supportive audience, ready to reward murder with honor.

Usually the killer is a brother, a father, a cousin, a paternal uncle, or a husband. In other words, the perpetrator tends to be a close kinsman of the victim, as we have seen in the cases of Sara, Pela, and Fadime. He comes from her family of birth rather than her family of marriage. Even after marriage, a woman's honor tends to be linked with her family of birth, and it is their obligation, since they brought her up, to effect a "cleansing of shame." But in some societies, Lebanon for example, practices are changing and the killer is more often a husband.[8] Due to the practice of intermarriage between cousins, husbands are often blood relations.

As to why a brother is usually preferred to a father, a Kurdish woman told me that fathers should be spared the experience. It is said to be too hard on them. The blood of a young man is hotter; he can more easily bring himself to carry out the deed. With age, men mellow.[9]

Some might object that it is meaningless to place honor killings in a separate category. Murder is not less terrible in particular contexts. But it must be said that systems dictating that a family should kill its own child—for the sake of honor—are special cases. Such a system offers the child no protection. It is also inhuman in the demands it places on the mother and father.

In the story I tell below, a father sits immobile at the site of his son's murder. It was an honor killing. The setting is the Indian state of Haryana and the year 1999.

"It's not worth getting upset about. This couple was guilty of a social evil. But it is over now. The village has already taken care of it."

This is a policeman speaking to journalist Barry Bearak, who had arrived in the village of Shimla in northern India to cover the murder of Desh Raj and Nirmala. Nirmala's family had killed them both on March 29, 1999.[10] Desh Raj and Nirmala had been lovers in secret for three years before 1999, when they decided to elope together. It was a fatal decision. Desh Raj miscalculated badly when he sought refuge with his brother-in-law, who lived in a neighboring village. The brother-in-law went behind his back and told on the young couple. They were hunted down two days later.

The girl's father and fourteen other family members were arrested and charged with the killing. A few days later, Nirmala's mother told the journalist: "My daughter ran away and our whole family was humiliated. We killed her to protect our honor."

Desh Raj was twenty-three years old, Nirmala seventeen.

One man said, "Whatever happened had the support of the village." Still, outside his house Desh Raj's father sat immobile from first light to nightfall, grieving for his son. The boy's mother, Reshma, blamed the girl: "Why did she go with him? It's always the girl who instigates these things. And she knew this marriage could never be."

"Such a marriage is a crime against nature," the boy's older brother said. "A man and a woman from the same *gotra* are like brother and sister."

This was the crux: a marriage between Desh Raj and Nirmala would have been thought of as incestuous. A *gotra* is like a clan, in which all the members are descended from the same tribal ancestor. It includes everyone living in a particular village—in this case, some seven thousand people. Regardless of how distant relationships between individuals are in reality, they are regarded as brothers and sisters. Because of this, young people must find marriage partners from outside the village. Any other choice would be "a crime against nature," as that man put it.

This is not traditional in all of India, or among all Hindus. It is a specific system or set of rules that apply in Haryana and certain other Indian regions.[11]

All communities develop rules about love and marriage. In India, these vary from region to region and from one village to the next. In the south, marriage between people in the same village is common, and even first cousins may marry. But Desh Raj and Nirmala did not live in the south. Their homes were in Haryana, where spouses must have been born in different villages.

Don't think, though, that honor killing was inevitable in this case. There were ways to avoid it. People in the village did what they could to find an amicable settlement. The moment the couple's hiding place was revealed, the village elders were called to an urgent meeting. Their judgment was that Desh Raj must leave Shimla and live in exile for five years. Nirmala was allowed back, presumably on the assumption that her parents would marry her off, which meant that she too would leave town.

The couple was told and the girl was taken back home. The young man despaired and eventually got very drunk. In this state he went to Shimla and stood outside the front gate to Nirmala's home, shouting, "I want my wife!" That's how the story goes.

The village council was called again, but before the meeting could start, the girl's family was on the move, picking up sticks and scythes on the way. Some say that members of the boy's family supported them, though they deny it. Some wondered later about the murder of the girl: was it part of the plan or an afterthought? One village elder said, "I think after they killed the boy they may have realized: if we don't kill the girl, people will think this is unjust."

The dead boy's mother said that both of them might well have deserved it, but the killings happened too quickly. People behaved like a lynch mob. "Even when you want to kill a dog, some people will oppose it. But when my son was killed, no one cared."

She also spoke of pressure on the family to withdraw charges against the killers. "We are told the important thing is that everyone live together in peace."

The policeman interviewed by the journalist opined that too much attention was being paid to a small matter. "Such vigilant justice is rare, but it happens," he said. "These things must be allowed to take their own course."

The story of Desh Raj and Nirmala is important for several reasons. It demonstrates the danger of stereotyping: it is not Hindus, or Indians, who typically kill for honor's sake. It is not even generally true of people from the northern states, or from Haryana, although the record for Haryana, admittedly, is not favorable. The story also shows that the local population did try to engineer a peaceful outcome. After five years in exile, Desh Raj would have been allowed back. However, the young couple would have to break off their relationship.

The forbidden love between Desh Raj and Nirmala had flourished for three years before they were killed, despite the families' suspicions. It was the public breach of norms that called for an urgent response. The affair could have ended differently if Desh Raj had not gotten drunk and insisted on seeing "my wife"—within earshot of everyone in the street.

Honor is a public matter. The recurring theme in all documentation of honor killings is how things are seen: "image" or "appearance" is crucial. As Samia Sarwar's father, a senior civil servant in Pakistan, put it, "We always tried to keep things covered." Samia was shot, at the instigation of her family. She died in the office of her lawyer, Hina Jilani, in Lahore, during a consultation about how to get a divorce to end her long-standing, violent marriage. The gunman was brought into the lawyer's office by Samia's own mother, a gynecologist. The family had taken Samia back and supported her—but would not let her seek a divorce. Her father is at pains to let people know that he is a liberal.[12]

And so he is, from one point of view. Taking a daughter back to protect her from an unhappy marriage *is* a humane thing to do, especially in a society where such acts are far from usual. Many insist that young women should learn to put up with misery and violence for the sake of honor. Suffering and endurance are woman's fate. Probably Samia, like Fadime, paid with her life for refusing to accept her family's ultimatum: she must lie low for the rest of her life and never divorce. "We always tried to keep things covered," her father said. Fadime had to disappear out of sight—that is, leave Uppsala. Desh Raj was stay away from Shimla for five years.

What do we know about the incidence of honor killings worldwide? UN estimates are that every year some five thousand persons die in honor crimes, but the criteria it uses are not clear. Cases of "passion killing" or "jealousy killing" may be included. This is understandable. In some areas, Latin America for instance, "passion killings" perpetrated by jealous or provoked husbands are clearly honor related, as are many murders of wives or lovers in Scandinavia.[13] But I have made a case, as have many others, for singling out as a special category the premeditated murders perpetrated by a person's, usually a woman's, collective kin group for the sake of restoration of family honor. Some estimates are that the numbers run to more than five thousand female victims a year. I have seen no attempt to count how many men die in honor killings worldwide.

problems in studying

There are several reasons the statistics are questionable. Murders are often not recorded by motive. Israel is one example: classification of murders according to the motive was introduced first in 1992.[14] Such classification still is not done in many of the countries where honor killing is a widespread practice. Many such murders are not reported or are covered up as accidents. The corpse of the victim is simply done away with and the name of the dead one not spoken again in the community. A Norwegian Kurd from eastern Turkey told me that in his home region, the saying "she's gone to Istanbul" was a euphemism for "she is killed." Everyone knew what it meant.

Honor killings may also be camouflaged as suicides. Indeed, "suicide killing" is emerging as another concept for honor killing. Both Turkey and Iraqi Kurdistan report an increasing, even accelerating, rate of suicides among young women since new legislation was introduced imposing more severe penalties on perpetrators. One observer notes: "Killers have, thus, adjusted to legal reform."[15] Also in Britain, where Asian girls have a suicide rate of three to four times higher than other girls, it is suspected that several of these deaths are covered-up honor killings, or girls driven to kill themselves.

A study from Palestine (the West Bank) illustrates the problem of researching the prevalence of honor killings: The district attorney had files on "deaths resulting from suspicious circumstances and criminal acts," but the research team's review of the files "did not yield a single crime classified as 'crime of honor.' Rather, three categories were used: 'fate and destiny,' 'murder,' and 'unknown.'"

Nearly 90 percent of the total female deaths in the files were in the first category—a broad category indicating that the person may have died a natural death because her time was up (God's will). But, the researchers note, ~~the girls were young, most in their early twenties or younger~~.[16]

Local police may well sympathize with the killers, even in societies in which honor killing is officially regarded as a crime. As our policeman in Shimla said: "It's a lot of fuss about nothing much."

Nothing much, an honorable act, an emergency response—these explanations don't seem to match up. Honor matters a great deal. The emergency is acute, a matter of life and death. But from a legal point of view—in certain countries or regions—to kill a woman or a man for the sake of honor is "nothing much." It doesn't attract any attention from the authorities. The media and the state shouldn't root around in such matters. The state has no call to act; it is up to the people directly involved. This is particularly so in places where the state is weak, but strong states may also choose not to interfere. Honor and law exist side by side, in a symbiotic relationship. The systems are opposed but often act in harmony. A man of honor is elevated above the law; he is a law unto himself. In many societies the punishments for honor crimes are light, a fact that makes taking the law in your own hands a relatively easy choice.

I have noted the UN working estimate: annually, about five thousand persons die in honor killings. Of necessity, the figure is approximate. This is also true of the statistics produced by certain countries—insofar as any are collected at all. Let us examine some examples that give an indication of the size of the problem in different countries.

In Britain, in 2006, there were twelve honor killings, according to the Home Office. Six took place in metropolitan areas. Most of the victims were of South Asian or Middle Eastern background. They were Hindus, Sikhs, and Muslims. The Metropolitan Police is now examining 117 cases suspected of being honor killings. They are classified as murders "motivated by perceived dishonor to a family or community." The murders took place between 1997 and

2005. Commander Andy Baker tells the media, "We are not reinvestigating or reopening the cases. Many have gone through the courts with convictions. It is a matter of looking at them, learning from them and working with agencies to prevent them in the future."[17]

The first man in British legal history to plead guilty to an honor killing was Abdullah Yones, who had killed his daughter Heshu, sixteen years old, in October 2002. The family was from Iraqi Kurdistan. Heshu had fallen in love with a Christian Lebanese boy. Abdullah Yones pleaded with the court to hand down a death sentence for him. He had been in hospital for four months after the murder, severely injured, as he had tried to kill himself by slitting his wrists and jumping from a balcony. The judge could give him only a life, not a death, sentence. Heshu's case shows the terrible price the community exacts of a man who feels bound to kill his daughter. But her fate is the more tragic. Her case became an eye opener. "Honor killing" became an established concept in Britain only after the case against her father.

In Germany, human rights organizations report that there have been forty-five honor killings in 1996–2004. Six of these took place in the course of four months, between October 2005 and March 2005. All were in Berlin.

Just as in Britain, the German experience involves a particular murder that had the effect of opening the nation's eyes. Hatun Sürücü, killed in February 2005, is the German "Fadime." She was a twenty-two-year-old mother of a young son, divorced from her violent cousin-husband from a forced marriage, and finishing her education as an electrician. Her seventeen-year-old brother killed her with his two elder brothers standing by. The two were charged with him but acquitted for lack of evidence. The case has raised an outcry and was to be heard in the Supreme Court in August 2007. The perpetrator was sentenced to nine years in jail plus deportation after serving the sentence. The family was originally from Turkish Kurdistan but had lived in Germany for more than twenty years. Hatun had been born in Germany.

In the Netherlands, twelve to thirteen honor killings take place yearly, according to the police. Ayaan Hirsi Ali has played a crucial role in the Netherlands in alerting the authorities to the problem of honor crimes.

In Israel, in 2006, twelve women were murdered for reasons of family honor. All the victims were Arab: Muslim, Druze, or Christian. In 1987, a case involving a Jewish community was reported. A rabbi tried to resist community pressure to kill his adulterous daughter; her husband too wanted her to live, but in the end the father gave in after being publicly condemned.[18]

The authorities in Israel have been criticized for turning a blind eye to honor killings among the country's Arab citizens. Several researchers and human rights and women's rights activists contend that political interests lead the authorities to look leniently upon such crimes in their Arab communities.[19]

In Palestine, in 2006, seventeen women were reported killed in honor crimes, twelve in the Gaza Strip and five in the West Bank. A case from April 1, 2005, involved a Christian girl, Faten Habash, murdered by her father. Like Fadime, she had fallen in love with the "wrong" man, in this case a Muslim. A Bedouin leader in the city of Ramallah who tried to mediate between the families of the couple observes: "Nobody from the Church has publicly condemned the murder. I believed that because of all the media attention, the Church would signal its attitude and distance itself from this kind of action. But I understand that the Church has chosen to turn a blind eye to Faten's fate."

In Pakistan, the number of honor killings is estimated to run to more than one thousand annually. In Punjab province alone, at least 1,578 women were killed during 1998–2003. The unrecorded deaths are likely to be many more. Amnesty International estimates suggest that thousands of women are killed nationwide every year. In 2001 Amnesty strongly criticized Pakistan's apparent lack of political will to curb honor-related crimes against women, such as murder and serious violence. "In Pakistan," the report concludes, "at least three honor killings are carried out every day." It also points out that "honor killings, forced marriages and other violent acts against women are on the increase in Pakistan, despite President Pervez Musharraf's repeated public statements that such crimes are against the law and that the perpetrators will be punished."

As with Desh Raj, men too can be victims of honor killings. In Pakistan, official figures indicate that roughly one-third of the victims are men, but that proportion varies from region to region. The ratio of men to women is highest in the tribal areas in the North West Frontier Province and Baluchistan. Here, male victims constitute about 40 percent of all cases. It is a telling fact that the courts convicted murderers in only about 7 percent of all cases.[20] Pakistan, like several other countries, has no state prosecution for family murder. It is up to the next of kin to decide whether they want to file charges. In cases of honor killings of women, they usually will not. I assume that most of the cases that received a court sentence were brought by the families of male victims murdered by the woman's family because of an illicit love relationship; the records do not say.

In Pakistan too, victims come from different religions. Tahira Khan, who has done extensive research in Pakistan and India, observes, "There have been many cases of honor-related murders of young Christian girls by their families reported in the media in the last twenty years."[21]

Speaking of India, should dowry deaths be regarded as honor killings? The view of Asma Jahangir, UN special rapporteur for freedom of religion and belief, is that dowry death is a form of honor killing because the bride's in-laws often stand silently by as the woman immolates herself, and they do not try to prevent it. If dowry deaths were included with honor killings in international statistics, the numbers would rise dramatically.

Reports from Turkey indicate that honor killings are on the increase there too. Official sources report seventy such murders a year, but it is estimated that the real numbers are much higher. The majority of honor killings take place in the Kurdish region in the southeast, but the conservative Black Sea Region also has a bad record in this regard.

As for the reasons for the increase, several researchers point to the increased migration from countryside to town and heightened conflicts between generations. During the last fifty years, the proportion of the Turkish population living in towns and cities has increased from 25 to 75 percent. The older generation stands by traditions, which are in conflict with young people's—notably young women's—wish to be liberated. Pinar Ilkarracan, leader of a human rights organization in Istanbul, has said, "Both urban settings and television have meant that young Turkish women are becoming steadily better educated and more exposed to a world beyond Turkey. Daughters rebel against parents who refuse to let them meet boys, make their own choice about whom to marry and be in touch with friends outside the four walls of the family home. Increasing social pressure on both generations has led to an alarming rises in domestic murders and other brutal forms of violence." A Norwegian newspaper rightly comments: "A bloody price for women's liberation."[22]

But the conflict is not just, or perhaps not even mainly, between generations. A recent, extensive study reports: "Most of the time young men were hard-liners while the middle aged seemed to be comparatively tolerant. . . . It was observed that with age came some degree of increase in tolerance." Further, "On the whole, women were not as sectarian as men, particularly young men, in matters of honor."[23] These are important findings, even though one should be careful not to generalize, as the study underscores. In other parts of Europe as well, it seems often the case that it is younger men, rather than the elderly males, who are guardians of honor.

The Turkish penal code regarding honor killing was changed in 2004. Before 2004, while the punishments for "ordinary" murders were either life imprisonment or execution, a killer was treated with more leniency if the deed was "a matter of honor." Minors were likely to get a maximum of two years in prison. In 2004, when Turkey was about to apply to join the European Union, it had to reform the law with regard to honor killings. Honor was no longer acceptable as an extenuating circumstance; murder is murder. However, there is ample documentary evidence that some regional courts continue with the old ways.

The Turkish penal code does not use the term *honor killing*. Instead, the term used is *custom/moral crime*. According to the new penal code, moral killings are seen as an aggravated circumstance for murder crimes. Imams have now been engaged to speak out against such crimes. But the evidence is that such crimes continue as a major problem. Murder trials are often hampered by a lack of witnesses. Canan Arin, member of the Istanbul Law Society and head of its Center for Women's Rights, states, "Witnesses refuse to speak up. The court has to rely on what the perpetrator says, and that means that the sentence is reduced to the minimum penalty, even though the charge is premeditated and cold-blooded murder."[24]

In many countries, state denial of honor crimes and honor killings is a major problem. Jordan is an exception. Jordan, where an estimated twenty-five honor killings take place yearly, stands out as a country where the authorities admit that honor killing is a major problem and make active attempts to deal with it. Queen Noor and the late King Hussein have both played crucial roles in the move to place the issue on the political agenda. So too have human rights and women's rights activists in and outside of Jordan. Special mention must be made of the journalist Rana Husseini, who has received several international awards for her work to cover, and combat, honor crimes.[25]

They have all had to deal with considerable resistance. The tradition is deeply rooted and seen as part of the defense against the secularization and immoral influence of the West. "I am accused of making our country promiscuous," Asma Khader says. Khader is a Jordanian lawyer who has led the push to strengthen the laws against honor killing.[26]

Empathy for honor killing is built into the law. A man can be declared not guilty if he has killed a female relative because she was unfaithful or had sex before her marriage. If he can convince the court that he killed in extreme rage (or "fit of fury") , the sentence may be exceptionally light: six months in prison. Premeditated honor killings rate a minimum sentence of one year in prison.

The Jordanian authorities have indicated that they intend to change such laws. King Abdullah II took the initiative, and the government put forward a proposal for criminal law reform twice during 1999–2000: all murders were to be judged on equal terms.

Clan chiefs and Islamists dominate the parliament, and on both occasions the reform program was voted down.[27] Bedouin chief Trad Fayiz put the majority attitude into words: "Within the family or the community, each woman is like a branch of an olive tree. If one branch of the tree becomes worm-eaten, it must be cut off to keep the rest sound."

When thousands of Jordanians demonstrated in the streets of the capital, Amman, in support of the reform, the Muslim Brotherhood—the largest party grouping in the parliament—declared a fatwa (a religious decree) to the effect that forbidding honor killing is contrary to Islamic law (sharia). "It would rob men of their right to react in a normal human way, should they surprise a wife, a daughter, or another female relative involved in sexual acts outside marriage," the fatwa stated. Zahra Sharabiti, a Jordanian barrister who has specialized in defending men charged with killing for honor's sake, has said, "We are convinced that the woman is responsible for the shame [in such cases]. She could have resisted the seduction."[28]

Such attitudes are widespread and cross cultural boundaries. We have observed that Desh Raj's mother accused Nirmala of causing the tragedy that befell the young couple. It is a widely held opinion that the woman is especially to blame for extramarital sex.

What makes the situation in Jordan so interesting is the openness of the debate. In this it differs from many other countries with a tradition of honor killing. One consequence is that we now can more easily discuss and analyze conditions relevant to both our general understanding of honor killing and the obstacles to reform. We have seen that in some sectors of the population and in Parliament there is solid resistance to criminalizing honor killing, that is, putting it on equal footing with other types of murder. The main reason is that honor killing serves a social good; essentially it is about self-defense and survival. "We don't think of this as murder," a twenty-two-year-old Jordanian man said, and his mother and sister nodded in agreement. "It was like cutting off your finger." He had killed his sister when he found her with a man. It had cost him four months in prison. A father who had killed his daughter in similar circumstances and been sentenced to two months in prison said, "Honor is more precious to me than my own flesh and blood."

Among those committed to bringing about a change in the law is a member of the royal family of Jordan, Prince Ghazi bin Mohammed. In a thesis on the system of clans and tribes in Jordan he writes: "Neither *sharia*, the Islamic law, nor the traditional laws of the Bedouins permit or defend so-called honor killings. There are no special allowances, for instance if a wife, daughter, sister, or other female relative had been proven to be sexually active before or outside marriage." Speaking of Islam and what it means, Prince Ghazi notes that although sharia does not exclude the death penalty for adultery, it sets strict standards for the evidence: four trustworthy witnesses must have observed the actual intercourse. And even when this criterion is met, "it is still not within the rights of the witnesses, the family, or any other layperson to carry out the punishment for adultery—it is the prerogative of the social authorities, in accordance with proper legal process."[29]

We will soon see that there are Muslim societies in which Prince Ghazi's statements are the established practice. One such is the Sultanate of Oman, an Arabian Gulf state. Women in Oman have a great deal of freedom. Honour killings are unheard of in Oman, just as in many other Muslim communities elsewhere in the world.

Regarding every woman in the family as family property is an essential premise for honor killing. To her family, a woman's worth depends on her chastity and respectability. Angela Pathak, who carried out a wide-ranging study on honor killing in Pakistan on behalf of Amnesty International, writes about "women as a commodity, like money, or cattle, or buildings." Shala Haeri, an anthropologist, uses a similar analogy: "In Pakistani society honor, *izzat*, is intimately tied in with the sense of a male 'natural' right to possess and control womenfolk. . . . Men possess honor, just as they possess gold and land—the three elements that are said to be the most sought-after commodities in Pakistan and therefore to be at the root of all conflicts. . . . It follows that women cannot own honor in the same way as men. They represent honor; they symbolize honor; they are honor."[30]

Haeri points to another problem: rape used intentionally to damage the honor of a political opponent. This is a familiar part of warfare: to rape an enemy's woman is to demean him utterly. But rape is also used in peacetime to humiliate another man and his family or community. It works every time, precisely because men's honor depends on the sexual purity of women. Raping a man's woman (or women) is the ultimate humiliation.[31]

I mentioned earlier that until recently fourteen Latin American countries had laws permitting rapists to go unpunished if they married the victim. Marriage restored the honor of the raped woman, and therefore of her family. In cases of gang rape, the law in Peru stated that if one of the guilty men married the victim, the rest of them would go free. In Costa Rica the rapist would also escape punishment if he offered to marry his victim, even if she said no.[32] Significant pressure was brought to bear by human rights organizations, and now the laws have been changed in most of these countries, though it is hard to be certain about how things are working out in practice. Popular concepts of justice tend to persist, and local courts can make their own bylaws. In Egypt, a similar law on rape was actively applied until 2001: a rapist went free if he married the woman he had violated. Leading religious authorities demanded law reform, and now rape is a criminal offense. In the Middle East, this reform makes Egypt a pioneering country. Many other countries only very recently got rid of laws similar to the old Latin American ones.

Such ideas about honor exist across religions and regions. It is also true that within regions, and among people of the same religion, differences in practices and beliefs can be huge. On the Arabian Peninsula, Saudi Arabia and Oman are neighbors but are as different as night and day when it comes to women's liberty and rights, including the right to protection against violence.

But it is also true that there are similarities across religious groups living in the same region. In Egypt, for instance, honor killings are reported among Copts as well as Muslims.[33] In India, they occur among Hindus, Sikhs, Muslims, and Christians, as well as among people of tribal religions. In Yemen, a Muslim society with a Jewish minority, honor killings were also reported among Jews.[34] The salient factor seems to be traditions, which are often shared in certain regions, regardless of religion.

The problematic aspects of honor are embedded in cultures, traditions, and power politics. We define culture as the sum of values, attitudes, and ideas—all that lies "behind" our acts and is expressed in our behavior. A brief definition of culture is that it is "your way of seeing, not what you see."[35] "Honor is more precious to me than my own flesh and blood" expresses one such way of seeing the world. Honor is a cultural prism, a pair of spectacles: looking through the lenses, you see specific circumstances in which honor is more important to you than the life of your daughter or sister or mother. This is a mode of being-in-the-world with its own internal logic. Others in your community agree, though not necessarily about everything. Nor is it true that one's lenses for observing the world cannot change. I am by no means implying that behavior is a product of culture. Individual human beings think, feel, reason, and choose—everywhere. Honor killing may be on its way out, as in some communities, or in, as elsewhere (the Nordic countries, for instance). In every case, this is the result of people's active participation.

Structures can be changed, as can mindsets. Culture is changeable. Fadime flew the flag of change. She lost. The race is not lost, though. As well as brave individuals, there are organizations and agencies working to stop honor killings and protect potential victims in Jordan, Pakistan, Palestine, Peru, and Sweden—among other places. Men and women support change. This is not about women's fight for liberation but about human rights, fought for by both sexes.

Next we will take a look at a Muslim society in which to be honorable means to honor others. In this country, honor is a matter of respecting others rather than demanding respect for yourself. It is a humane concept, part of the culture of an exceptionally tolerant and charitable society.

In the mid-1970s I carried out the fieldwork for my doctoral degree in Oman, a sultanate in the southeastern corner of the Arabian Peninsula. Oman had been a kind of "Tibet of the Middle East": the country had been ruled by an eccentric sultan, Said bin Taimur, who distrusted everything modern and kept his country closed to outsiders for decades. In 1970, his son Qaboos bin Said removed the old sultan in a coup supported by the British. The country was still as traditional as any Muslim country anywhere. When I was granted a visa in 1974, the sexes were kept separate to an extreme extent. Women wore black facial masks (*burqa*) and long black cloaks (*abbaya*) whenever they had had to leave their home. When they went outside, they had to stay in quiet lanes, because main streets and market squares were male-only territory. A Western observer would assume that Omani women were uniformly virtuous, obedient, and submissive; but behind the facade I found a many-faceted reality. Women had a great deal of freedom, and breaches against the norms of chastity were not sanctioned for the simple reason that according to the general idea of honor, it was shameful to criticize others. Honor entailed showing respect and being hospitable. If anyone were to intervene when a woman had been unfaithful, that person should be her husband. But the absence of gossip usually meant that he did not know what was going on. Or if he did, he might well pretend ignorance and save his honor. That was the common scenario.[36] The "will not to know" is a well-known way of retaining honor, in Oman as in many other societies.

Things were different at the wedding ceremony, because that was the time when evidence of honor must be made public: virginity and manhood were both central. Even so, the reality was quite unlike my expectations. Oman surprises us—and challenges our ingrained perceptions of honor in Muslim societies.

6 / *Virginity, Virility, and Honor*

In the spring of 1974, my husband and I were living in a town called Sohar in Oman. Sohar is the reputed birthplace of Sinbad the Sailor.[1] One day marriage celebrations began next door. The house was the groom's family home, and we were invited to join the splendid three-day feast. On the third day, the party reached its high point: the groom and his companions drove down the coast to fetch the bride from her home. Safiyya was just thirteen years old, a girl who had never before even caught a glimpse of a man not related to her. Clothed in green from top to toe, her face covered by a veil, she was presented to the assembled guests. We could only guess at what she was feeling as she was carried off to this unknown place in order to take center stage in a drama that would end in marriage to an unknown man. No turning back now, we thought and felt for her. In most parts of the Muslim world, divorce is the husband's privilege. Like other women, this child bride had to get used to her new life and settle in—or she would have, had fate not intervened.

During the preceding three-day feast, the bride's family had had a parallel celebration at their home. Now the couple was escorted to the wedding hut, the *kille*. This was the place where they were to spend their honeymoon and get to know each other. Bride and groom had never met before: as tradition dictated, their first meeting was taking place now, after their guardians had signed the marriage contract. They would be considered properly married only after meeting in the *kille*, face to face for the first time, and consummating the marriage. A palm-leaf hut had been built for the occasion and splendidly decorated with textiles in glowing colors, mirrors, and silver jewelry loaned by the groom's female relatives. All this was to create an atmosphere of joy and abundance, which should favor the young couple's getting on well together. The silver jewelry would also keep away the *jinn*.

The couple would be left together in the *kille* for up to six days and seven nights before ordinary life caught up with them. In the *kille* they had no duties. All their meals were brought to them, and someone from the bride's immediate family was on hand to help. No duties—except one: they must be able to produce a blood-stained handkerchief, or preferably two: one for the groom's family and one for the bride's. The blood would prove that the bride had been chaste.

When, after five days, the bride's parents had not been shown a blood-stained handkerchief, they swung into action and marched into the office of the governor of Sohar to demand a divorce for Safiyya. The marriage contract was annulled and the bride's marriage gift (*mahr*) returned. The groom, who had paid for the wedding feasts, forfeited a great deal of money.

The test told against Safiyya and Abdullah. But Safiyya was blameless. Safiyya's "shame" was intact; that is, she was still a virgin. The thirteen-year-old girl had not had any opportunity to prove it though, because the groom had failed her. He couldn't pass his side of the test.

The girl has to show that her hymen is intact, but the boy must penetrate it. *Must*, at least in Oman, at least at that time. In the literature on virginity and honor, the fact that at the time of marriage the groom is under scrutiny as well as the bride tends to be disregarded. He is tested. He has to prove himself a man.

It is not easy for a man to meet everyone's expectations when an attentive public is following his every move. True, the walls of the *kille* are hung with plastic mats and lengths of fabric, and these dull the sounds a little. But knowing that the wedding guests are lined up outside the hut, eagerly awaiting a happy outcome, is unnerving enough to undermine a man's virility. My informants tell me that the audience cheers on the groom (I couldn't observe this, because it would have been improper for a young woman to spend the night with the men). The bride herself can be frightening: she is said to defend herself tooth and nail against the intruder. "But the next day she loves him, because she's his wife," my Omani women friends assured me.

It could be that my friends' stories about the cheering audience and marital skirmishes were exaggerated. But I was left in no doubt about where their sympathies lay. "Imagine, five days! Five days was all they gave him!" Twenty-five-year old Latifa was full of pity: "It's so hard for a man. Abdou didn't manage it for a whole week. But he said to me, Look, you aren't my wife just for an evening. We have a whole life in front of us." (Latifa's Abdou went on to prove the point: thirty-three years later, they are still married and are proud parents of twelve children.)

Did Safiyya's husband, Abdullah, speak similar words of wisdom? We don't know. Her family sent him packing regardless, with the blessing of the state. Under Islamic sharia law, impotence is a valid reason for a woman to divorce; in many societies, in fact, impotence is just about the only reason that permits a woman to divorce her husband. In Safiyya's case, it was a matter of annulment rather than divorce. She was a virgin afterward. Islamic marriage practices have several stages, and, as noted already, the process is not regarded as complete until the bride and groom have had full sexual intercourse. The marriage contract is a purely legal document. Marriage proper demands more than that.

My female friends were Saffiyya's cousins, but they still insisted, "*Lots* of men fail. Abdullah isn't the only one!" They added, "It's dreadfully shaming for a man. He won't dare to marry another woman from Oman. He'll pick someone from Egypt or Jordan. They're more modern."

This was true. By that time, a public test of virginity and potency was well on its way out; at least in the Cairo districts that I have known since 1969, many Egyptians, also of the lower class, had become "modern." Many couples were given an opportunity to sort things out between the two of them, as long as they could produce the evidence of the bride's chastity—two blood-stained handkerchiefs—in the morning. This approach to marrying was called the foreign (*afrangi*) way, as opposed to the people's (*baladi*) way. How the married couple had gone about producing the blood was their affair (this is still true today, because the demand for proof has not gone away). They have quite a few options, apart from the real article: blood from a nosebleed, for instance, or a cut finger. Even chicken blood will do. But this presupposes an agreement between the two partners, which is facilitated if they have chosen each other and want to live together. This is true of most couples nowadays, and such change was on its way already in the early 1970s. The old customs have shifted steadily in one direction, from arranged marriage (promoted with varying degrees of pressure and force) and toward the love match (*gawaz ilhubb*). A love match means that groom and bride have chosen each other and that before the marriage they have had opportunities to meet and get to know each other, even if under the watchful eye of a chaperone. They spend the wedding night alone in their own rooms, a relief for bride and groom alike. My friends in Oman call it "the modern way."

Of course, to deflower their bride in public had been a struggle for Egyptian men too. I have heard many stories about men who could not, for the life of them, rupture the hymen, with a finger—as was the norm—in the full view of a team of female relatives. Then, to deafening applause, one of the women would step forward and watch as the blood flowed. With any luck. If the family had suspected that all was not in order, perhaps because the bride-to-be had confided in one of them, there were other solutions: an artificial hymen, maybe a blood-filled plastic bag pushed up the vagina. No one wants any trouble.

[handwritten margin note: Can avoid divorce.]

My intention with these stories and examples is to cast a new light on honor and chastity. Safiyya's case is not unique. Virginity and virility are two aspects of the same phenomenon. It generates a range of problems in most societies where public proof of virginity and manhood is required. My research in Oman (1974–76) opened up a new world to me. I observed hitherto unreported aspects of marriage customs. In Western perceptions of the Middle East, chastity was—and still is—the crucial issue. The real picture has many more shades and complexities. We need inside information from behind the social facades in order to detect and get the measure of men's dilemmas and agonies. My women friends in Oman pitied Abdullah. "Five days! Imagine, only five days . . . the poor man."

To report failures of virility is obviously not in men's own interest. Analyses of gender roles in the Muslim Middle East bore the hallmarks of masculine bias until well into the 1970s; most researchers were male. Then more and more women began working in the field, and by now the stereotypes are coming apart. In literary fiction, plays, and films, "insider reports" by both men and women have been just as important challenges to Western conventional wisdom. But even today we know very little about the real dramatic tensions and anxious choices that emerged in my telling of Safiyya's story.

Practices in Oman have been changing since then. It wouldn't surprise me if men had driven these changes. But I had no opportunity to return to Oman between 1976 and 2000 and observe the process. I have seen only the end result: a traditional set of south Arabian marriage customs disappeared, and with them went a truly demanding trial of manhood.

If the groom failed, he was badly shamed. A foreign marriage partner was in the cards, and he would also have lost out financially. True, his bridal gift would be returned, though here I'm on uncertain ground: possibly he got only the portion that was not "under the table." Already early in the 1970s, Oman and the other Gulf states had introduced an upper limit on bridal gifts, to stop what had become rampant inflation in response to excessive demands by brides' families. This law had only limited effect. Many evaded it and paid on the quiet. But because such deals are sensitive matters, I have had no chance to check what actually happens in the case of a groom's being sent packing because he is impotent. What options would he have in negotiations with his ex-wife's family?

What we do know for certain is that his honor was lost—honor, that is, in the sense of social standing. Presumably his self-respect also suffered. Here the relevant honor concept is the extended or vertical one: honor as worth in one's estimation and that of others. All the same, it is worth repeating that the audience was not united in making this judgment and that, in particular, the young women I talked with seemed genuinely sympathetic.

On the other hand, Safiyya's future looked bright. As a divorced girl and a virgin, she could carry her head high. She was a girl still, not a woman. In Arabic, the word for girl or maiden (*bint*) also means virgin. It was right for Safiyya. Until the next suitor turned up and succeeded, that is. Safiyya was only thirteen years old. Time was on her side.

(Some more fragments of her story: Safiyya did get married and then divorced. That time it was her fault. After some time as a married woman, she fell in love with another man. It is characteristic of social mores in Oman that her husband's family did not argue much: forcing the woman might be risky, as she might be unfaithful. I have heard that Safiyya is happily married now, for the third time.)

But in another case, a bride without a blood-stained handkerchief to prove her innocence had only herself to blame. It was said that she had had secret assignations with one of her cousins, while ostensibly going off to a grove of date palms on calls of nature (custom demanded segregation, so the women went to the palm grove while the men used the beach). She failed her test of virginity. Her would-be husband went off to see the governor and demanded a divorce. The judgment was straightforward: Let her go in peace. You, the groom, have a right to get the bridal gift back, but not the cost of the wedding. After going public, the man decided to keep her as his wife.

The code of honor in Oman is no stricter than this. It is not up to individuals but to society—the public authority—to intervene and, if called for, to punish breaches of the code. Oman's rulers exert powerful, authoritarian control and do not allow private acts of revenge. Humane ideas have gained ground. Since 1970, when Sultan Qaboos bin Said took over as head of government, the country has adopted a liberal, humanistic interpretation of Islam, which within certain limits allows women many freedoms. As some of them said back in 1974, "Even when the man has the right [*haqq*], the woman is given the right."

It is an essential part of the story I just told about the unchaste bride that, as time went by, she had to cope with her husband's taking two more wives. I haven't met a single Omani woman who would wish for such a fate. I cannot be certain whether the man gains honor, in the sense of prestige and reputation, from taking more wives. My best informants were women, and they disapproved. Still, women are not the most important audience for men.

Safiyya's story is worth telling in the context of a Scandinavian debate about hymen surgery. In 2001, ten ruptured hymens were restored in the Volvat Clinic, a large private medical center in Oslo. The practice was stopped at the request of the Norwegian Medical Ethics Council, but it was reintroduced a year later, also then against the request of the Medical Ethics Council but in response to the demands of girls in fear for their lives. A public discussion followed: some argued that the health authorities should pay for artificial hymens at the going rate of about 10,000 Norwegian kroner apiece (about $1,800). Others, both with and without immigrant background, argued that such practices must be banned. It is true that provision of hymen restoration "on the welfare" means that the state is lending support to ideas and actions that should be opposed. The goal should be to change the minds of parents and also of the young men, born and reared in Norway, who want to enjoy what life has to offer while denying their sisters and female cousins the same pleasures.

Rasool Awla, a male social scientist with roots in Iraqi Kurdistan, argued in a Swedish newspaper column that Fadime was not a virgin and that it was this, rather than her going out with a Swedish man, which sealed her fate.[2] The true cause of her family's dishonor was that her love for a man, with whom she could have had a sexual relationship, had become public knowledge. The point Awla wanted to make is clear enough: for girls to lose their virginity in secret is one thing, but it is quite another if they go public with the fact. When an affair of the heart becomes common knowledge, it amounts to "going public."

Safiyya's story tells us that honor does not follow the same pattern everywhere. In some traditional societies, including Muslim ones, humane attitudes can prevail, despite the strict rules about sexual behavior of girls and women. The problem is not inherent in Islam, or in Arabic or Kurdish culture, but exists in some localized groups—and these groups defend their views and abuse power in ways that must be curbed. In modern Europe, the lives of some young women are under death threat from relatives who insist on being in total control of their bodies. This is extremely serious. At the same time, it is important that we make such problems our own, without generalizing. They belong to particular places and are not simply "Muslim problems."

Or Christian, for that matter: Anna is a Swedish-Syrian young woman with an Assyrian Christian background. As a girl, she was not allowed friends of her own, she had to come home immediately after school, and so on. Anna says, "I am grateful for the upbringing I've had. But I wish that I had had a childhood more like other girls' and that I could have been a normal teenager. Among us it is not unusual for girls to be married off when they are only ten years old or, anyway, as soon as they reach puberty. You must be a virgin when you marry; it's an absolute rule. If you're not, the entire family is dishonored. Even nowadays the couple must be able to show a blood-stained handkerchief the next morning to prove to the bride's family that she had been chaste. Using tampons is totally forbidden."[3]

It could well be that attitudes among Assyrians in Sweden are more conservative than attitudes in Syria. In 1991 (six years before the interview with "Anna"), Bouthaina Shaaban, a Syrian professor of English literature, wrote, "Today, young men's attitude to virginity is changing (though no man would openly admit this), and is becoming quite relaxed and understanding." However, Syrian law grants the man immediate divorce and the right to a full return of his bridal gift if the bride is not a virgin.[4]

Shaaban's book begins with a scene that is etched in her mind. It reflects life in a small rural village. In the spring of 1968, Shaaban is on her way to school when she spots a classmate named Aziz. He is "joyfully descending a hill in the centre of the village, waving a dagger dripping with blood and chanting: 'I've killed her and saved the family's honor!'" He walks to the police station, hands the dagger to two policemen standing outside it, and says, loudly enough for everyone to hear: "I have killed my sister and have come to hand myself over to justice." The three of them stroll into the police station, chatting cheerfully.[5]

Aziz's sister Yasmin was fifteen years old. She had been sent off to Lebanon to work as a servant and eventually was "in a family way." The family was poor, and her wages had been a crucial means of support for her mother, a widow, and Yasmin's three older brothers, who all went to school. Yasmin had started in service at the age of seven. When she was brought back home, she was smartly dressed, as smart as any city girl, Shaaban tells us. The village girls admired her. Then the rumor that Yasmin was pregnant started making the rounds. No smoke without fire, her aunt said to herself; she went off to talk to Shabaan's mother about what to do next. Her advice was that Yasmin be seen by a doctor straightaway. The pregnancy was confirmed, and Yasmin was sent away again, this time to seek refuge in the home of the village chief (al mokhtar) in a neighboring village. She should have been safe there. Arabic custom dictates that a man must do everything, even risk death, to save the life of a person who has sought refuge with him. At night Yasmin slept between the man's two daughters in a shared bed. But *celebrate honor killing*

Aziz got in, and her companions awoke to a terrifying sight: Yasmin lying dead in a pool of blood.

Shabaan reports: "Unlike most criminals, who try their best to leave no traces behind, [Aziz] dipped his hands in the warm, innocent blood and went out triumphantly to celebrate publicly the cleansing of his honor."

His sentence was just six months in prison: "What is more, he emerged from prison with a mysteriously heroic air." As time went by, Aziz became one of the most important men in the village. After a trip to the Gulf to earn money, he returned and opened a bakery, "feeding the village people with bread made with the same hands that had cut his sister's throat and had been dipped in her blood."[6]

Yasmin was not given a funeral. Shaaban confirms that burial ceremonies are not normally held for victims of honor killings; they are outcasts, even after death.

In Shabaan's account of Yasmin's life and death, the women seem to be on the girl's side. The aunt finds a refuge for her—or at least so she thinks. Yasmin's mother gives her some sound advice.

This is a recurring theme in tales of honor killings: women try to protect women. But such is not always the case. Mothers are known to have entered into conspiracies to kill their daughters. Examples include the mother of Samia Sarwar from Pakistan (p. 76) and the mother of Basma from Palestine (p. 20). But it is hard to be certain about what people truly want and what they say after the fact of the murder. There is much to suggest a deep ambivalence: grief mixed with resignation. In the Indian case of Desh Raj, his mother is in this typically divided state of mind. "Maybe he deserved to die," she says, but then she adds, "It shouldn't have happened like that, without anybody trying to do something about it."[7] Fathers too often despair. Desh Raj's father remained immobile at the place of his son's death—it was stained red with blood that he could not see. He was blind. Maybe that was a kind of blessing. Could he have endured the sight?

A mother's tale of her anguish when her daughter risked losing her virginity and the dishonor that her behavior brought the family has been fixed in my mind, ever since the time when I spent several years living in one of Cairo's poorest areas as a "member of the family."[8] It was a story I was told several times, and I actually witnessed some of the events as they were unfolding.

Afaf was sixteen when she started staying away from home in the evenings. Her family had no idea where she might be and combed the streets to find her. Sometimes they would find her just sitting around in the home of a friend or relative, but at other times they searched in vain. When she came home, often very late, they punished her.

Her mother said, "She drove us crazy. We all had a go at her, me too. Her father beat her with his belt or one of his clogs. Her two older sisters pulled her hair and boxed her ears. Her brothers beat her up soundly. Nothing helped. We'd ask all these questions. *Where* have you been? Nowhere. What did you do? All we got was more nothings. When we asked why she's drifting about like that, she said home was sheer hell. Now I understand her better. She didn't know what she was doing. She suffered from a sickness of the nerves.

"We were terrified about what might happen to her. And ashamed that we should have to walk the streets and ask people if they had seen her. She made everyone of us into a laughing-stock. People would think that she was no longer a virgin. God forgive me, I am not sure myself any more."[9]

Did the family arrange to have Afaf checked? They did not, unlike the family of Swedish-Assyrian Anna, who was taken to a gynecologist to get the state of her hymen confirmed. Afaf's family took a more relaxed view. Maybe her mother simply told herself, "Tomorrow is another day." Maybe she thought they might as well wait to have her checked until Afaf was about to marry—it could be many years down the road. In the end, it was Afaf herself who decided to get official proof of her virginity. She wanted to marry in the traditional rather than the modern way; this meant that a witness would be present when her husband "took" her honor. I did not ask who actually performed the test: her husband or a female relative using her finger. As it turned out, Afaf *was* a virgin. This was in 1989, and Afaf was twenty-seven years old. She had chosen her mate herself, but she had listened to the advice of her brother and a brother-in-law, who was a friend of her prospective husband.

The stories in this chapter have been brought together to suggest the breadth of the spectrum of attitudes to virginity and honor in certain areas of the Middle East. Another aim has been to set our Western ideas and our public debate in a wider perspective. Also, I wanted to show that the tragedies of Fadime, Sara, and Pela must be understood within a specific context—not as reflecting the teachings of Islam or of some "traditional culture" but rather as the results of judgments made by people in certain specific situations, defined by a patriarchal social system and a tribal structure in which women are seen as the property of men.

What is honor? It is question that a young Egyptian journalist remembered from his schooldays. His biology teacher put it to the class but went on to answer it himself, after turning to a poster showing the female genital apparatus and pointing to the vaginal opening: "Here is the site of the family honor!"[10]

Such attitudes are widespread, found in societies in many parts of the globe. They are spreading in the Scandinavian countries—countries that rank at the top of international measures of gender equality.

A Turkish researcher observed that in her homeland the liberation of women has been paid for in blood. This is equally true of the Nordic countries today: some young women pay a bloody price for freedom. The conflict is between, on one hand, principles of gender equality and ideals of liberty and human rights and, on the other, collective clan structures that celebrate patriarchal rule. The sense of being embattled feeds on what many immigrants (and their native-born sons) consider an immoral society. It confronts them directly when their girls and young women want to be free and enjoy their basic human rights.

We are about to turn back to Fadime's story. It will help us to understand what is at stake and what path we must follow to avoid further tragedies.

III / *Fadime's Case*

7 | At a Trial

"Fadime is one of the martyrs of our time. Let us thank God for Fadime, that with her fearlessness, strength, and love of life she has given courage and strength to so many."

The canon's words must have sounded like blasphemy to some of those who attended the ceremony. The Sahindal family made up some 250 members of the congregation. At the court proceedings against Fadime's father in Uppsala District Court, no one in the family, with one exception, would testify. The exception was Fadime's sister Songül, who had broken with the family and appeared in court with police escort. She had been urged by the family, including her mother, not to take the stand. Songül, her little sister Nebile (thirteen), and their mother had witnessed Fadime's murder, which was committed in Songül's flat on January 21 that year.

The trial in Uppsala District Court took place between March 11 and 14, 2002—only seven weeks after the murder.

Their father, Rahmi Sahindal, admits in court that he shot his daughter. His account of his reasons and of the events leading up to the killing is coherent and consistent. He insists that Fadime was a whore. Her behavior shamed the whole family. To kill her was "the final solution." He knew that he could never rid himself of her by any other means. "The problem is over now."

But he is a father too. Surely no father wants to kill his daughter! He must be ill. He pleads with the court that he should be treated as a sick man. The court considers the psychiatric report in public: Rahmi Sahindal is not mentally ill, not even clinically depressed, but his emotional and intellectual development is poor. He reacts primitively and naively and lacks the ability to empathize.

No one in the entire extended family is prepared to step forward either to support or to criticize this conclusion. Three witnesses are called. All refuse to make statements. Rahmi had telephoned one of them, a cousin, to tell him about the killing. The cousin had contacted Rahmi's brother-in-law, who in turn phoned the police. This cousin now tells the court that he cannot testify against his own uncle's son, who is also an old mate of fifty years' standing. The judge explains that his refusal could be regarded as contempt of court and perjury. The cousin decides to stay in the witness box but remembers nothing, not even how and when he learned that Fadime had been killed.

The public prosecutor pushes him. "You must remember. That Fadime had been killed was a special event." The cousin replies, "There aren't any special events in my life."

Fadime's mother does not want to testify either. She can't bear it, she says. Besides, she has already told the police everything she knows. She is informed via her translator that the bench relies exclusively on what is said in court and will not have access to the police records. She won't budge. Songül glares furiously at her mother as she returns to her seat among the family members in the public part of the courtroom. During the next break in the proceedings the mother is seen weeping in the corridor, and the following days she stays away.

Fadime's maternal uncle backs out, stating correctly that he is too closely related to the accused.[1] The prosecutor exempts thirteen-year-old Nebile from testifying.

Now only the older sister is left to stand up for Fadime and honor her memory.[2] Songül creates a verbal portrait of Fadime as a courageous and thoughtful woman whose only sin was to want to live according to her own lights. She was twenty years old in 1996, the year she fell in love with Patrik. They wanted to marry, and in January 1998 Patrik's father and grandmother paid a visit to her parents to ask for their consent to the marriage. Rahmi seems to have been prepared to consider the match, but his wife was not. Relatives, both in Sweden and in Turkey, were consulted. Asked who exactly, Songül confirmed that they were all in on it: "You can't name them one by one."[3] The mother's brother advised against the marriage, because if Fadime were to be allowed her Patrik, all the girls in the family would want to marry Swedes.

The court is shown a TV interview from 1998, during which Fadime reveals that she was under pressure to marry a relative. Her meetings with Patrik had to take place in extreme secrecy. Patrik, who was interviewed too, says that at first he had exclaimed, "We aren't fourteen anymore, for God's sake!" Fadime understood that the make-or-break moment had come when her father saw them in the street: "If I chose Patrik, my choice would take me away from my family. This terrified me. Was I prepared to follow that road?" She talks of what a nightmare it was for her father to see his daughter with a Swedish man: "He would've broken my neck if he had got hold of me. . . . I know I've ruined the life of my whole family. No one will want to marry the girls in my family—they're all whores now."

She knows—it's no speculation, she truly knows—that she will have to live with murder threats "until their last breath. That's the only way for them to regain their honor, their pride." Fadime's insight into her family's mindset and culture meshes perfectly with her father's declaration in court: "It was the only way. The problem is over now."

She knew the risks but must have been hopeful; if not, she would hardly have made that journey to Uppsala four years later (January 21, 2002). Fadime had arranged to go to Kenya for six months of practical experience, a requirement for the final exams in her course in social work studies. She was ready to leave but wanted to say good-bye to Songül, Nebile, and their mother. Everything else was done and ready.

The murder took place in Songül's flat. The four women met there in great secrecy, as they had three or four times earlier that year.

It was important that the men in the family not know about their meeting. Her mother had baked Fadime's favorite pies for supper. The atmosphere was relaxed: they chatted and laughed together.

Rahmi Sahindal turned up on the landing outside the flat at about 8:30 p.m. He hammered on the door and shouted at them to open up. Fadime said they should let him in, but first she would crawl under the bed and pull the bedspread down. Her mother thought that locking herself in the bathroom might be a better idea; they could always say that the lock had jammed. Songül thought both options too risky. She was terrified of what Rahmi might do. They switched the lights off, hoping that he'd think no one was in.[4]

This exasperated him even more. He went back home and phoned Fadime's Östersund number four times (according to the records of his mobile phone company; Rahmi denied trying to contact her). Next he checked on his wife's whereabouts. She was not with a cousin she liked to visit. He pocketed a handgun and five cartridges before setting out again for Songül's flat.

Nebile and Fadime were leaving (their mother was to stay the night), but first Nebile peered through the peephole to make certain that all was safe. As she opened the door, her father stormed past her and shot Fadime at close range. The first shot hit the back of her head and killed her. She fell. He bent over her and placed another shot close to her mouth. Then he fired at her again but missed.

"You rotten whore!" he shouted, both before and after his deed. "Why did you have to come into my family?"

Rahmi admits to having been preoccupied with thoughts of murder during the previous five or six months, but he claims that "what happened," which is how he speaks of the killing, was spontaneous. He had no idea that "she, Fadime," was in Uppsala. He had gone to see Songül, who was unwell. Normally he visited her every third day (Songül states that her father had not been to see her for three weeks). By chance he carried his gun. He had owned that gun, a gift from his father, for thirty-two years; it was important to him. No, he can't think why he took it with him just that night. He never uses it, except at New Year's, when he goes outside to fire it in the forest (members of his family say they did not know he owned a gun). When he saw Fadime, he instinctively pulled out his weapon.

The prosecutor, Anne Sjöblom, asks Rahmi how the killing happened.

"It didn't take long after she opened the door. I saw her and fired." He never knew if the shots hit her. He remembers her falling and also that he saw his youngest daughter, his wife, and Songül inside the flat.

"Did you say anything? Did Fadime or anyone else say anything?"

"No. What was there to say?"

"Did anyone do anything?"

"No. What was there to do?"

But everyone started crying, he adds.

After the murder, he turned, ran downstairs (the flat is on the first floor), and then outside. His wife and Nebile caught up with him. He doesn't remember what they said. He stood under a tree nearby and watched as the ambulance came and then drove away with "that daughter who was dead." He hid in a small wood, called his mate Haydar (who remembers nothing at all in court), and told him, "I've done it now." Haydar asked him to go to the home of an acquaintance and stay there. Next Haydar phoned Cemal, Rahmi's brother-in-law and the head of the family. Cemal called the police. "That's how they arrested me." The time was around three o'clock in the morning, five hours after the murder. The records show that Songül had called emergency services at 9:54 p.m.: "My sister is dead! My father has shot my sister!"

The official tape is played in court, and they hear the screaming of terrified women in the background.

"Previously you've mentioned [in a police interview] your suspicion that Fadime visits Songül," the prosecutor points out. "You have also stated that Fadime called you two days earlier and threatened you with bringing her Swedish boyfriend to Uppsala and taking him to see you. Also, that she would notify the police, ask them to charge you and take your youngest daughter away from you."

"No, no," Rahmi protests. "I didn't know she'd be in Uppsala. She lived so far away. I didn't know." Later he repeats the story of how Fadime terrorized him over the telephone, not just two days before coming to Uppsala but frequently. She harassed him, even in the middle of the night. She persecuted him. When the prosecutor confronted him with the fact that there were no telephone records to support his claim, he stuck to his story: "She knew how to get hold of secret telephones!"

The prosecutor asks: "For how long had you been planning to kill her?"

"I never thought of doing anything like that," Rahmi replies. "But it's true that if she was there I had made up my mind to shoot her. There was no other way. It was the only thing I could do." He felt tormented and persecuted. Fadime had shattered the family. "She showed us up in the media for four whole years. I told her to go easy. Please, I said to her, don't go to the police and accuse us. You have your boy there, you're studying. . . . I kept begging her for two years. She wouldn't let up, it was she who kept destroying our family, she kept telling the media about us, she told the whole world. My son, who's only seventeen, was put in prison. All these Swedes came by and threw stones at my window. They shouted things. 'Fucking blackhead, go back where you came from!'

". . . It was the final solution. I knew I'd never get rid of her. . . .

"Afterward I thought of how I had hoped to talk to her and how maybe this wouldn't have happened if only . . ."

The prosecutor asks, "When did the problems start?"

"The problems started four years ago . . . when I saw her with that boy for the first time. . . . I begged her to come back home, but she never did . . . she tormented us all the time. . . . We all begged her to come back to us, all the time, but she wouldn't . . . then, no more contact. . . . Look, you have your boy to be with you, I said. Take it easy. But she kept going out with different men. I told the municipality and the police that she must stay away from Uppsala. But she came here and got my boy into prison and then she made my daughter Songül, she's twenty-three years old now, go along with her. . . . Later on, I said to her: 'My daughter, you do as you please!" She carried on and ruined our lives . . . all the time, she stirred up trouble.

"What would *you* do if your daughter kept going out with different men?" he bursts out to the prosecutor. Fadime provoked him. She kept calling and threatening him.

"She said, 'I'll come home and introduce my boyfriend to you!' It was just two days before she turned up in Uppsala. I'm not stupid, you know. Her behavior was awful. She said she'd take my [youngest] daughter away from me."

In Rahmi's version of events, Fadime is the perpetrator and he her victim.

"Listen, that Fadime . . . the way she behaved—if you had a daughter like that, you would have wanted to shoot her too!" he exclaims.

Rahmi's defense lawyer, Johan Åkermark, asks his client to explain more about the original conflict between father and daughter. Rahmi denies that he wouldn't accept a relationship between Fadime and a Swedish man—however, that was what he had stated in the 1998 trial, which ended with his and his son's conviction for threatening to kill Fadime. This time he insists that he never stood between her and marriage to a Swedish man. On the contrary: "I told her a hundred times, calm down. She had picked him on her own, she can marry him. . . . I said to her, if that's what you want, off you go to church and marry him! But she was only twenty." He addressed the court, appealing to Swedish culture. "A Swedish girl of twenty getting married, did you ever hear anything like it?"

Surely Fadime was too young? Surely she was utterly unreasonable?

The families disagreed about who should pay for the wedding, Rahmi claims. Fadime wanted a big wedding with three hundred guests, just like her two older sisters. She demanded that her father should pay. Patrik's family thought he should too. But the Kurdish tradition is that the families share the costs.[5] Patrik's father had acceded to this, says Rahmi. "The boy's father said he agreed, but he didn't stick to it." The bench wants to know if it was true that

Fadime's family objected to the marriage. "No, not at all. . . . But it's nothing I've experienced before . . . that a foreigner marries a Swede!"

"People have wondered whether it was an honor killing," prompts his lawyer.

"No, that's not true, I'm not out for honor in Sweden . . . she has offended me badly and so I've gone and shot her."

He described himself after the shooting as remorseful. "No father draws a gun on his child. But when I saw her my thoughts went wild—that's why it happened."

More than four years passed between the first death threats against Fadime on September 3, 1997, and her murder on January 21, 2002. For Fadime, these were years of fear and anguish, but also of hope—hope that by going public she had increased her chances of survival. Four years that brought grief and pain. Patrik died in a traffic accident on June 3, 1998. He was driving from Stockholm to Uppsala in the streaming rain when his car went off the road, and he died instantly. It was the day that he and Fadime were to have moved in together.

The year had begun hopefully. On January 4, 1998, Patrik's father and grandmother had visited Fadime's parents to propose on his behalf. Fadime's parents might have accepted (as a matter of fact, Fadime's mother and two older sisters had been parties to her secret relationship with Patrik), but it was not for them to decide. The larger family, the clan, turned the refusal down. One week after their pronouncement, her mother told Fadime that the family had cast her out and she had to leave Uppsala.

Four months had passed since that fateful day when her father had seen her with Patrik, September 3, 1997. Afterward Fadime did not dare to go back home. Two policemen escorted her when she collected her passport and other personal things there. She was saved by her social work course in Sundsvall, a three-hour train journey northward from Uppsala, although, as she said, "in my case, leaving home to study is just as big a crime as having a Swedish boyfriend." (Songül tells of how the family had hid the letter from the university that confirmed Fadime's admission.)

After the marriage proposal from Patrik was refused, Fadime's father and brother started phoning her and threatening her life. She reported them to the police, and on February 4, the police brought charges. Her father and brother were convicted of threatening to kill her. The sentence was passed on May 7, 1998.

Earlier in the spring, Fadime and Patrik had agreed to be interviewed on Swedish TV about their forbidden love and the threats against Fadime. The program was broadcast on May 6, the day before the verdict against her father and brother. Less than a month later, Patrik died.

One week after Patrik's death, her brother attacked her again, this time in Central Square in Uppsala. If passersby had not intervened, he might have killed her then. She was taken to hospital with severe injuries. Another trial followed in August, and this time the brother was sentenced to five months in prison. Damages of 20,000 SEK (3,300 USD) were to be paid to Fadime—a sum that was also due to her according to the sentence passed on her father and brother the previous time. She had not forced the damages issue, in order not to subject her family to additional stress.

Songül had moved with her sister to Sundsvall, in September 1997, and later followed her when Fadime had to complete her studies in Östersund. Fadime adored Uppsala; it was the place she wanted to stay. But as noted, her mother had let her know that she was expelled. Now, in court, Rahmi admits to having said that he'd kill his daughter if she showed her face in Uppsala.

Her father defends himself by saying that he had told the police Fadime mustn't come back to Uppsala. The bench asks for clarification.

"What I said was, nothing will happen to her for as long as she doesn't turn up in this town."

"And if she did?"

"I was sick then . . . I didn't feel well. That's why I said what I said. And let the police know."

Fadime must not come back to Uppsala—this had become a theme, which is repeated once more when, at the last minute, the trial takes a dramatic turn and one of Rahmi's nephews suddenly claims to be the true murderer. The drama starts just as the prosecutor and the defense lawyer are preparing to plead. The trial has to be interrupted, which is exceptional at such a late stage.

The police report of the interview with Murat Sahindal, the nephew, states:

> He had wanted to shoot Fadime since 1997–98, when her brother was imprisoned and all the media uproar started. He had been out looking for her several times. Fadime was a whore. Rahmi had warned her that someone would kill her if she returned to Uppsala. She kept harassing Rahmi. She had said to him, among other things, that she would move back to Uppsala. She was a dishonor to the whole Sahindal family in Uppsala. Now their honor is restored. *Nothing would have happened if only she had stayed in Östersund.* Fadime shamed all of them. Murat has no regrets and would do the same thing again. Songül is a whore too.[6]

This declaration is not believed, and Murat is not asked to appear in court. Some of his relatives explain to the media that he stepped forward because he admired Rahmi and wanted to be regarded as a hero by the family. That's why he tried to take the blame on himself.[7]

His behavior is in line with "proper" honor traditions: it does not matter who takes the punishment; one is as good as the other. To take on the blame on behalf of someone else is a rational choice that can make a man a hero.

It is also true that Murat belongs to the inner circle of the Sahindals: his parents are a brother and a sister of each of Fadime's parents. Some members of the family think that he is a black sheep. He was on probation when Fadime was killed and stated that a mate had helped him disable the electronic ankle-tag so that he could go to Uppsala without the knowledge of the police.

Songül has testified that her father fired the shots, but she knows that the family is in on it. He acted deliberately. The murder had been planned. She had herself overheard several discussions between relatives, agreeing that Fadime must be killed. "That one should be done away with," her (maternal) uncle had said at one family get-together. "That whore must be put down," her father had said while out driving a year ago, overheard by Songül's mother, brother, mother's brother, and two sisters. Clear-eyed, straightforward, and poised, Songül explains the background story along the same lines as Fadime herself had done in the TV program four years earlier. She had said that killing her was "the only way for them to regain their honor, their pride." This was not one man's judgment but a view held by a whole group.

"It has to do with honor," Songül says. "Now that she's dead, they think that their honor has been restored."

During her time in the witness box, she never takes her eyes off her father. She outstares him, and for most of the time he looks down on the table in front of him; he also keeps his eyes lowered while a video with Fadime (and Patrik) is played.[8] Unless required to, he will not even speak of Fadime by name; instead he refers to her as "that daughter" or "that daughter who is dead."

Songül describes her father's voice as determined, but not angry, when he shouted outside the door of her flat that they were to let him in. He did not sound like a man driven to act by his flaring temper. "He had made up his mind."

By then, Songül says, Fadime had been made the scapegoat for everything that went badly for the family. Fadime had done no harm to any of them, but they blamed her all the same, even for Songül's illness. Songül suffers from bipolar disorder but says she knew it had nothing to do with Fadime. She thought it had to do with family intermarriage, like cousins marrying. Besides, she has had the illness since she was little.

Songül claims that she too had been pressured to marry a Kurd. That was why she left home in 1998, first to live with one of her older sisters and later with a friend, before moving in with Fadime. They had lived together until a year ago, when Songül was admitted to hospital. Since then she had stayed in a sheltered apartment in Uppsala. It was there that the murder took place. During the past year, Fadime, her two sisters, and their mother had met in her flat three or four times.

During Songül's statement, several male relatives roll their eyes heavenward and shake their heads helplessly. I had been shown to a seat in the family rows, and some of the men speak to me spontaneously afterward. All lies, they tell me; Songül is chasing media celebrity, just like Fadime. "The media have only managed to find one true thing to say about this business," a prominent member of the family insists. "Fadime is dead. The rest is lies." The whole thing has turned into a nightmare, not only for the family but for all Kurds in Sweden.

Other relatives have heard this and join us. They agree that the media aren't interested in their side of the story. They have tried to speak out, but there's no point. I suggest that maybe I could help—they shake their heads. Whatever they try to do backfires, they tell me. The media present them as monsters. It's tragic that Fadime was killed. Everything else is untrue.

One of Fadime's sisters dares to hint that being a woman isn't always easy, of course . . . Her remark isn't heard in the clamor of criticism of the media and their lust for celebrities.

How can the court take what Songül says seriously? She is sick in the head, after all. While Songül has made a deep impression on most of the listeners with her courage and her calm, thoughtful, and lucid statement, her relatives have heard a madwoman's tale. The media pretend to trust what she says only because they need a replacement celebrity to keep up their stream of abuse of the Sahindals and Kurds in general. Songül is playing to the audience.

"You have a look at this," one of the men says to me. "This is how they portray us in the paper!" He is pointing to a press photo in *Dagens Nyheter*, which shows one of the Sahindal men undergoing what is standard procedure for everyone attending the court: a strict security check, including a body search.

"And did you see Songül yesterday?" Songül's sister adds. "Walking past us under police protection! As if we would threaten her in any way!"

For a family intent on recovering its standing in society, I can hardly imagine a worse scenario than the intervention in the trial by the

nephew of the defendant. How wrong can you get? But the nephew's performance was in line with the traditional code of honor. As
we know, it has certain distinctive features: honor is a collective,
not an individual, property; clearly defined acts can cause the loss
or the recovery of honor; the alpha and omega of the family's honor
is the sexual propriety of its women, actual or by reputation; and in
the final instance honor can only be regained by getting rid of the
woman—that is, by executing her; an honor killing is conditional
on applause, or at least support, from the group audience.

Murat Sahindal may have counted on playing to his audience.
People have commented that he simply wanted to be a hero. True,
he may have misjudged the group's feeling about him: as someone
had said, he was the black sheep of the family. But even so, no one
stood up and contradicted his claim, which was so absurd it would
have come apart if just one of the summoned witnesses had spoken
up in court. Such a statement would have added significantly to
Songül's testimony, Rahmi's admission, and the forensic data indicating Rahmi as the perpetrator. As it was, reasonable doubt existed—enough for the court to make the extraordinary decision to
interrupt the trial and continue the police investigation. Whether
the nephew's initiative signified just the mindset of one "black
sheep" or the calculations of a group on whose advice he relied, its
effect was to diminish respect for the Sahindals among Swedish
people. The issue of social standing runs like a red thread through
the fabric of Fadime's case.

Rahmi Sahindal reminds us over and over again that it was the
media attitudes and Fadime's use of public channels—including
the legal system—that added up to her mortal sin. "It's about one's
honor, you know," he said, elaborating on how he was humiliated
in the eyes of his relatives, his neighbors, his friends and acquaintances—the eyes of the entire Swedish people. He had begged her
to spare him: "Don't show me up like this, to the media and the
police! At least fifteen people spat at me!" He no longer could bear
to get on the bus between his job and his home; he wanted to move
to a new place. He couldn't bear going to work, developed a heart

Physically deleted few. — (handwritten margin note)

condition, and in 1999 was declared disabled and unfit for work after sixteen years in full employment.

Rahmi addresses the court: "A grown daughter, twenty-six years old and studying at university . . . it is she who should help a father in my situation. What she has done to me, I don't know how I can explain it to you."

And I find it in me to sympathize with him, a human being who is a victim too, caught in a clash of cultures almost without precedent. I understand why Fadime said, "Poor Daddy!"

The prosecutor probes: "You tell us that the problem is over now . . . ?"

"I have many things in my thoughts," Rahmi replies. "The problem was Fadime, but now the problem is—what will happen? I'll be put in prison—and then what?"

"Do you feel relieved at all?" the prosecutor asks.

"Not relieved. Not so. But it was a problem. And the problem is over now."

I was shaken by the trial in Uppsala. Watching cultures on a runaway course toward collision was a thought-provoking experience. It brought home to me the sheer amount of *work* that remains before integration will be possible. I found it frightening, but as I saw it, the case was not enigmatic. Its very lack of mystery made it more terrifying. Even when the nephew stepped in and heightened the drama, his act was part of an overall, crystal-clear logic. And when the psychiatric expert reported that the accused was "primitive" and "naive," that too fit into the overall pattern. "Primitive"—in whose opinion? Rationality has many faces.

Uppsala District Court met again on April 3, 2002, to pronounce judgment. Rahmi Sahindal was convicted as charged and sentenced to the most severe punishment available in Swedish law: a life sentence.[9] He was also to pay Songül damages of 50,000 SEK (about 8,500 USD). The judge agreed with the prosecutor's pleading. The judgment states that the murder had the character of an execution and also that it took place under aggravating circumstances: a defenseless young women was killed in front of her mother and sisters, one of whom was only thirteen years old.

Rahmi Sahindal's conviction and sentence were truly disappointing both to him and to his family. They had hoped that Rahmi would be referred to the health service for continued care. Rahmi's entire defense had aimed at this: recognition that he was ill and needed care. The psychiatric expert did not agree.

Rahmi protested: "I am ill, but the doctor doesn't believe me!"

8 Little Sister, Thirteen Years Old

Nebile (pronounced 'Neh-bleh) was an eyewitness to the tragedy. She and Fadime had been about to leave together when their father suddenly appeared in the doorway. She cannot remember who opened the door. At first she tells the police she did it herself, but then she becomes uncertain—maybe it was Fadime. Anyway, Nebile had looked through the peephole to make sure that it was safe to go outside. And then there he was, in front of her.

"It was like, he was a ghost . . . I was so shocked . . . his hair was all messy and he looked kind of yellow and his eyes were red."

Her father had been shocked to see her.

He was mega upset, really shocked to find me there, I screamed and then, I can't remember properly if I grabbed hold of him and pushed him, or what I did, anyway then I caught sight of the gun, and I thought, well, I believed, just then I thought it was a toy gun . . . he was so pale, I didn't recognize him at all, I thought this man isn't my dad, it's someone else and then I thought, like real fast, what am I to do now and then—you know, when he grabbed her [Fadime's] hair, then my mother came running and pulled at his arm with the gun so it pointed at her and said, don't kill my, you see, what she thought was, don't kill her, you can kill me, kill me instead of her, and then I thought I'm dreaming, I said to myself, I pulled at my hair and it wasn't a dream and I was like, now what do I do? And I didn't know what I should do, but I went over and clung to him and everyone was tugging him, kind of trying and then there was a bang, and I thought there are balloons, like a balloon had burst, you know what I mean, if you take a pin and prick it, anyway I don't know if he shot her in the head, but what I heard was three shots, though in the news they said two, but I heard three, he fired three times, and then, I don't know if she fell but my mum says she fell straightaway. . . . I don't think she suffered, I don't think so, I think she died at once, and then, and then, when he stood there and I hadn't a clue what to do, but anyway, I went up to him and clung to him, and I thought he was going to fire, shoot again, and I held on to him and said "Fadime, run!" I said, "Fadime, go away!" She didn't go, she just lay there, and I thought, I thought, perhaps she's scared, she is in shock maybe, she won't get up, I wasn't going to kick her, but I touched her a little with my foot, I said "Fadime, Fadime!" She didn't get up and next, next, Mum ran outside, I don't know why she ran . . . I thought, where's she going now? I figured maybe she going to get help or something like that, and I thought . . . I thought she was shocked, I thought, perhaps she's going to kill herself now . . .

Nebile runs after her father, who has run out too and down the steps but stopped outside the block of flats. She catches up with him and grabs hold of him.

"There were so many thoughts, there was lots I wanted to say, but it wasn't the right time and not the right place, I just held on to him, I looked into his eyes, he too, our eyes met, no, I felt, no—he isn't my dad, it's another man, I thought, that's what I thought, he was totally unlike himself . . . he had tears in his eyes."

She wasn't afraid of him.

"I knew somehow, deep inside, that he'd never want to harm me or anybody else, I think he didn't want me to be there, he was ever so surprised that I was there . . ."

This idea of hers, that she shouldn't have been present, mattered a great deal to her. Later in her statement to the police, she returns to the theme:

"I heard that he had phoned Fatma, you know who I mean [one of her aunts] and told her that he'd wished, you know, anyway he said, 'I didn't really want Nebile to be there,' and he was like, 'I'm sorry she was there and had to watch all that,' he said . . . he wanted to do it on his own, but it didn't work out."[1]

Nebile had run after her father and grabbed hold of him, then released him. The police want to know what made her let him go.

"What made me let go of him? That's when I suddenly thought of Mummy, like, where's my mum now? And that's when I let go of him and he ran away."[2]

She describes her father running away: "He kind of flew, he flew, you know, he did fly, almost, and I walked about outside and I thought, where is Mummy now and I shouted and kept looking, behind stones and bushes and things, and I thought what I could do, Mum has gone . . ."

She returned to Songül's flat and phoned her sister Elmas: "I called, I said, she didn't get it at all . . . I said, 'Dad has fired his gun!' I tried to get her to understand, but she didn't, I said 'Dad has shot Fadime!' I told her 'Mum has gone away, she isn't here any more,' I said . . ."

Nebile had to let go of the phone because Songül needed it. She had contacted the police and was waiting for them to call back.

"I put the receiver back, I didn't even look at Fadime, well, I saw that she was wearing her light brown coat and that there were dark stains on it, or I don't know, where he shot her I guess, I saw that, but I don't think it [the bullet] got through, that jacket was too thick, I think, anyway I didn't really look at her, but I did in a way, I saw her face and there was blood in her mouth, it looked like blood I thought and then I just stood there for a bit and then I looked around. I said, 'Mum? Where are you?' No, you see, I didn't know where my mum was . . ."

It does not take long before the mother is back: "She came and comforted me, and said, 'Don't be afraid, nothing has happened,' she said to make me feel better and she said 'Don't be scared, because she isn't dead,' that's what she told me."

Fadime's light brown coat was new. Just a few minutes earlier Fadime and Nebile had been standing together, admiring it.

"She put on her coat, it was new, light brown, she had just bought it, she said 'Look, isn't it nice?' and chatted about it a little and then she looked at herself in the mirror and said 'It's nice,' and then she went over to Mum and kissed her and said 'All the best!' And then she picked up my present to her and I peeped through the peephole, had he been sitting on the stairs I think I would've seen him, but he wasn't so I opened the door and then there he was, standing in front of me . . ."

She had described her father's appearance as "his face looked yellow and he had red eyes." Later she explains what she meant: "I take a look and his skin is yellow, he has tears in his eyes, he's, his eyes kind of twitch, not like usually, you know, when his pupils twitch, but on that day they twitched more than ever."

"What do you mean by saying he looked yellow?" the police interviewer asks.

"He was so pale, you see . . . the color of his skin wasn't like it should be, it was odd, like yellow in an odd way, you know, it wasn't really yellow at all, I don't know what to call that color, but anyway, he was so pale, his face was such a weird color."

Nebile does not believe that the murder was planned.

"They keep saying he had planned this thing, but if he had planned it, then he would have planned to have someone being there, waiting for him and helping him escape. No way had he planned it."[3]

Nebile leaves you in no doubt that she lost a sister whom she loved. As she grew up, Fadime, who was thirteen years older, had been more like a mother. By the time Fadime left home Nebile was eight, almost nine. But Nebile is also critical of Fadime, who has caused the family grief and pain: "We were ever so close and I love her, but at the same time I'm mega angry because she had lied, she did do that, lied *so* much, all the things she said and she lied, I'm ever so disappointed and mad with her for that, but at the same time I love her as well."[4]

Nebile believes that Fadime was lured into telling lies because she wanted to become a celebrity. The girl has bought into the family's narrative—as told by thirteen of the fifteen family members interviewed by the police. Nebile says that Fadime wanted a career as a celebrity and claims that when she challenged her big sister, Fadime herself admitted that she had told lies:

So I said "Fadime, why did you do it?' I said, "Fadime, why have you told such a lot of fibs on TV?" I said, "Fadime, was it worth it," I asked, "really—was it worth it? Truly, truly worth it?" I said, "Was it really worth it that you spoke to the media and . . ." Anyway, she was in all the media, in all the newspapers and things, all that stuff made my dad sick, he became sick because she was in all the media and especially because she lied and she described us like a family of monsters, she really did.

She lied and lied and in the end my dad went crazy, like he got sick, and she says these things, anyway she had been somewhere on the twentieth of December, wherever, in Parliament or whatever, and I heard this tape of when she told the people there that our dad had beaten her with a rolling pin and hit her thirty times . . . and we have this rolling pin, a wooden one, you see, it's made of wood, and she says that Dad has hit her with it at least thirty times, but he has never touched her—I mean, thirty times! Goodness, if I take it and hit your head with it thirty times, I don't think your head can take it, I think your head will break, don't you?

(The story about the rolling pin can be found in a police interview from 1998. Fadime said that her father had hit her on at least thirty different occasions and had used a rolling pin, which meant that she had been badly bruised. When Nebile retells the story, the thirty incidents have become thirty blows, one after the other—perhaps because this is how the family tells it. Nebile tries to show, with faulty logic, that Fadime must have been lying.)

Another story about Fadime's lying concerns virginity:

You see, with us you got to be, like when you get married, you must be quite pure, and she has said that when my sister, you know the one, she, they forced her to marry her cousin . . . anyway, whatever, she says that girls should be pure when they marry and she says that when they [the sister and the cousin] married, then loads of my relatives and my aunt were sitting in one room and the cousins, or anyway, the father and rest of the relatives, you know, just the men, they were in another room and then, when it had happened they bring the sheet out and show it to the men, and they look at it and go "yes, she's pure, she's a good person," and so on. But we don't do stuff like that, we aren't into that . . . what do you call it, into that kind of culture, it doesn't happen anymore, well anyway, not nowadays, girls don't have to be pure, we don't make a fuss about it. If one looks back at when my father, at his time, then maybe it was different and it mattered, but it doesn't now, boys and people who live in society here, it doesn't matter to them if it is . . . everyone doesn't bleed, that's what I'm trying to say.

("We aren't into that . . . what do you call it, into that kind of culture": Nebile, who was born and brought up in Sweden, may well have said this in good faith, or else in order to show that she is in no way exotic or peculiar. Young people of her age don't want to stand out from the crowd, especially not in ways looked down upon by the rest of society. In Sweden, nothing is gained by announcing that you belong to a "culture" that requires bloodstains as evidence of being a virgin on your wedding night. "We're modern too," she seems to say when she insists that boys nowadays don't care about that kind of thing.)

"What you've just described, who says it's like that?" the interviewer asks.

"It's Fadime, she has written it and said it too . . . she has said it on TV, I don't think she wrote it for the papers, but she did say it on TV . . . and I said 'Fadime, is it worth it?' And I said 'A family is worth more than a [boyfriend], friends matter much more than a mate, much more than a boyfriend,' that's what I said and I was like 'Was it really worth it?' And she said 'I know, I lied,' that's what she said to me, straight out. She said, 'Forgive me for all that,' she told me 'You see, I didn't know what to say.' She wanted, that's what I think, she wanted to do this to make a career . . . she wanted to become a celebrity, have microphones in front of her, be in programs on TV."

In Nebile's opinion, the problems in the family all began with Fadime and Patrik's relationship.

"Everything, I mean this problem, began in 1998 when my sister fell in love with a Swedish boy, actually he isn't Swedish, he is Iranian, he's half Swedish, but we're trying to make the crappy papers write about that, but they don't . . ."

"How old were you then, back in 1998?"

"I was nine I think, she was in love with this Swede . . . anyway, she wanted a wedding party and in our, you see, we usually . . . anyway, in Sweden do the girls usually pay for the party or for the wedding or how is it done? For Swedish girls?"

"In the old days they did, but not nowadays."

"OK, I don't know, but everyone says they do and among us it's the boys and she wanted to . . . Loads of people come to our weddings, a thousand maybe or eight hundred, and that's what she wanted, like a super-huge party and we were to pay for it and we were like, 'No Fadime, we don't want to, we'd rather have a small party' and that's when it all began, because she went on about 'that kind of party' and 'this kind of party' and on and on, and that's when it started, she got in touch with the media and she lied about everything. I am totally mad with her about that, it was a crappy thing to do, I mean I've read the papers and watched TV, but there's not one effing sentence or one effing word that's true, what she says about our family, nothing fits in . . . you see, I read and watched and read and not one single sentence or anything is true about my family, and the thing is, she rang my, you see, after my dad got a heart problem, after 1998, and he had sleep problems and kept talking to himself in the shower and in the bathroom and watching TV . . . but we didn't make much of it, we thought it's like he's worn out, talking to himself, but not to worry, it's nothing really, a sleep problem, that's not so special, it's nothing, well I don't know, but old people often have a thing about not sleeping . . . he was old, a bit, so that's maybe why he couldn't sleep and it had nothing to do with all *that* and my sister [Fadime] phoned and Dad said hello, she put the phone down and then she phoned Dad, said hello, at six in the evening and at four and at three o'clock at night, phoned and phoned . . . and my dad said 'Do what you like, just leave me alone' . . ."[5]

The police interviewer wanted to know how Nebile could be so sure that Fadime was lying.

"What I've been telling you, I mean how lots of what she says isn't true, it's because I live in this family and I haven't ever seen anything like all what she says, never, I've never seen, look, of course we've all had some bad times, but not like she tells it, in our family we always stick together, we cry sometimes and we have fun, we've had our moments, we have, but not like that, you know."

"You said 'We've had some bad times'—what do you mean by that?"

"Look, it's like we've had different times, we've been together and maybe if something happened, I don't know, like a relative had died or something, then we'd cry together . . ."

She is positive that, in general, they have had a good time together: "We always have a good time, I've never felt like that [the way Fadime describes it] and she tells the police that . . . Dad has hit her, stuff like that, why didn't the police ask if there aren't other children in this family, why don't we go and find how they are getting on, why don't we, you know?"

"Now that's a good question," the interviewer admits.

Nebile is critical of the way the media have been exploiting Fadime:

> She says "The family beat me up, they planned to do these things, they hit me, I've been abused and my sisters have been abused." Why didn't the police, why didn't they try to help us then, we phoned them, you know, the newspapers and kind of tried to speak to them, but they said no because then they maybe won't sell any more copies, they have used my sister.

The policewoman wonders if Nebile can be certain about what has happened. Couldn't Fadime have been subjected to bad treatment without Nebile's knowing?

"No, no, no!"

"Are you telling us that you're with your family all the time?"

"I've been with them since I was born and besides there are my other sisters, do you think they're lying or what?"

"I can't tell."

"You can't tell, you can't tell, but I know that they don't lie!"

Nebile is also sad and upset on her mother's behalf: "My family isn't like that and my mum says that when they came here, she was hardly more than . . . she couldn't have known anything about our culture . . . she was like four, maybe six years old and all the same she says . . ."

"Who says?"

"My sister, it was when she came here. She says that . . . Mummy told her, well, she made them write in the paper that Mummy told her she mustn't play with the Swedish girls because they're whores, every one of them is a whore and they're like this and like that. Mum had never said anything like that and she was so upset when she heard about it, she went 'How can she say that?' Obviously she thinks that if they write that in the paper and Swedish people read how my mum has told her that she mustn't play with the Swedish whores . . . obviously they'll think, like, you know, fuck that, why have we opened up and let them in? They come here, and eat, and are given everything they need and then the grown-ups say to their kids that they mustn't play with the whores! They'd be really mad about it, it's easy to see that, and what we want is to tell them the truth, it isn't true, just falsehood, she says."

According to Nebile, the truth is that her father and brother have been wrongly convicted of subjecting Fadime to physical violence. Her brother acted in self-defense and also in order to protect his parents: "My brother couldn't stand being around and watch when my parents cried in front of the TV set, in front of Fadime, just because she was lying . . . Daddy had this job at Sala-something and they did all these things to him, like throwing snow at him, they called him bad names, they said to him 'You're a fucking homo, you're a fucking abuser, you're a fucking' oh I don't know what, they believed lots of things about my dad . . . and my brother, he stood there, he watched Fadime on the TV and he was like . . . she needn't be on TV, she needn't go all out to be in the mass media . . . I mean, like stuff happens . . . she herself did all that . . . and then, you know, when it happened, when you say that my brother hit my sister, kind of thing . . ."[6]

"Please use people's names so we know whom you're talking about."

"Mesut and Fadime. Be cool and I'll tell it properly, you see, they were at, I tell you . . . anyway, it was about a week after he, Patrik, died . . . or maybe it was two or three weeks, or maybe a month, and my brother sat there, he was with my other sister, her name is Elmas and they waited for the bus and Fadime had shopped and bought loads of stuff... actually, I'm not sure that she had bought anything, but anyway, she had been to the shops, as far as I know and anyway, there she was, walking along... my brother has seen her, I mean my brother saw Fadime but he didn't do anything, he doesn't even look her way, like he just doesn't take any notice and then she walks up to him and sneers at him and says 'How's it going, Mesut? How are our parents?' and then she says 'You fucking homo' or, you know, things like that to make him angry, so he gets up and does whatever and she goes... ha, ha, ha! Laughing at him ... My brother takes no notice, but she kind of smacks him and goes 'You fucking homo.' That's makes him, it's the last straw, and he gets up and hits her.[7] And since then she has phoned my brother many times and said lots of things, you know, when she talks about all this in that film."

"Which film?"

Nebile explains that she means a TV recording. It is probably the documentary film made of Fadime and Patrik in the spring of 1998.[8] It includes a taped recording of Fadime's being threatened by her brother, who says he'll kill her. According to Nebile, this is how it came about: Fadime keeps phoning, deliberately provokes her brother, and "then she phones back and he, my brother, is furious and says lots of things to her and that's when she presses the button and gets it all on tape."[9]

Nebile never believed that her brother wanted to kill Fadime. However, she describes how worried her mother was in case he should find out that Fadime would spend her last night in Uppsala. When he offered to drive her to Songül's flat, she replied, "No, I'm not going there tonight. My foot hurts to much." He said, "Anyway, hand me the pies you baked, and I'll take them round to Songül." "Don't bother," the mother told him. "Songül is bound to come here later on."

When Mesut had left, Nebile asked her mother, "Why won't you go?" "And then Mum said maybe 'Don't be silly,' or more like, she said 'Imagine if something happens to her, I wouldn't take that risk.'"

Next Nebile says to her mother, "You know that Mesut would never do something like that, you know he's in prison for all that, but it was she who said, you know, you fucking homo and things like that to him, all that wasn't my brother's fault."

The police interviewer asks her if she thinks her father and brother knew that Fadime would be visiting Songül that evening.

"No, they didn't, but I think my brother kind of guessed, maybe he sensed something was going on, that's just what I think, but what I know for sure is that my brother would never touch her, like when I was talking to him on Monday, no, yes, yesterday . . . I sat in his car with him and we talked and I said, 'Look, if you, if we say that you, anyway this is just something I was thinking about so I thought I'd ask you, if Mum had said "Yes, please drive me there" and you take Mum there and . . . you say "I'll come in with you" and you see that Fadime is there, what would you have done?' And he said 'I wouldn't have touched her, just have looked at her and been like "Fadime, what have you gone and done?" And then I would have walked back to my car and driven off.' . . . And then he said 'What she wants is to see me put away in prison and I just won't give her the pleasure.'

"He said, 'I wouldn't have touched her, only looked at her and said "Fadime, what you've done—was it really worth it?" And then I would've been off to the car and away.' . . . He said, 'She wants to see me in prison, but she never will!'"

Nebile struggles with the thought of whether the murder might have been prevented. The police question her more closely about any sense she might have had, without necessarily realizing why, that Mesut knew of Fadime's visit to Songül. Maybe he had guessed without having been told?

She says no, she believes he had no idea: "No, I don't think anyone thought that, my brother didn't have a clue, besides, if I had known I would've stayed at home, because Dad wouldn't have gone there then, but I didn't know, if only I had, you know, had a sense that she might be, then I'd never have gone there."[10]

Nebile reflects, in retrospect, on what she and her mother and Songül would have done if they had known that Rahmi was waiting on the other side of the door: "Phoned the police maybe and then we might have thrown her from the balcony, it isn't that far to the ground . . . we could've made a hole in the wall and pushed her through it so Dad wouldn't have caught sight of her, whatever, we could have done all sorts of things, but we didn't know, we didn't know he was there."[11]

Nebile has no idea how her father got hold of a gun. Neither she nor her mother had ever seen it before, and there was no hiding place, not even in the cellar, where it could have been kept without their knowledge. Rahmi Sahindal himself insists that he cares for the gun very much, that it is a gift from his father that he has kept for thirty-two years, and that he has been using just once every year, at New Year's, when he goes out into the forest and fires two shots.

When Fadime was shot, Nebile stood almost shoulder to shoulder with her. They were on their way out and the passage was narrow. Their father fired at close range, some thirty to forty centimeters away (or so she thinks), after grabbing hold of Fadime's hair with his other hand and aiming the muzzle at the back of her head. It was quick, but not instant. Their mother, who had been resting on the sofa in the sitting room, managed to reach them and tried to stop him, to knock the gun out of his hand. Did he speak at all? "Maybe he mumbled something when he fired, or something like that, but everyone was screaming, so I don't know if he said anything."[12]

Nebile is haunted by the thought that Fadime might have suffered before she died. "There's something I want to know, you see I don't know if she was shot through the head and wherever—do you know?" she asks the police.[13] Talking about why her father fired several times—Nebile remembers three shots—she says: "He must have thought, I guess he went like 'If I'm going to kill her and end up in prison, she had better be properly dead,' that's what I think he thought."[14]

The court was told nothing of what has been quoted here. Nebile Sahindal was on the list of trial witnesses, but it didn't take long to decide that she would not be heard. Earlier her mother and her mother's brother had stood down as witnesses, and another uncle had more or less followed their example: he remained in the witness stand but remembered nothing. In such circumstances, hearing a thirteen-year-old seemed pointless.

But Nebile followed the trial right to the end, unlike her mother, who had had enough after the first day in court. The two of them had arrived together and burst into tears simultaneously when Rahmi Sahindal was escorted to the defendant's seat.

Later they both got their feelings under reasonable control and were able to follow the trial with apparently stoical calm. On the second and third days, Nebile turned up in the company of her sisters, aunts, and other relatives, dressed in a bright red padded jacket and black trousers.

She had worn a red T-shirt on her last evening with Fadime. Having come straight from a training session at the gym, with the red T-shirt she had worn orange tracksuit bottoms and trainers in the same color:

"And if you want to know what kind of jewelry I had on, well, only this one and this one, and then I was given this one." She points to a gift from Fadime. Suddenly she insists she must find out about something: "Do you know, have you got the things she gave me so I can have them back?"

"We'll sort that out, come time."

"I want them, I must have them back."

"Of course you will, just wait for a while."

"OK, but when?"

Just before her sister died, she had given Nebile a brooch and matching earrings, a lipstick and other makeup, some money and a dress shop voucher.

Throughout the police interview Nebile is very keen to be believed. She wants the police to understand that she has good grounds for her statements.

For example, the police wants to how well she really knew Fadime, who moved out of the family home in 1997, when Nebile was only eight years old.

"I knew her ever so well."

"Did you?"

"Really well. She and I were close, always. I used to call her Mummy, you know, and she called me her little sweetheart."

But surely there had been times when Nebile wasn't around to listen to what was said between Fadime, the other siblings, and their parents. "You must've been going to school like everybody else?"

"Of course I went to school, but you know, I don't know how to say this, you'll never believe me . . . you think I was just little then and didn't understand anything. But I knew what was going on, I've lived in this family always, so don't you think I know what has happened and that? My sister, she used to come home like at four or five, why shouldn't I have been there then?"

"Sure, but I wondered if there weren't things going on that you didn't know about. It happens, doesn't it?"

"OK, you can think what you like about me."

"I suppose all eight-year-olds don't know exactly what goes on in a family?"

"So that's it, you think my dad was horrid to my sister and beat her up?"

"No, I don't think anything of the sort, I'm just mentioning how things might've been. But you say that you knew everything, one hundred percent?"

"I know, I know, I mean I don't and I don't believe that, but whatever I say, that I know for sure."[15]

Nebile asks if she will she be allowed to see her sister before the funeral.

"I don't know," the policewoman replies.

"OK, no, because I wanted to put a little something in her hand . . . anyway.

9 A Mother's Story

Mother uninvolved (handwritten note)

Fadime's mother is not a witness at the trial. She asks to be excused and says that she has told the police everything she knows. They inform her that the court relies only on what is said in the courtroom and will not learn of the evidence from the police investigation. She does not budge. Speaking through an interpreter, she says that she couldn't bear it.

As her mother settles down among the relatives in the public gallery, Songül sends her a murderous glance. Her mother stares straight ahead, trying to seem unmoved by her daughter's piercing gaze. I didn't see her expression change once during the trial—except when the defendant was brought in and she burst into tears.

She hears only a fraction of his explanations because it is discovered that a mistake has been made and she should not be there. Witnesses are not allowed to be present during the trial before they have made their statement to the court. She and Nebile must wait in the passage. But she hears Haydar, Rahmi Sahindal's best friend, who remembers nothing. She stays away from the next two days of the trial.

Haydar has said to the police that when Fadime's mother phoned him and told him about the killing, she asked him what she was to tell the police. He had replied that they had to tell everything.

He wants to make this very clear, he repeats: the women sought his advice about how they were to behave and he told them to be completely frank. More than once after Fadime's death, he had said that there was no way to defend what had happened and it's a great tragedy.[1]

But as we know, the courtroom resounds with the silence of Fadime's relatives. Had it not been for Songül, no one would have testified. Her eyewitness account is the prosecutor's trump card. They tried to silence her too, she tells the court: several members of the family, her mother in particular, pleaded with her to refuse to stand witness. Her relatives told her that they would reject her if she spoke up in court. Already on their way to the hospital on the night of the murder, her mother said to Songül and Nebile: "Don't say anything to the police, what can we do, it has happened."[2]

The relatives leave an impression of unspoken unity: everyone must avoid informing the authorities about what happened, that is, about the murder of Fadime. It would seem that the entire family has taken the defendant's side. On the other hand, it is also possible that the silence should be understood as family members' getting out of taking sides; they avoided speaking ill of Fadime, as well as condemning Rahmi.

And now, after Fadime has been given a "state funeral," criticizing her seems riskier than ever.

Besides, Songül steps into the breach. Her solicitor, Leif Ericksson, argues that Songül takes the witness stand in order to spare her mother and Nebile. At this point, the three women are still talking to each other.

In the case dealing with Fadime's murder, her mother is a nonperson—at least this is how the media portray her (until she testifies in the court of appeals). It is easy to see why. She has hardly said a thing. It is impossible to get a grip on her. Even her police interview is meager reading, just four and a half pages as against her daughter Nebile's thirty. She comes across as quiet, someone of few words.

But she was a central figure in Fadime's life. In her 1998 TV interview, Fadime said that what had hurt her most was that her mother, "who gave life to me and has always loved me, rejects me now." She said that her mother hated her. When the journalist argued that "love doesn't just die," Fadime declared it had, once she became seen as someone who had ruined the lives of the entire family. In her talk in Parliament a short time before she was killed, Fadime said that her mother had been blamed when her daughter broke away from the family. Two sides of the same issue: rejection and blame. I assume that the mother had been under heavy pressure to distance herself from "that daughter of hers" who had caused the family so much damage. And that she felt forced to demonstrate whose side she was on by the only means at hand: she had to throw her daughter into the void. This act had nothing to do with her feelings for Fadime, which were probably dominated by motherly love—still. It had to do with her other children and the responsibility and loyalty she felt toward them. It also had to do with the fact that hers was a nodal position in the close-knit network of family ties: generations of marriages between close relatives had forged iron links of loyalty and mutual obligation.

Fadime's mother, Elif Sahindal, looks strikingly like her dead daughter. Her appearance and manner suggest strength, decisiveness, and an upright, dignified persona. But she would not announce her thoughts and feelings in the marketplace. In line with traditional Kurdish culture—with Middle Eastern tradition in general—one's private life should be shut off from the eyes of the world outside, that is, from people who do not belong to the immediate family or the wider circle of relatives. This was what her mother saw as Fadime's main offense: she used the media to expose the hidden life of the family and, in that way, brought misery on them all.

I base this on her statements to the police. She told them how she had been saying to Fadime that "at first there was nothing special, but then Fadime herself had created problems." She was referring to the court case brought by Fadime against her father and brother and the sentences they had received, and to Fadime's appearances in the mass media. The rows began after all the public attention.

According to police records, Elif Sahindal insisted that the media spectacle nearly made her husband ill. He started brooding about a lot of things and felt particularly bad about being described as some kind of monster—he didn't even dare seek medical help. The media were blackening the reputation of an entire community. Fadime exaggerated and lied about so many things.

For almost three years, mother and daughter had no contact with each other. Elif had missed Fadime very much. They got in touch again during the year before she was killed. Fadime called to tell her mother that she had missed her immensely too, but she also said what had happened couldn't be undone and besides she could never backtrack. During that year Elif and Fadime met three times, including the last time. They got together in Songül's flat twice, and once Fadime visited Elif in hospital, where she was waiting for an operation. Only Elif herself, Nebile, and Songül ever knew when Fadime was in Uppsala, Elif says.[3]

But this was not the case that last time. Several others were in the know. Apart from the mother and two sisters, Haydar's wife Fatma knew that Fadime was in Uppsala, because Elif told her as she drove Elif to Songül's flat. Kemal, Fadime's cousin and confidant, knew too. Fadime had asked him to pick her up when she left Songül's place. Another cousin, who lived in Stockholm, was also informed, because she had kept Fadime's things in readiness for her upcoming trip to Kenya.

As for the question of Fadime's male relatives: did her brother Mesut, and possibly others as well, know about her visiting Songül? Her mother had gone to extremes to *keep* him from finding out. She may not have trusted her son. According to Songül, her mother had responded cryptically when Songül phoned to say that Fadime had arrived, and furthermore, it had been Mesut who initially answered the phone. He had probably stayed on the line and listened to what his mother was saying. This sequence was repeated when Songül phoned back with a message from Fadime that her mother mustn't bother to come if her leg was painful (Elif was plagued by a sore knee). Again Mesut had picked up the receiver, again their mother spoke as if the call was about something different in order to avoid raising suspicions.

Nebile suggests that her mother suspected Mesut of having guessed the true reason for the phone calls. That was why she turned down his offer to give her a lift to Songül's place. When Nebile asked her why she didn't go along with Mesut, her mother said something like "Don't be silly" or "Imagine if something happens to her, I wouldn't take that risk."[4]

Had her mother had an inkling that Fadime was in mortal danger? Possibly not. But she must have feared what *might* happen. Fatma, who drove Elif to Songül's, admits that she herself had been afraid when she learned that Fadime was in Uppsala. Fatma feared that her niece would be beaten up, not killed. Years earlier, she said, her fear would have been of something more serious, but not now. "The family had become whole again."[5] If so, Fadime's mother had played an important role in bringing it about. It is up to women to make their families "whole." But below the surface strong forces were simmering, and Elif knew better than to challenge her son, Mesut. Several relatives told the police that, in their view, the real threat had come from Mesut rather than from Rahmi. Kemal, Fadime's cousin who was to collect her that last night, said, "Fadime's brother would have killed her if he found her."[6]

It is not known where Mesut was at the critical moment that evening. He lacks an alibi for the period between 9:00 and about 9:45. This was when Rahmi left his flat (when he had failed to gain entry to Songül's flat, he had gone home to phone Fadime's home number in Östersund), traveled to Songül's house, and waited outside her door until it opened on his defenseless victim.

Three-quarters of an hour during which Mesut has no alibi. It seems that a white Audi was observed outside the block of flats at the time when the murder was committed. Rahmi had neither a driver's license nor a car, but Mesut drives a white Audi. Several family members doubted that Rahmi had been able to get hold of a gun on his own; Songül believes that Mesut must have helped him. The woman who gave Mesut his alibi tells of how he kept watching the clock to be ready to leave at 9:00 in order to meet someone off a train due at 9:00. She found it odd: why leave at nine to pick someone up at nine? Mesut spent the night in this woman's flat. The following morning they heard on the news that a Kurdish woman had been murdered in Uppsala. Mesut's only comment was "Did you hear that?" He went straight back to his parents' home. Between 8:00 and 9:00 that morning, his sister Fidan tried to get in touch with him there. Her mother came to the phone and said, "Mesut can't speak now, he just cries and has locked himself into his room and keeps knocking things over and hitting out and weeping and he's in despair and quite alone in his room."[7]

Both Songül and Nebile speak vividly of their mother's reactions that last evening; Elif herself has little to say. Her account is brief and to the point, but perhaps she uses words sparingly because the police interviews are mediated through an interpreter, an outsider. She tells of how she said, "No, don't open the door so they don't find you" (note her use of *they*, not *he*), when her husband wanted to get in. She relates how Fadime said "Poor Daddy" three times. And Fadime's idea that she should hide under the bed.

Elif had been resting on the sofa when she heard screams from the hall and ran out. Then she saw that Rahmi had grabbed hold of Fadime's hair and was pressing a gun to her head. Fadime fell and Elif tugged at Rahmi's gun-hand, turned it toward herself, and said, "Shoot me instead, shoot me!" She ran off to the neighbors' doors to ask for help. Down the stairs, then outside and up other staircases, without shoes on. When she came back she saw the ambulance and lots of police. She asked to see Fadime to find out if she was alive, but the police stopped her. She asked if Fadime lived, but the police didn't know.

According to police records, "Elif did not know where the weapon came from. She had no idea that Rahmi owned anything like that. Elif had never heard before about him going out shooting to mark the New Year."

Furthermore:

Rahmi had said nothing to Elif [i.e., before the shooting, about his plans?], but he was angry and dejected because he was in all the media. Elif told Fadime she must stop speaking to the media and Fadime had said she would, and then went on doing it after all. The media are to blame, they had blown up this small thing into a big affair. Afterward Rahmi fell ill and had nightmares. He woke up in the middle of the night and talked to himself and became bad tempered. Elif does not believe that Rahmi phoned anyone or spoke with anyone that evening or night. She only saw Mesut the following day, when he came home, and then he wept and hugged her and said "What has happened to us?"[8]

Fadime's mother acted in ways that from "our" point of view present her in a bad light: there is her withdrawal from testifying in court, combined with Songül's statement that her mother asked her not to be a witness and also that on the evening of the murder she had said, "Don't say anything to the police, it has happened." The impression that she betrayed her daughter was reinforced when the court listened to the tape recording of Fadime telling of how she feels rejected by her mother. How could a mother do this? How could she bear it?

Elif Sahindal had many responsibilities to consider, especially toward the thirteen-year-old Nebile. Nebile describes running around and looking for her mother after the murder, fearful that her mum wouldn't come back and might commit suicide. Her story leaves us in no doubt that at least this daughter panicked about her mother's reaction after the crime. What would happen to Nebile?

I walked about, went out [of the flat] and back in all the time. I didn't know and I was so scared something had happened, that Mum perhaps, I wanted to be with my mummy, and then I went outside, no, I didn't go out, I went out once and shouted and then I realized that it was pointless to shout, of course Mum couldn't hear me, because if she had heard it then she would've come.[9]

Fadime has confirmed that Elif was blamed for her daughter's breaking away from the family. It is quite natural, after all: mothers do carry the main responsibility for the children's—and especially the daughters'—behavior, not only in Kurdish culture but also in many others. But in this case it is clear where the responsibility lies, as it is the women who embody family honor. Fadime had far overstepped the mark in her family's eyes: it must be her mother's fault. Elif might well blame the mass media in turn, just as many of her relatives do. It does not mean that she is not responsible.

Grief, doubt, and guilt go together. Doubt: Did she do the right thing that evening? Shouldn't they have contacted the police when Rahmi hammered on the door? Guilt: if it hadn't been for her, Fadime wouldn't have come to Uppsala.

"I did it. It was all my fault!" That is what she told Fidan when she phoned to speak about the murder.

Elif trusted Fidan, one of her daughters who had responded to her wish to make the family "whole" again. Fidan, Songül, and Nebile had stayed in touch with Fadime. Fidan's brother-in-law Ismail states that Fidan and Fadime were in close contact by phone after the events of 1998, which was also true of Fadime and her mother during "the last year."[10] Fadime is described as the one who pushed to make her relationship with her family more normal, but her mother stood by her, despite her husband's express prohibition of any contact and despite her second daughter Elmas's strong resentment of Fadime. Elmas could not forgive Fadime for the hurt her media appearances had caused the family. The two sisters had not spoken since 1997. Songül explained to the court how badly it had upset her when, on the night of the murder, as they sat in the hospital together, Elmas had said, "Why didn't you cut free from that rotten whore? You all were running after her like little chickens." Elmas seems to have had a similar outburst when she was on the phone to her uncle (her mother's brother) Cemal. That she was prepared to say such things, especially under the tragic circumstances, was part of the reason that Songül broke with the family and asked for police protection.

We see a mother whose children are at loggerheads. Two of them, both important to her—her second daughter and her only son—reject Fadime totally. One daughter is in secret telephone contact with Fadime. Another left the family and moved in with her sister. Yet another—the family's lastborn—has met Fadime in secret, even when her mother was not around. Fadime had said in public that she hopes her little sister will one day be strong enough to break away. Perhaps it was a good thing that their mother couldn't read and understand Swedish. Perhaps it spared her a little suffering. True, it also meant that she had no defense against what the others told her. Maybe this was worse still.

Fadime's mother has lived in Sweden for more than twenty years but has only minimal insight into Swedish society. When, after the murder, she ran off to the neighbors to get help, she found it difficult to explain what she wanted in her very broken Swedish. She speaks only a local Kurdish dialect fluently and is surrounded by a large extended family tightly bonded through intermarriage between cousins; her roots are in a place where the state is regarded as an enemy. All of this conspires to make it hard to comprehend Swedish legal traditions. Fadime had been killed. Her husband had confessed to the killing. What more was there to say?

This woman, whose looks are strikingly like Fadime's and who radiates strength and intelligence, is handicapped in the context of Swedish society, which she does not understand. Further, she is trapped in a life situation that nobody would wish on themselves.

Speaking on the phone to Fidan, she shouted into the receiver: "The mad bastard, he took my child!"

10   *Naive and Primitive?*

During the trial of Rahmi Sahindal, the bench considered expert psychiatric evidence. It was set out on four pages of typescript. The full text was read out in court. It begins with an account of Rahmi Sahindal's early years in Turkey and his arrival and later experiences in Sweden. Concurrently, it provides an expert evaluation of the defendant's character. Terms such as *naive* and *primitive* are used.

Rahmi Sahindal was born in Elbistan, in southeast Turkey, on January 1, 1946. He was the youngest of eight children. His parents were farmers and lived in a village. Rahmi spent most of his childhood as a herdsman for his parents' sheep. He did not complete his basic schooling. During his childhood and youth he was subjected to physical violence; beatings were common in his upbringing.

When he was thirty-one years old, Rahmi went off to work in Saudi Arabia for a couple of years. Later, he went on to Iraq, where he made a living as a construction worker. He arrived in Sweden in 1981 as a political asylum seeker. By then several of his relatives, including his wife's brother, had already made their homes in Sweden. His wife and five children—one of whom was seven-year-old Fadime—joined him in 1984. They settled in Uppsala, joining members of the family. By 2002 the Sahindal headcount reached about three hundred.

The expert report clarified what living in Sweden had meant for Rahmi Sahindal. He spent one year in a training course, including, among other things, instruction in Swedish, and soon afterward landed a job in a laundry (most of the staff were Swedish). Work went well until 1998, when he was granted incapacity benefit. The reason was the problem with Fadime, which grew during 1997–98. Rahmi had a heart condition, felt depressed, and began to drink more heavily, though he did not feel dependent on alcohol. He isolated himself at home with his wife and two youngest daughters, avoiding Swedish people. In his eyes, Fadime had left him exposed, compromised, and subjected to a media witch hunt. He thought Fadime was persecuting him. His daughter took on the shape of evil incarnate in his mind, his sleep became interrupted by nightmares, and he sank steadily deeper into despair.

The psychiatric expert characterizes Rahmi Sahindal's psychological and mental capacity in the following terms: His emotional side is stunted. He sees himself in negative terms, and his capacity for empathy is poorly developed—all of which is a consequence of deprivation early in life. Intellectually, he is also underdeveloped; he is inflexible and avoids dialogue. He starts every interview with a monologue about the media witch hunt and his daughter's harassment of him; his ability to adjust is low, and his reactions are naive and primitive.

"Naive and primitive"—a characterization that would in normal circumstances have angered the liberal-minded public but is accepted this time, in the full glare of publicity. The defendant and his legal advisers do not object. The liberal public and the defense probably have a joint interest here. Establishing that the defendant is naive and primitive gives his lawyer a chance to trigger sympathy for the perpetrator as an awkward figure of below-normal ability. Meanwhile, good citizens are anxious not to vilify "a whole culture." Those who are keen to stress that the individual rather than the honor code is the key to this murder are well served by "naive and primitive."

Jealousy-driven murder is of course a matter of one individual's act. Is that not also true when someone murders for honor's sake? Is there really a difference? This debate has raged in Sweden more intensely than in Norway. Some left-wing intellectuals react angrily the moment anyone dares to suggest that honor killings have something to do with culture, or vice versa. Those who hold the opposite view are mercilessly critical. On the former side, "Swedes" predominate, on the latter, "immigrants."

The same polarity was seen in Sara's case: people who have felt the problems "inside themselves" insist that culture must be taken seriously and that honor killing is a reality. It is secure members of the privileged group who refuse to take such experiences seriously.

Honor killing is a dangerous category. The risk is that a whole culture or community is branded as having a tradition of "honor" that can lead to murder. Asked by his lawyer whether honor killing is part of Kurdish culture, Rahmi Sahindal replied that it was not—maybe a hundred, or fifty-sixty years ago, but not now. "What had happened" was pure chance. True enough, he had played around with the thought of killing Fadime maybe some five or six months earlier, but when he shot her he must have been ill. It made his head swim. "How could I shoot dead my own child if I hadn't been sick?" he asks the psychiatrist—without getting a reply.

"Naive and primitive" is as close as the psychiatric expert comes to a diagnosis. The doctor denies that Rahmi is ill. ("I'm ill, but the doctor doesn't believe me," he complains.) The report states, "There are no symptoms of a depressive condition," nor of any other mental illness. It follows that Rahmi Sahindal loses the chance of being placed in an institution rather than jailed.

It is odd, in my view, that the phrase "naive and primitive" was never questioned. "Primitive" by whose standards? The logic behind this honor killing becomes clearer as the trial progresses. One witness after the other avoids testifying, the family protects the murderer, and one relative suddenly steps forward to declare that he shot Fadime.

The circle is closed when Fadime's father, at the last moment before the right to appeal against the district court decision runs out, withdraws his admission of guilt. Honor confronts law. Justice, it would seem, is not respected. This case follows a steely logic. There is nothing primitive and naive about it. Seen from a certain perspective, it is shrewd and rational. That perspective does not depend on the values of one individual but of a collective view of human beings, society, and law.

Let it be unsaid how large that collective is.

The trial, like so much in Fadime's story, will likely make Swedish history: in defiance of the family, a single sister testifies; three other close members of the family withdraw; the perpetrator's nephew insists that he is the real murderer, while the murderer, against whom there is overwhelming evidence, who once pleaded guilty and was sentenced accordingly, now pleads not guilty.

We shall later see what the outcome will be. One thing is certain: the family considers it untenable that the court should trust Songül—a sick woman. Remember, they say, she has been diagnosed bipolar. Fadime was the first to charm the media and portray the family as a lot of monsters. Now Songül does the same. Is there no end to this chasing of celebrity status? What will it take to end Swedish society's witch hunt of the family? That Rahmi retracts his guilty plea is a last desperate attempt to say, "Listen to me, I'm ill." A last attempt to raise sympathy for what has been his line of defense throughout the trial. Fadime is dead, so that's one problem out of the way, but at what cost? Five or six months in prison will be enough to kill him, he insists. The family is suffering. The Sahindals, Kurds everywhere in the country, are harassed. Grandchildren are bullied in school.

What is to be gained by retracting? Self-respect and also respect from the many who see a sentence as a gross, ruthless act against a sick man, who had been forced to kill because he had been betrayed by the authorities. Had he not told police and municipality that Fadime must not be allowed to come to Uppsala?

Unless new information relevant to the evidence in the case becomes available, appealing the sentence would almost certainly be pointless. To withdraw the admission of guilt is a step in that direction. It is a countermove that could cause the court a great deal of soul searching. Could an appeal on that basis also contribute to a rehabilitation of the Sahindals and of Kurds in Sweden by establishing once and for all that this is not an honor killing? Hardly. If Rahmi Sahindal did not shoot Fadime, who else could have done it? Another relative, who had also been dishonored? However, the Sahindals feel they will be more respected, in the public eye as well, if they act according to the code of honor: just as you learn not to pick your nose, you know better than to give Songül the last word. A system of justice that takes that girl seriously is not worthy of respect.

The scene is set for a confrontation: honor versus law.

In court Rahmi Sahindal seemed a rather helpless figure. Confused and contradictory statements marred his defense. The murder was not planned, but had been all the same. He had never thought of killing her—but sure, killing had been on his mind. He had gone that night just to visit the sick Songül—but sure, he had decided that if Fadime were there he would take her life. The gun was fired because he lost control, but he had actually made up his mind to shoot. And so on.

"If you had a daughter like that, you would've wanted to shoot her too!" That's how desperate you can get, he seems to say, not realizing that he is shooting himself in the foot. This sentence of his will bounce back and hit him with a bang. He carries on like this, piling up trouble for himself, while at the same time pleading for sympathy. He is an ordinary working man, he hasn't been to university. Who ought to have stood by him? "That Fadime, what she has done to me—I don't know how I can explain it to you!" he says and then hammers home the point about how there was "only one way out."

But if you examine his statements to the police and compare them to his court presentation of his motives and thoughts, another Rahmi seems to step forward: this is a man who is logical, opinionated, consistent, and wholly able to account for his situation and his reasons for acting as he did. The apparent messiness and chaotic thinking that characterize his explanations in court and make him come across as inarticulate and "of below-normal intelligence"—all that is gone.

Fadime harassed him. She persecuted him. Because of her, the whole world was turning against him. She showed him up. That's why he felt compelled to shoot her. The police had questioned him about the situation before. This daughter, who is now dead, had been living with a Swedish boy, who is now dead. Then she moved to Östersund. And since then, father and daughter had not had any contact, but she had carried on harassing him. The day before "what happened," she had phoned him to say that she was coming to Uppsala and, once there, she would complain to the police about him. With deep feeling he had begged her not to come because he was unwell. Around one o'clock on the day of her arrival in town, she phoned again to tell him that she was moving to Uppsala and she would come along later to rent a flat quite close to his. This upset him very much. He was beside himself. He got his gun out, loaded it, and went off to Songül's flat, where he fired twice at Fadime, aiming at her head; he isn't entirely sure but knows that one shot hit her in the head. In summary: he didn't know what he was doing, and then he lost the weapon, and then he was arrested.

He had never harmed anyone in his life, but this daughter, she was awful, she did so many bad things. She caused him to be talked about on TV and in the papers, the mass media got hold of him, and everyone was told a lot of bad things. He has a large family and many friends but was ashamed to meet up with them. Fadime behaved like a whore. She had been going with a lot of boys. This made him suffer dreadfully and finally go and shoot her, that is, on account of all that.

When she was still living in Uppsala, she was off with some boy every single day, and at the time his son was just sixteen years old. His son had said to his sister: "Why are you doing this? Why are you going out with a boy every single day?" And that was the reason she complained to the police and his son went to prison for seven months.

"This isn't good for me."

"What do you mean?"

"Well, I don't know what I'm to do."

"You felt there was nothing else for it except to do what you did, is that what you mean?"

"It simply was the last way out, wasn't it, I mean usually you don't shoot your daughter dead, you just don't, and, anyway, now there is grief at home—my wife cries, my children cry, it's no good, if you see what I mean."[1]

Rahmi confirms that he was aware of Fadime's presence in Uppsala, because she had told him over the phone that she was going to complain about him to the police. That was how he came to bring the gun with him to Songül's flat. He wouldn't have shot anyone if Fadime hadn't been there. Anyway, as usual he intended to see Songül, who wasn't well.

"What were your thoughts as you entered Songül's house?"

"Because she [Fadime] had phoned me, I thought, she's sure to go there, so I'll bring my gun."

"Yes?"

"You see, I had made up my mind . . . if she's there I'll shoot her."

"You had no other thought in your head, then—other than to shoot her?"

"You see, I had decided, there is no other solution . . . you see, it was that last way out, I had to shoot her."

Had he tried other ways of dealing with the situation?

Rahmi replies to this question by explaining yet again how "that daughter, who is now dead," persecuted and harassed him.

In which way did she harass him?

She would phone, even in the middle of the night, and threaten to complain about him to the police until he was put into prison.

In prison, for what?

She was going to tell the police that she was scared her father would shoot her: "It made me suffer very badly and, so you see, it was my last way out."[2]

He had not been drinking alcohol on the day when Fadime was killed but had consumed a bottle of whisky the previous day. In court too, Rahmi talks about his alcohol intake. He drinks because he's in despair.

"Well, how do you feel now, when your daughter is gone?"

"Terrible, I feel terrible. I thought it maybe would've been just as well if I had shot myself too, you see, it would've been better."[3]

The police wanted to know if he admits to committing a murder.[4]

"This whole event as you described it to me, it's what we call—as a crime, that is, we call it murder—is that how you see it? Do you admit or deny it?"

"Yes, I admit that I've done it, but without wanting to, it wasn't what I set out to do, you see."

"What do you mean by that?"

"What I think is that if I hadn't had my head full of these thoughts I wouldn't have shot to kill and that might have been better."

"What were these thoughts of yours?"

"Because of her behaviour . . . I was so ashamed, you see, I know many people and I have many relatives in our community and she did these awful things to me. You see, she was with a boy every day."

"For how long have you been having these thoughts?"

"Ever since the problems started."

"And when did the problems start?"

"About one or two years ago. If all had been well for me, no troubles or anything, why would one, you know, when it is like that, you don't shoot your own child and kill her, you just don't."

It is more precise to say that Rahmi's problems started some three or four years earlier. His sense of time was out of order. In his mind only one year, or maybe two, had passed since his son Mesut went to prison, but that was in the autumn of 1998; his father says he spent seven months inside, but it was actually five. What matters to Rahmi is his experience of time: the prison term was very long, and it must have happened just last year or maybe the year before. "You see, my son was just a young boy, that's no age to spend seven months in prison."

This interview begins first thing in the morning after the day Fadime was killed, lasts about an hour, and ends with Rahmi's being asked to describe his personal feelings after the event.

"You see, on the whole, I feel not so good at all."

"So you don't feel some kind of relief now after what has happened?"

"I'm feeling a lot of remorse that I did it, you see."[5]

It is said that nothing is as coherent as a paranoid person's account of his persecution mania. Rahmi Sahindal's narrative of how *he* was persecuted, and of his persecutor, is just as coherent, even if we don't rely on a psychiatric diagnosis. His story hangs together. From a certain perspective at least, it is logical—that is, from his vantage point. It is reasonable to assume that he is not alone in seeing things this way; his wife's statement fits in with his views. So does the story told by his youngest daughter and those hinted at by other, officially mute voices. Voices of summoned witnesses who refused to testify; of potential witnesses, who were never called, like his son Mesut—but fundamentally, they would have shared Rahmi's version of events. So is he of below-normal intelligence? emotionally underdeveloped? Does he lack capacity for empathy?

Or is this a feature of a certain way of relating to the world that characterizes many of the people around him and has influenced him, made him feel at ease?

Several relatives have described Rahmi to the police as a good, well-meaning man. "He's very kind, calm and composed," a male cousin says. "Very kind and very considerate," a niece says, but goes on to add: "But he isn't really that bright, kind of intellectually." Rahmi's daughter Fidan comments: "You felt sorry for him. We were pleased that he could manage his way between his job and home." People who knew him well project an image of someone who is awkward in some situations—as are many others, particularly men, who are illiterate in the setting of Swedish society. But even if he didn't seem intellectually sharp, none of those who spoke to the police have ever doubted that Rahmi and his family were haunted by nightmares because of the hostile media image of them. Many who were disposed to be kind toward Fadime would still sympathize with Rahmi. "The way Rahmi sees it, every Swede knows all about his daughter Fadime," according to one source. For anyone whose cultural background entails putting the interests of the family above that of the individual and preventing insight into private matters at any cost, Fadime's behavior was intolerable. "All about his daughter" stands for "all about his shame, humiliation, dishonor." Naked, exposed, and shown up—who would like to be in his shoes?

Rahmi realizes that he is straddling a cultural divide: on one side the Swedish camp and on the other the Kurdish one. When asked to describe what the differences are, he denies that there are any. For instance, the way children are brought up in Turkey is no different from the way they're brought up in Sweden. His own children grew up in Sweden and were left to do their own thing, to play and socialize with whomsoever they liked. When it came to marriage, his daughters picked a husband as they pleased. Any objections he might have had would just have washed off them. They need take no notice of what other members of the family or relatives might say. "In other words, Rahmi Sahindal believes that every one of his daughters has a life of her own and has always been free to chose whom to marry," the police interviewer notes.

Furthermore: "For Rahmi and his family, the problems began with Fadime's meeting a Swedish boy some three or four years ago." Rahmi tells of how he was out on his motorbike when he caught sight of Fadime in the company of a Swede. Surprised, he had stopped and asked her why she hadn't told him that she was going out with a Swedish boy. Instead of answering, Fadime and the boy hurried away. Rahmi had not been upset at all at this point, just stayed rather neutral. Why could he be sure that Fadime and the boy were more than friends? Because they walked arm in arm.

Rahmi had nothing against his unmarried daughter's being seen on the arm of a young man. What angered him was that they were in too much of a hurry to get engaged, or so he thought. In his opinion, she should complete her studies first. He had not threatened her at all back then. The trouble between Rahmi and Fadime began afterward. Fadime had complained to the police that he had threatened her. She kept going back to complain about him. The outcome was the media witch hunt. In the end, world opinion turned against Rahmi's family.[6]

Why didn't Rahmi himself go to the police and file a complaint against Fadime for her harassment? Because she got in first and he felt that they wouldn't trust him. But he became steadily more unwell, and that was why he had been drinking a good deal from the time the problems started; it was his reaction to being under all that pressure.

A confrontation about the costs of the wedding is part of the narrative about "the unreasonable Fadime." In Rahmi's opinion, the row starts when Fadime insists on a big wedding. This is the core of the problem. Rahmi had agreed to the marriage, but not to her entering into a relationship before the marriage. Now she wants as grand a wedding as those of her sisters. Then the groom has to pay, Rahmi tells her. Patrik's father refuses. Rahmi claims that they reached a compromise, but then Patrik's family reneged on it.[7] Nebile's account in the police interview suggests that this is the story in circulation at home. Nebile asks about who pays for the wedding in Sweden and thinks it is the bride's family; on the other hand, in their community the groom bears the costs.

This story adds to the image of Fadime as demanding and uncompromising. But according to Songül, it is pure fabrication. There never was any talk about wedding expenses. The discussion between the two parties never reached that point. She knows because she was present at the meeting when Patrik's father and grandmother came to her parents to ask for Fadime's hand in marriage. What happened was that her father said, "I'll see what I can do," and then, after some thought, her parents agreed to the marriage. But the family council, which had to be consulted, said no. Hence the matter of wedding expenses never arose. Negotiations were broken off before it came to that, says Songül.

never got to wedding discussion

Rahmi's story is not believable. In two earlier trials both he and his son had been convicted of uttering death threats against Fadime—his son was also convicted of inflicting grievous bodily harm—and at the time he gave a quite different account of what it meant to him to see his daughter with a Swede. This time the stakes are higher. The tactic he follows is to produce a *normal* explanation of his own and his family's situation. As a family they are in no way unusual, nor are they part of a culture like that Fadime sold to the media. Like his daughter Nebile, so also Rahmi; like her, he protests against the family as presented by Fadime. His message is "Don't think we're like that." "We aren't into that . . . what do you call it, into that kind of culture," as Nebile put it. Or, reading between the lines: "Don't stigmatize us! Fadime is lying."

But the police have a job to do. What could be the motives for the killing? They dig deeper. In a third interview, they ask about marriage customs in Rahmi's home territory. Rahmi tells them that he and his wife Elif chose each other; they are cousins. Asked to describe an ordinary relationship between two young people, he explains that the young man has to do his military service first. Next, if he's interested in a girl, he asks his parents to visit her parents and ask for her hand in marriage. Should the request be refused, the boy can always elope with the girl. If so, they have to go and live somewhere else. Later, there may well be reconciliation, and then the young couple would be allowed to return home.

Is this of any use when it comes to understanding why the theme of Uppsala keeps turning up? Fadime must not come to Uppsala. He had told her so, he even begged her to stay away. He had warned the police and the municipality in the hope that they would keep her out of town. In his fourth and last police interview, he also admits to having threatened her: "If you come to Uppsala, you won't live long!"[8] The nephew's intervention in the trial also emphasizes

Fadime come back => defied father.

this: if Fadime had only stayed in Östersund, he says, the murder wouldn't have happened. Why was her return to Uppsala such a provocation?

Probably the provocation was extreme: she showed no sense of limits—and that meant she had to accept the consequences. Honor demands nothing less.

In his own view, Rahmi had already bent over backward to be reasonable. He had agreed that Fadime would be allowed to marry the Swede, on condition that she vanished from Uppsala and severed all contacts with the family. And then the boy died—the wedding was off, but she had been issued an ultimatum that was still in place: exile from Uppsala and exclusion from the family. The decision had been made in a major family conclave and conveyed to Fadime in a phone call from her mother. Her brother said to the police, "Fadime was allowed to leave on condition that she stopped harassing the family." That is, she was "allowed to leave" or given free passage—on one condition. It was definite: expulsion into exile.

This was a "cultural" solution, in line with what applies in the family's tribal homeland in cases when a couple marries against the will of their family. "Eloping" is institutionalized. It is a "solution" that gives the young people a measure of freedom without great loss of respect for the girl's family; honor is retained and lives are saved through this compromise. This kind of expulsion is regulated along the same lines as political exile: whoever is in authority decides if and when it is to stop. Exiles can be shown mercy, but they *must not* demand rights.

Fadime was also provocative because she set up an alliance with her mother and sisters. Rahmi tells of his fear that Fadime would take his youngest daughter from him, as she had already taken Songül. He suspected them of being secretly in touch, although Nebile always denied it. He had ordered his wife to cut any contact with Fadime, because he was afraid that "the problems would just continue." When asked to explain this, he said that if the two women talked to each other, Fadime might well turn up in Uppsala again. He says that he dreaded the possibility, which might harm his son and himself. Harm—in which way? "Because he might be violent toward Fadime?" the interviewer asks. He doesn't know. But *the problem* is that it is as if something evil hangs over the whole family now that the world, through the mass media, has come to know about what has taken place inside it.

Rahmi tells the police that it was concern for his son Mesut that led in the first place to the decision that Fadime must leave Uppsala and not come back. Mesut must not run the risk of meeting her in town. And what was "the risk," exactly? Why be afraid of this? Was the whole family afraid, perhaps?

Rahmi claims that he could not accept seeing his daughter in the company of a young man when they were not married—here he is contradicting what he said earlier about how it was fine with him that she walked about arm in arm with a man. In his third interview he admits that he felt ashamed in front of his relatives when they found out about this. He had also emphasized earlier that Fadime had plagued him with her complaints to the police and that she was the cause of Mesut's and his being tried in court. Later he admits that what he calls "the problem" had begun earlier—that is, when he saw her with the Swede. He had felt ashamed in front of his family, his neighbors, and everyone he knew, everywhere in Sweden. Even world opinion was informed. He had come to feel some sort of hatred toward Fadime. Probably her brother, who had grown up in Sweden, felt the same.

So the "Fadime problem" is over now. Does Rahmi feel relieved?

No, he weeps every day. He would like to ask the entire Swedish people for forgiveness for the deed he has done.

Rahmi honors Sweden. As he says in his last statement in court: "This Sweden is a good country, so how could I carry out an action like the one I did?"

And here it comes back once more—the despairing outburst declaring that she was the perpetrator, he the victim. He wanted to kill himself but could not bring himself to do it. He was not under pressure but stresses all the same: he was sick, sick, sick. Can no one understand?

Is this the talk of a man with below-normal intelligence? lacking in empathy? A man who reacts naively and primitively? Or is this a desperate expression of emotion arising from a desperate situation?

This is how I understand his case: the official diagnosis was mistaken, and instead Rahmi's reactions fit into a rational and consistent pattern with an internal logic. This is uncomfortable for us to accept. But it is dangerous not to.

Honor killings have their own iron logic. One man had been charged with killing Fadime, but the Swedish system of justice, as Nalin Pekgul points out, is not suited to dealing with this type of crime. The focus is on the individual perpetrator. But in crimes carried out for the sake of honor, several people are responsible. Such crimes are acts of collectives, based on their analyses and conclusions.

Rahmi Sahindal cut a poor figure in court. The psychiatric report confirmed this impression: Fadime's father had had a deprived childhood and youth. His life as a shepherd meant that animals were his best friends (he has spoken of how he confided in them), and his upbringing had been beaten into him. He is nearly illiterate and lacks ability to adjust. He is stiff, unyielding, monomaniacal in his view of himself and those around him—which is not surprising, given his negative self-regard.

The psychiatric report is contained in four pages of ordinary typescript. It is a condensation of an entire human being. That human being is fighting for his life in court and becomes involved in a contradictory rigmarole to explain what he did or did not do, thought and did not think, felt and did not feel. Seen from this perspective, he is "one of us." The difference between him and most Scandinavians, and most Kurds too, is that he has taken the leap and made reality of an idea of honor that he denies: it was not an honor killing; he is not looking for honor in Swedish society. But she insulted him. That is why he went to find her and shot her.

This is a clear enough tale. "World opinion" reflected his self-image, as it would when the next battle started in the Swedish Court of Appeal.

11 *Strength Born from Grief*

Murderers too must be given a voice. It is no use just to condemn, we should also try to understand. Only when we attempt to follow the chain of thought that led to the crime—for it will entail a kind of rationality, however perverted and terrible—can we hope to help prevent similar tragedies.

This is why Rahmi Sahindal has been allowed to hold forth at such length. "What happened" has been told from his point of view and in his words.

The family has also been allowed to speak—Fadime's mother and sisters. This is how I have responded to the relatives' criticism that the media and the public don't want to listen to what they have to say. Spokespersons for the family claim that they are misunderstood, that whatever they say is taken the wrong way. It's actually useless for them to try to tell *their* story. The media are all out to blacken their name.

"They see us vampires, whereas she is just a little immigrant lass who they feel sorry for. But she is the strongest now. She has got money, education. Her father is completely broken; her mother cries all the time. We sit with them every night, trying to comfort them and help them survive," one relative said at the time of the 1998 trial.

It is instantly obvious why Fadime should be so appealing to the media. Beautiful young women easily grab attention. How could her father, a worn-out working man, compete? Or her younger, semi-criminalized brother, or her nearly helpless mother? Is there a grain of truth in the family narrative about Fadime, the media's pet sacrificial lamb? Could it be that she was carried away by her eagerness to be a celebrity? That her portrayal of the family was based on fantasy and exaggeration?

Now it has been said. The questions are on the table. The voices of the relatives have been heard. One might elaborate their version by letting other voices join in. Twelve members of the family were interviewed by the police, besides those already quoted—Rahmi, Elif, Songül, Nebile, and Haydar. Their statements to the police fill some 150 pages of typescript, but none of them testified in Uppsala District Court. However, I feel that it is unnecessary to present their stories here. In total, the statements by the family (about two hundred pages) add up to a consistent picture of a father, ill and forced to act despite himself, pushed into depths of despair because his daughter has put him and his family into the media spotlight. To be on display, exposed to the scorn of the world at large, would weigh heavily on most people. Fadime was an oppressor. She and the media together turned her father into a killer.

At this point, Fadime must be allowed to speak. Her side of the story has never been properly told. From time to time it has been visible between the lines, as it were. The case begins and ends with her, but her testimony has been chopped up into scattered sentences. Maybe it once seemed all that was necessary. But now we have paid enough attention to the views of her nearest and dearest; hearing Fadime's voice again feels like an acute necessity. The victim must have the last word. Listen to her as she testifies in an interview on July 25, 1998.

In the streaming rain on June 3, 1998, the day before Fadime and Patrik were going to move in together, Patrik's car went off the road between Stockholm and Uppsala. He was killed instantly.

"I still cannot grasp that he is gone. We lived for each other. I still wait for him, expecting him to come through the door. You see—Patrik was my first love. He taught me so much."

"Do you feel it is unjust?"

"Yes, it feels like a punishment. Like we must have done something terrible to deserve this. That's what my family says—that it was the hand of God. 'Not even God is on her side,' they say."[1]

Fadime was not invited to Patrik's funeral, but she attended all the same. His family believed that his relationship with her had caused his death. The accident was investigated for possible criminal intent, but no evidence was found. Fadime herself did not think her family was behind it. After Fadime's murder, the investigation into the circumstances of Patrik's death was restarted but was again inconclusive.

Patrik's family didn't accept Fadime while he was alive. "They were Iranians and against intermarriage with Kurds," Fadime says (Patrik's father came from Iran; his mother was Swedish). It is a measure of the strength of the young couple's love for each other that, even so, Patrik's father and grandmother went to ask Fadime's family to let her marry Patrik. It also shows how much the family cared for him.

Patrik was never to meet Fadime's family. In the spring 1998 interview—part of a TV documentary on Fadime's life—he admits that he is irritated and angry with her relatives. "You are condemned out of hand. They don't want to know why I care for Fadime. They're totally ignorant about me. They just go 'we, we, we' all the time. They aren't interested in how I see it at all."[2] But most of all, he is angry about the way Fadime has been humiliated by her family. How did he feel about the responsibility that rests on his shoulders, the journalist asks, after Fadime was expelled from her family? Patrik says that they have thought and talked a lot about it. The feeling holding them together is very strong. But what, wonders the journalist, if things go wrong? They have thought and talked about that too. The future cannot be guaranteed. But they stand by their choice.

Fadime and Patrik should have started living together on June 4, 1998—in Uppsala, the city from which she had been expelled. One can imagine the outrage this would have caused in her family. Whether Patrik's death was accidental or premeditated, it is understandable that his family blamed Fadime. In any case, given how fragile Patrik had felt for so long due to the inhuman pressures he and Fadime had endured, his reactions may have been dulled.

They had been granted two years as sweethearts. Patrik and Fadime met on a course in computing in 1996. Patrik later spoke of how Fadime held back at first, how hard it was for her to show her feelings. She knew what she risked if she fell in love with a "Swede." She warned him in good time of what a relationship with her would mean for them both. During their first year together, it was an "indoors only" affair. Patrik had said: "For heaven's sake, we're not fourteen!" and later they were less cautious.

Then, on September 3, 1997, Fadime's father spotted them walking along the street together. We have already heard Fadime admit that seeing him scared her silly. "I was so frightened! I thought, this is it!" From that day on, she couldn't go back home. Her father would break her neck the moment he got his hands on her. In the street, he had to be content with raging, calling her names, threatening her, and spitting at her. With two police officers as protection, she went home to collect her passport and personal belongings. This was her exit from the family—from that day she was on her own. Only her sister Songül and a few cousins supported her. Songül moved in with her for a period of about two years.

Fadime moved to Sundsvall in order to study, but Patrik stayed in Uppsala. She had been accepted at the Sundsvall Institute already before the fateful encounter with her father. Now the chance to study was her salvation. Her further education had been much against her family's wishes. In their view, Fadime said, living on your own was just as bad as having a boyfriend. But ever since she was little, she had been determined to study something, to work and live like her Swedish friends. She wanted to train, gain knowledge, and use what she learned to do her best for other people.

On the other hand, the road her family had wanted her to take would have led to marriage with a cousin from Turkey. She had always been aware that her marriage would be arranged by her family. "You just know. Such are the rules," Fadime says and goes on to explain: "When the girls are sixteen years old, they are taken for a holiday in Turkey.[3] The girl knows what it's about, that she may be married off, but aloud she says it's just a visit to the old country and that she'll say no to any offers of marriage. But she marries, all the same, because of the pressure she's under."

"Isn't the girl scared? The man is a stranger after all," the journalist asks.

"Of course she's scared, but she is forced into it. It's not what she would choose for herself."

"But isn't the girl dreaming about a different future?"

"Of course she dreams, exactly the same kind of dreams as Swedish girls. It just doesn't work out like that. She has no choice." Fadime adds that the marriage unites two families, not two individuals. "Anyway, they [Turkish people] would do anything to send a son over here."[4]

Fadime's brother travels to Sundsvall, confronts her, and issues death threats. By January 1998 it is obvious that her family will not accept her marriage to Patrik, come what may. During the winter and spring of 1998 she receives a series of phone calls threatening her with death. Other family members phone to harangue her. Her nine-year-old little sister calls her a "fucking whore."

"It makes you sick at heart to hear a nine-year-old girl's voice say: 'We'll kill you, you're a whore.' But it isn't really my little sister speaking, she doesn't know what she's saying. She's strong, though. I hope she'll break free of them one day."[5]

Fadime says that she has chosen to tell her story to the media because she hopes it might help others in the same situation, as well as protect her life. "Perhaps they won't dare to kill me now that so many people know who I am!"

But she felt it necessary to turn to the media for another reason, which was that the police did not take her seriously the first time she reported the death threats against her, on January 11, 1998. This was why she went public on February 4, in an interview for the Stockholm-based evening paper *Aftonbladet*. The interview triggered further death threats, Fadime complained to the police again, and this time the case was heard in court (April 1998). The trial made history. It was a Scandinavian first: a father and a brother charged with threatening to kill a girl on the basis of *her* report. Fadime was offered the option of the court hearings' being conducted behind locked doors. She refused. The public must know of her situation, a knowledge that she hoped would help others and frighten off her family.

Just as the trial is about to begin, Fadime is asked if she is afraid.

"I'm most afraid of their hatred," she replies. "But I'll go through fire and flood if it helps just one individual."

During the trial, her brother's hatred runs out of control. He rages against Patrik and, in a break, attacks Fadime. It is heartbreaking to hear their mother scream. When Mesut is charged with contempt of court, his defense is straightforward: if there is a conflict between Swedish law and Kurdish tradition, he will follow Kurdish tradition. Because he is seventeen years old, he is legally a minor and his sentence is mild: like his father, he is fined 20,000 Swedish kronor (ca. $3,500). Fadime's lawyer, Leif Ericksson, had argued for damages of 60,000 kronor to be paid jointly by her father and brother. One of the journalists asks if that wasn't too large a sum, but Ericksson replies, "No, rather too low. What has taken place constitutes an unbelievable violation of Fadime. She has lost her entire family. If Patrik goes, what would be left for her?"

One month later Patrik dies. Fadime is as brittle as glass, according to her friends. One week after his death, Fadime's brother beats her up in the middle of Central Square in Uppsala. "It was sheer luck that I wasn't killed," Fadime said afterward. "Had I met him in a place with fewer people around, he would have killed me. I'm certain of that. He is perfectly capable of murder."

In August 1998, a new trial starts. The brother is sentenced to five months in prison and criminal damages of 20,000 kronor. The judge's summing up stated:

> On June 11, 1998, Mesut Sahindal encountered Fadime Sahindal on Central Square in Uppsala, where he subjected her to physical abuse, that is, he head-butted her in the face, pulled her hair, and then kneed her in the face. When Fadime Sahindal fell to the ground, Mesut Sahindal hit her head with his fists and kicked her body. This beating has caused not only severe pain, but also headaches, bruising of face and body, and continued ache in her chest and on the right side of her abdomen.
>
> This is grievous bodily harm. Specifically, Mesut Sahindal behaved ruthlessly as he, without provocation, set about abusing the physically weaker Fadime Sahindal in a public place and, once she was on the ground, continued to kick her. Furthermore, this abuse is part of a history of repeated and serious attacks on her.[6]

As we have seen, Fadime deliberately staked everything on courting publicity. One aspect of this strategy was the TV documentary in which she and Patrik collaborated with the journalist Marianne Spanner in spring 1998. It included film clips showing Mesut as he attempted to attack Fadime during the trial and had to be forcibly restrained. The documentary was first shown on May 6 that year, the day before the sentencing of her father and brother. It offers a moving and terrifying insight into what Fadime (and Patrik) had to live with but probably also served to stoke the anger of her relatives. It is impossible to judge whether Fadime would have used the same media strategy if Patrik had not stood by her. As it was, she had to bear the consequences alone, in a situation totally different from what she had imagined.

Fadime became a national celebrity. Everyone wanted a piece of her life, and she felt beleaguered by the media. She received endless invitations to feature in all sorts of events. She was also asked to

Not done for attention.

comment on Pela's murder but refused. "No more broadcasting, no more newspapers. I've done my part," she said. She stood firm. The talk she gave in the Old Parliament Building, which was not meant to be publicized, was an exception.

Fadime never judged her parents. She tried to understand them. In the *Aftonbladet* interview in February 1998 she said, "All this begins and ends with my parents' fear of Swedish society. They are both illiterate and find Swedish people hard to understand. They live surrounded by their own people and the satellite dish which allows them to watch only Turkish TV. I don't know how many times I've tried to persuade my mother that Swedish girls are not whores. Mummy simply says that she knows what she sees with her own eyes." Fadime put it as clearly in her last public engagement, her talk in the parliament building in November 2001: her parents were victims of poor integration, and she sympathized with their plight. They had lost both their honor and their daughter.

Fadime was too deeply rooted in Kurdish culture not to understand what her parents were going through and why. Her refusal to marry her Turkish cousin was regarded as a cardinal sin. *She had valued her own happiness more than her loyalty to the community.* Or as the chairman of the Kurdish Association in Malmö said later, when asked to comment on Fadime's death: "In the Kurdish culture, the girl can choose whom she wants to marry, but her parents must approve of it. . . . If the girl has been brought up properly, she accepts our judgment of her choice. If she does not, you may have to make your own daughter an outcast."[7]

bad daughter = bad parents.

Fadime rebelled against this kind of "culture." "I can understand . . . my parents, who have grown up in quite a different reality. But I do not accept it. This 'culture' my parents claim we must take care of—it's just nonsense. They're frightened to lose control of the family."

Fadime believed that many immigrants find the contrast between their Swedish present and their past so great that they invent rules, which they call "their culture," to protect themselves. For instance, the rule that girls must be strictly brought up while the boys can do as they please. "My brother had a Swedish girlfriend who lived with us for half a year. But I am ostracized for going out with a Swedish boy. It's not like that in Turkey, you know. There, girls are allowed to study and live away from the family and have a life of their own."[8]

Fadime had plenty of support. Many, both men and women, have argued that in immigrant families girls are kept under stricter control abroad than in the parental country of origin.[9] The Swedish Kurd Masoud Kamali says, "Many of the traditional values are reinforced in exile. For the ethnic group it is a matter of marking their territory."[10] Fadime crossed the line when she chose a Swedish boyfriend and a Swedish lifestyle. The Norwegian Kurd Sükrü Bilgiç has confirmed that among Turkish people in Norway the segregation of the sexes is intensified and that the result is restrictions on the freedom of women.[11] This holds true for other ethnic groups too. "Culture" legitimizes your customs and becomes the catch-all word for what you want to protect. Fadime, and many with her, have protested that this process is always at the girls' expense.[12]

When you feel pressured by outsiders, you naturally tend to retreat and hide among your own people. Some immigrants to northern European countries think that they are surrounded by sinfulness. Safeguarding your beliefs and identity becomes urgent. In most societies, and especially those with a strong code of honor, women are the carriers of tradition and family reputation. We have already observed that honor crimes are on the increase in large Turkish cities, due to the population influx from the countryside and the increasing liberation of women. Many immigrants to European countries remain deeply rooted in rural cultures established several hundred years ago. More recently, the growth of religious fundamentalism has promoted cultural conservatism—and in some instances extremism—in a number of countries and regions. In some cases, political oppression has had the same effect. Brutal living conditions have been imposed on the Kurds during the last twenty or thirty years of their battle for the independence of Turkish Kurdistan. Fadime's parents came from that part of the world.

Fadime did not regard what had happened to her as in any way extreme. "It is the same for most girls from the Middle East, Pakistan, India, and Iran." She knew many stories like her own.

We know that Fadime feared her brother more than her father. She did not believe that her father would ever take her life, but she felt sure that her brother might try to.[13] Many of her close friends have confirmed that Mesut would have killed her if he had got hold of her. He seems to have tried to when he saw Fadime in Uppsala on that day in June. Bystanders intervened and rescued her, but she was seriously injured.

We have also heard Fadime's father say that she had to leave Uppsala for Mesut's sake.

Mesut had been three years old when he arrived in Sweden. By the time he attacked his sister, he had had a Swedish girlfriend and moved in with her. Some things single him out: for instance, he was the only boy among six siblings. From the moment when a boy was born at last, after four girls, the family would have indulged and pampered him. Sons carry on the family line, and it is their right and duty to protect and control the girls.

Fadime understands her little brother. He is bound by customs and practices demanding that, as the next head of the family, he must undo the dishonor she has brought on her family and on the Kurdish community. He cannot act independently, given the pressures on him and expectations of what he will do. She realizes that if he kills her, he would become a hero in the eyes of the entire family.

This is what she has to say about the time after Patrik's death:

> I was completely apathetic after the accident. I couldn't manage to do anything. It was actually my brother's beatings that woke me up. How could they believe that I'd care about a few bruises? I, who had lost everything and had hit rock bottom. Nothing could be worse. And then they trample on me in such a situation. It ignited me. It maddened me. I felt like

shouting loudly, wildly. I thought, I'll be damned if they are going to break me. I'll show them, I'll manage.

So ironically, it's those who are trying to kill me who are keeping me alive.[14]

But they won in the end. They won by ambushing her. Even Fadime could not hold out against a gun. Three men, one after another, claimed to be her murderer. This courageous young woman had become important enough for three men to have a motive for killing her. We have come across two of them. The third man turns up in the Court of Appeal. There may well have been other supportive figures, someone who actively helped Fadime's father to get hold of a gun and transport him to the site of the crime.

During the appeal hearing, the court watched a videotaped police interview of her father as he explains in detail how he committed the crime and where the shots hit his victim. The man on the tape is apparently thrilled and proud over what he has done. He does not glory in the deed, but there is no regret in his face. I would characterize him as rather upbeat and excited.

Father doesn't show remorse ⇒ doesn't want jail. Wants to be treated by Turk law.

IV Norwegian Lives

Intermission:
   Honor in the Courtroom

Have honor killings like these happened in Norway? People—
Swedes especially—sometimes ask me this. The answer is no, at
least not the same kinds. The Swedes have Fadime, Sara, and Pela in
mind, and in Norway we have not had to deal with similar cases—
thus far.

The Norwegian experience is different from the Swedish. Honor
killings have taken place in Norway, as in other European countries.
But there has been no high-profile case of a father or brother being
tried for murdering a young woman for honor's sake. However, a
case is under investigation.

A case of triple murder was due to come before the court in the
autumn of 2007. A man of Pakistani background killed all three of
his sisters; they were twenty-six, twenty-five, and thirteen years
old. The girls were axed and shot to death. The family are long-
time residents of Norway. The youngest girl was born there. The
perpetrator claims to have been "of unsound mind." He had been
clinically depressed for the previous four years. It may well be that
the murders were not premeditated; it remains to be seen what
the court will decide. But it is well known that there had been severe honor-related conflicts in the family. In 2002, the eldest girl,
then twenty-one years old, went to court to obtain a divorce from

her violent husband from a forced marriage; he was also her paternal cousin. Her father, and the brother who is now charged, strongly opposed her decision. The ex-husband was then deported to Pakistan.

The three sisters were unusually close; their mother was dead, and the eldest was like a mother to the younger. She was just to begin working in an organization set up to help young women of immigrant background. She also wanted to move with her sisters from the family abode into a flat of their own. On the day of the murder, she had received the deed for the flat.

The sisters had also appealed to an organization helping immigrant women for support and advice regarding family problems.

The case was bound to attract huge attention when it opened in court, as it already had at the time of the murder in October 2006. Swedish courts are recognized to be much more efficient than Norwegian courts. In Fadime's case it took less than two months from the murder until the trial in the district court, which was especially fast. The very special circumstances made high efficiency both important and possible. But overall, the Swedish judicial system is noted for its efficiency.[1] A problem with the triple murder is that the Norwegian police could hardly find witnesses who were willing to testify. There was no Songül, no Breen, nor any other family member who would talk. Other potential witnesses, unrelated to the family, also resisted because of fear of reprisals. The police investigators contacted me to seek some advice regarding how to handle the problem of "complicity of silence." This is one of the crucial problems confronting law and order in the new Europe. Ways must be found to ensure that witnesses can give testimony without incurring revenge for themselves and their families. This is not the place to probe that problem further. But it *is* worth reflecting on the fact that the murder of three young women silences a community—at least in regard to the judicial process.

As of this writing, no one had yet been found guilty in this case; it remains to be seen what the outcome will be. There is a widespread opinion in the Pakistani community in Oslo that the perpetrator suffered from a mental illness, but also that the violence was in part due to problems of honor: the shame inflicted by the eldest sister's divorce and the court proceedings connected to it.

The perpetrator, who was the eldest of three brothers, was the head of the family in Norway, as the father mostly stayed in Pakistan. Whatever the outcome of the court case, the family honor will be restored in the eyes of *some* members of the larger transnational community. The girls are gone. Shame has been wiped away. It may be seen as God's will.

By the time Fadime died, I knew of only one Norwegian instance where it was proved that a woman was murdered by her own family in an honor killing. The murderer, her brother, stated in court that he had killed her and her husband for the sake of honor. The couple had married without the permission of the men in the bride's family, although her mother had approved. The bride's brother had acted to avert dishonor. His punishment was imprisonment for life (normally thirteen or fourteen years), then deportation. The prisoner protested against deportation on the grounds that in Pakistan, members of his dead brother-in-law's family would be out to kill him. He had good reason to fear revenge. The rules demand it, to use Fadime's expression. The case raises an interesting question of legal principle: no one can be deported from Norway if it is proved that he or she runs a real risk of being killed as a consequence. The logic of reprisal demands that men be killed in order to avenge murder. Is this sufficient reason to let a murderer stay in Norway after having served his sentence?

We have observed that honor killings are tactical acts. As a rule, they are premeditated and well planned. This can also be said about other honor crimes. The perpetrator is not picked at random. Within the family, assignments will usually be made. As Fadime said in her talk in Parliament, it was her brother who "was given the task to kill me," because he was under age and would not be punished as severely as an older man would. The fact that young perpetrators are picked to carry out honor crimes is well known. Under Swedish law, Sara's two killers were sentenced to three and a half and four years in prison, respectively. In 2006, another young man received a similar sentence in Sweden. He had killed his sister's boyfriend in an unusually brutal murder. His sister escaped and later testified in court for the prosecution. Both the victim and the perpetrator were of Afghan (Hazara) origin. The case raised outrage in Sweden because the culprit's parents, who had also been charged, were acquitted. The verdict from Göta High Court states that the culprit could hardly have carried out the murder alone, according to the evidence, but that it could not be proved that it was his parents, and not others, who had participated in the actual slaughter, although the parents were proved to have been in the location.[2] So the verdict served precisely the interests that accomplices in an honor killing have: to assign the job to someone who will be lightly punished. "Honor" outwits the law, so to speak.

Could it be that the humanistic tradition of northern Europe has had the "side effect" that honor killings of men are committed here rather than in, for example, Afghanistan or Pakistan, while women are preferably killed abroad, where sentencing for that crime is lenient? Such questions are hypothetical. It is impossible to generalize on the basis of the evidence we have; and there will be contingencies and deliberations of various kinds in actual, concrete cases. Still, it is worth reflecting on the case of the man who, after committing murder for honor's sake in Norway, protested against deportation to Pakistan on the grounds that there he risked being killed for honor's sake.

When this man was tried in 1993, the case did not attract much attention, nor did it trigger a debate about honor and killing for honor's sake. The time had not yet come, and the two victims belong among those who were "killed too soon." The whole affair was regarded as a curiosity, of no account to "us."

Let us remind ourselves that "honor killing" was not established as a category in Sweden until after the trial of Pela's murderers in December 2000.

The Scandinavian public was shaken by what happened to Sara, Pela, and Fadime because the girls were so very normal; in the words of Breen, Pela's sister, "You want to decide things about your own life, like a human being." Young Norwegian women *may* have been killed abroad for wanting precisely that, as we shall soon see. But so far, no cases in Norway have caused a stir on anything like the scale of the murders of Sara, Pela, and Fadime.

In Norway we have seen honor killings of a different type: wives murdered by their husbands. In 1996 a Norwegian-Pakistani woman was killed by her husband (also a Pakistani), who declared in court that the deed was an honor killing (see chapter 15).

In May 2002 the murder of the Afghan woman Anooshe Sediq Ghulam shook the country. Her husband shot her on the steps of the city courthouse in Kristiansund, a town on the west coast. Anooshe had filed for divorce, and the court was about to hear the custody case regarding the couple's two young sons. When Anooshe's papers were examined after her death, certain circumstances came to light, including the pattern of her husband's threats, which suggested an honor killing.

In June 2002 the District Court in Skien pronounced sentence in the case of the Norwegian-Palestinian Gamal Hosein. Hosein was found guilty of having murdered his Norwegian wife, who had had an affair with Hosein's much younger nephew and, according to witness statements, wanted a divorce. Hosein denies this. Was it an honor killing? It is hard to be sure. The murder might have been motivated by jealousy. It is sometimes difficult to draw a demarcation line. Honor killings do not always fit into an easy-to-identify category. I have shown that the background and motives need to be known, not only of the individual who kills but also of the collective that is more or less involved. If the perpetrator is to regain his honor, his group must back him. Indeed, the honor of the group is also at stake, since honor is a shared quality and not just a personal matter. In some cases, members of the group might lend active support by helping to plan and, occasionally, carry out the murder. Or else they might stay on the sidelines and applaud—or stand there lamenting what has happened while at the same time sympathizing with the perpetrator.

Honor killings are difficult to identify in a northern European context because the judicial system, in theory as well as practice, does not regard "honor" as any kind of mitigating circumstance. One consequence is that neither the defendant nor his legal team is likely to bring up the subject of honor. On the contrary, everyone tries to deny that honor is relevant. This at least has been the pattern in the cases I have followed, in the media or as an observer: honor is underplayed in our courts because it gains the accused no favors. Tor Erling Staff, the defense lawyer acting for the Afghan man Zahiredin Nasrudin Shamsi who was accused of shooting his wife Anooshe, moved quickly to deny that the deed was an honor killing. Now what did he mean? What, in his view, is an honor killing? Staff was only doing his job. Clearly, he had decided to insist that honor had nothing to do with the murder, because it would serve his client best. "Honor" has a primitive ring to it. It has been stripped of the more heroic connotation it once had. "Honor" has become a compromised notion, so it is better if it is not thought to have anything to do with the defendant.

Rahmi Sahindal denied categorically that Fadime's murder was an honor killing. "I'm not after honor in Sweden," he said. In court he used the word just once: "It's about one's honor, you know," he said and went on to explain how disgraced he felt in front of his relatives and neighbors and friends—in front of world opinion, as he called it. At all other times he stuck to describing what had happened and the persecution and harassment he felt exposed to, rather than his emotional reactions. Such reactions were packaged as "being sick": rather sick than ashamed. Rahmi bypassed the rhetoric of honor, even though indirect references turned up in many of his addresses to the court.

If the trials had taken place in the United States of America, it is possible that the defense would have pleaded that the court should consider the defendant's cultural background. In the United States, the concept of a "cultural defense" is established within the judicial process.[3] But it is thought controversial because of the many problematic questions it poses. I will cite one famous example: the case of *The People v. Kimura*.

A woman called Fumiko Kimura tried to kill herself and her children by drowning after she found out that her husband had been unfaithful. The children died, but Fumiko Kimura survived. She was of Japanese origin but had lived in the United States for fourteen years. In Japan, an unfaithful husband traditionally brings terrible shame on his wife and children. The "solution" attempted by this woman is not unknown in Japan, where there is a special word for it: *oyako-shinju*. It is now illegal.[4]

So did Kimura act as a Japanese woman? And if she did, should it count in mitigation of child murder charges? When her case was tried in 1989, this question was raised in court. Her legal team argued that the answer must be yes, that is, the crime was motivated by cultural factors. Experts on Japanese culture were called in support. To commit suicide and protect the children from the shame brought on them by the husband's treachery and betrayal was a taught response, part of the wife's "cultural baggage." Kimura had acted according to "her cultural tradition."

Or had she? When the judge pronounced on her guilt, he limited his review of the evidence to circumstances with a bearing on the accused woman's mental state at the time of the crime. In other words, he eliminated the option of using the full scope of a cultural defense. But the psychologists in her defense team, as well as her extensive grassroots support, must have swayed the jury: they decided that at the time of the deed her mind was temporarily disturbed. She got away with just one year in prison, followed by five years on probation. In addition, she had to receive therapy.

The experts called by the defense argued that a mother's killing her children and/or herself is a tradition in Japan, giving the wives and children of philandering men a way out of the humiliation that living with shame and degradation would entail. Kimura was "a traditional Japanese woman, strongly influenced by her early cultural experiences."[5]

In both the media and academic writing, the Kimura case triggered a wide-ranging debate. One of the fundamental issues is what saying "Fumiko Kimura acted according to her culture" actually

Use culture as a way of getting out of punishment

meant. What was her culture? She had lived for fourteen years in the United States and was in many ways well integrated: she had worked outside the home for years and was attending college. In Japan the cultural tradition said to condone mother-and-child suicide and murder is dying out. Arguably, it was never a general rule. Perhaps such shame-killings were exceptional in the past, as in the present?

"Tradition" is a difficult concept. Traditions can be invented, discarded, and reinvented. They can also be contested: people can *Honor killing isn't agreed upon.* disagree about what was truly traditional at different times and in different places. This is the case with "honor" as well. There are those who claim that a tradition of honor killing exists among the Kurds in Turkey, Iraq, and Iran and among the Palestinians and the Arabs in Israel. Others deny all or some of these claims. Fadime's father said that honor killings used to be common in his region of Turkey but that was a hundred or maybe fifty years ago. Turkey's human rights advocates contradict him and state that honor crimes are still common in that region. A witness in the trial of Gamal Hosein declared that she had never heard of honor killings being carried out in Israel. Another source states that there are about twelve such killings annually, a figure supported by several independent reports. "Honor killing" is a sensitive issue and the numbers are hard to pin down definitively, for the reasons we have seen.

The concept of "cultural defense" also raises other problematic questions. What are the implications of arguing that a particular crime has been influenced by culture? How does one go about defining a culture, or drawing boundaries between cultures? For instance, are all Kurds, or maybe all Turkish Kurds, part of one culture? No, definitely not. Where a culture of honor killings has been identified, is it true that all those brought up in that culture—or at least all the men—are likely to commit honor killings under certain circumstances? Where is the borderline between influence and conditioning? If murder is a learned cultural act, are some people programmed to kill whenever the "right" conditions apply? Is this truly the case? Do we act like that? Do we not have a number of degrees of freedom to choose?

Another key question: for how long can someone who has left his or her original home be assumed to belong to its culture? Rahmi Sahindal had lived in Sweden for twenty years, almost half his life. After all those years away, would it be meaningful to regard his roots in traditional Kurdish culture as a mitigating factor?

Before the start of the trial of Rahmi Sahindal, Swedish journalist and author Jan Guillou wrote in his newspaper column about the likelihood that the defense would try to use exactly this kind of argument: that the accused man's culture or religion should count in his favor. Guillou warned against this and argued that murder is a murder, regardless of motive.[6]

Rahmi Sahindal's defense lawyer, Johan Åkermark, knew all this. Bringing "culture" into the case could only harm his client. Worse still, it would provide him with an obvious motive for killing Fadime. The cultural defense was not used. Instead he argued that Rahmi was ill and, besides, the evidence was not technically good enough to convict him. That Rahmi had pleaded guilty was not sufficient: Åkermark reminded the court that around two hundred individuals had claimed to be the murderer of Olof Palme, the former Swedish prime minister. None of them had been convicted.

Later on, I learned that many Kurds in Norway thought the Swedish legal system unjust to Rahmi Sahindal because his culture had not been taken into account. The judge should have asked, Why did this man kill his daughter? What had she done to force him to be a killer? How had Fadime's decisions affected her father's *namus* and *shirif*—two aspects of honor dependent on, respectively, a woman's modesty and his social status? The trial was just a spectacle, or so many Kurds claim; it should have focused on the essential themes of *namus* and *shirif*.

It is easy to agree with them about the spectacle, at least up to a point. As we will soon see, I am referring to the appeal proceedings in particular. However, I also have in mind the way Rahmi's nephew intervened in the District Court trial by insisting that he was the killer. Again, the defense team saw to it that honor did not feature. They could have chosen other options, but that is easier when the killer is a young man. Sara's murderers got three and a half and four years in prison. A brother, twenty years old, who stabbed his sister twenty-one times with a knife and paralyzed her for life, was sentenced to six years' imprisonment. He screamed in court: "She's a whore! She doesn't exist for us anymore! Don't you get it? My entire family is dishonored, my life is ruined, my mother's life is ruined!"[7] Fadime's brother challenged the court when he said, "If there's a conflict between Swedish law and Kurdish cultural tradition, then I am right to follow the tradition."[8]

Young men will carry on like this. The law favors them. Rahmi Sahindal had to rely on a different strategy. Mesut Sahindal had reached the age of twenty-two—he was an adult—by the time Fadime was murdered. It is not unlikely that Mesut's adulthood freed him from the "duty" to kill her.[9]

In Swedish and Norwegian courts, defense pleas based on "culture" are much less likely to be made on behalf of adults today than in the past.[10] In the early to mid 1990s, lawyers sometimes asked me to appear as their expert witness. I was to explain acts of violence in terms of "culture." When I refused, I was asked on two occasions: "Do you think we'll be able to find someone else who is prepared to state that the accused did it because of his culture?" I had to reply, "Probably!"[11]

There are no objective criteria for what "culture" is. Culture is what you choose to see at a given time. Rahmi Sahindal provides good examples of this when he addressed the court. One moment he denies that the Swedish and Kurdish cultures are different in any way, and the next, he claims that they're like day and night. His reasons are strategic: he says whatever is in his interest at the time. A detached outsider might contribute a clearer vision of the real issues, but even an expert witness has a position, a standpoint from which he or she evaluates the world. *Culture is one short word that can take on many meanings and serve many purposes.* Fadime and her parents disagreed about aspects of Kurdish culture. Nebile protested wildly against her sister's view of the family culture. As an expert, I can understand what they all mean and will then attempt to explain why they see things differently. But I cannot be completely neutral. There is no high ground from which matters of morality, values, and judgment can be dispassionately observed and evaluated. No one can be entirely objective; we are all influenced by our experiences and our subjective interpretation of them. As they say, there is no view from nowhere.

That said, I feel I can add a comment based on my own experience. During the past fifteen years, I have often been asked to appear as an expert witness on "culture" in Norwegian court cases. The request has sometimes come from the defense, sometimes from the prosecution. One thing I have learned is that my initial, moral response to a particular crime matters little when I am in court. As I listen to the attorneys and the witnesses, I try to identify the point of view of whoever is arguing or testifying at the time. To me, a social anthropologist, this is second nature. Anthropologists are trained to engage with "the native's point of view" and then to record "the point of view of the others in the group," that is, always to be aware of the potential for differences within any group of people. My training serves me well in court because it makes it easier for me to remain neutral than one might otherwise expect.

In other words, my training has instilled a mental discipline that allows me to see both sides of an argument. The following brief account of a court case illustrates my point.

I was an expert witness in the Anooshe Ghulam trial, noted above, which took place in the spring of 2004. Anooshe Sediq Ghulam was twenty-two and the mother of two young sons. Her husband had shot her the year before outside the Kristiansund District Court, where the custody case of the couple's children was being heard. He went straight in to the police afterward, arms over head, and gave himself up. Detailed information about Anooshe's life that became available after her death made it seem clear that the murder was an honor killing.

Anooshe had lived with death threats; she had a secret address and was terrified of the revenge her husband's family might wreak on her parents in Afghanistan. Her husband, Zahiredin Nasrudin Shamsi, belonged to a very powerful, military clan, whereas her own family was politically weak; education was its forte. The couple had been married since she was thirteen and he twenty-three; her family had been compelled to comply. The couple reached Norway by way of Iran, Russia, and Ukraine, having stayed one year in each country. Anooshe was used to marital violence, but it increased in Norway, where she took the lead. Language courses and training were offered to both husband and wife, but Anooshe benefited much more, since she already knew English and was well educated: she learned Norwegian quickly and easily adjusted to her new surroundings. Shamsi spoke only Dari and was a shy man; he grew depressed and felt threatened in his manhood. Then, after an incident when her husband urged their seven-year-old son to slap her in the face, Anooshe rebelled. She didn't want her sons to grow up to be violent men. She wanted to break the cycle of violence. Seeking help from the social services, she divorced and filed for custody of her sons.

It was a dauntless act, as seen from her native perspective, an act doomed to bring revenge: not just Anooshe but her family was in danger. It is telling that her parents would not be able to attend her funeral in Norway. Her father, Ghulam Azarakhsh, later wrote me thus from the family's place of refuge in a Western country:

> We very much wanted to attend the funeral, or at least, visit the burial site of my daughter, and help our young grandsons cope with their terrible loss. However, we were told (by the authorities at the Norwegian embassy) that that would not be possible, as your government could not guarantee our safety. So we were denied the right to say goodbye to our beloved daughter.
>
> Next, I wish to make it clear that Anooshe loved her adopted country and chose to stay in Norway, despite the threats on her life from her husband. That choice cost Anooshe her life. The authorities were unable to protect her, even though they were made aware of the dangerous situation.[12]

Why would the murderer's lawyer ask me to appear for the defense? I was surprised. After all, my conclusions could have implicated the defendant further. As it happened, what I said may have helped a little, because Zahiredin Nasrudin Shamsi got eighteen years in jail rather than a life sentence.[13]

Were there any mitigating circumstances? The defense attorney, Tor Erling Staff, is one of the best lawyers in Norway. Staff tried two lines of defense: one was that Shamsi was "of unsound mind," and the other, that his cultural background had made him unable to grasp that his wife would and could divorce him and claim custody of their sons. The mental instability plea was similar to Rahmi Sahindal's. The "cultural" defense implied that the murderer's Afghan upbringing and life experience had rendered him unable to cope with his wife's decision, which had consequently plunged him into despair.

Culture makes killing okay?

Indeed, what Anooshe had done would be unheard of in the homeland of her ethnic group, the Uzbeks, in northern Afghanistan: the right to divorce is for the man alone, who keeps custody of the children. Social workers report that when Shamsi was informed of Anooshe's decision, he crouched in a corner and cried. Though Shamsi told the court that he, too, had been forced to marry—in his homeland marriage is not for individuals to decide—he was attached to his wife and children. She had not told him she was leaving, she just left. He hadn't realized there were any serious problems between them before he was informed by the authorities that she was not coming back. The police told him that she had filed a complaint against him.

Police told of tension, not wife.

He claims that he brought the gun to the courthouse to commit suicide in public view: he wanted the world to know about the injustices of the Norwegian system. During the first year after Anooshe left, he didn't even know where she and the children lived: "For over a year, I could not see any human being in the face, the whole world laughed at me!" he says, reminding us of Rahmi Sahindal's reference to "world opinion."

Norway had been, to Shamsi, a devastating experience. "I thought I would be a free man," he said. He had never expected the *public interfering w/ private matters.*

authorities to interfere in his private life. They didn't do so in Iran, Russia, or Ukraine.

His story of the planned suicide was less than credible when it came to light that the year before he had offered two criminals a large sum of money to kill Anooshe. Also, he had bought the gun many months before and buried it in the ground not far from the district court. He dug it up in the morning of the murder and shot Anooshe in the back with six bullets. Then he slammed the gun down on her dead body.

Insight into the cultural background of a defendant can help make the circumstances and context of the crime more intelligible and hence shed light on his motives. Staff, Shamsi's lawyer, tried to do this. His strategy was to focus on the person, the human being, who must be seen for what he was: "Afghan and Muslim." Staff underscored that he was not thinking in terms of honor killing: "I have never used the term *honor killing*, but as Afghan and Muslim, my client has been humiliated to the core of his person. He must be judged according to Norwegian law, but should he morally be judged in terms of Afghan or Norwegian culture?"

To create sympathy for the defendant, Staff tries to expose the dilemmas and predicaments Shamsi experienced. He asks him a series of questions regarding his cultural background—questions regarding marriage, divorce, child upbringing, and male-female relations. "Honor" is not mentioned, as the primary stance of the defense is that this is not an honor killing. "Culture" seems a better approach. Shamsi gives short answers; he is taciturn, used to handling weapons, not words (he is a military officer by vocation). He weighs his words, though. He will not generalize about Afghans or Uzbeks (his ethnic group) but qualifies his statements saying he can tell only what he knows from his own experience; families differ. But yes, he and Anooshe hardly ever spent any time together before coming to Norway; it is not the practice for spouses in his home region. He has never heard of a wife's divorcing her husband in Afghanistan. If there is a problem between a couple, then "white-bearded men"— tribal elders—will mediate between the two families.

And then suddenly he tells Staff to stop, stop asking about culture. The interpreters convey the message, which is explicit: no more talk of culture. Put otherwise: no cultural defense, thank you.

What was at stake? To my understanding, the pride of his tribe or clan. Shamsi is not a lone individual. He has been brought up to always consider the collective good before his own well-being. Loyalty to the group comes before everything else. The integrity and worth of the group's traditions is unquestioned. It is a matter of honor to defend them through thick and thin. It is quite acceptable to try to obtain a lenient sentence based on extenuating circumstances or mental instability or self-defense. But to have your culture exposed as so many quaint customs in court is quite another matter.

Your lawyer's intentions may be the best, but the effect is to paint a negative picture of your traditions in light of Western ideals of freedom and equality. Shamsi risked dragging others with him into the pit.

It is not given, in other words, that a client will see his best interests served by a cultural defense. In this case, as in some other cases I have observed, there was a clash of interests between the defendant and his attorney. The man on trial is not just what he appears to be: an individual out to get acquitted. He is also a member of a particular clan or ethnic group which demands that he show pride, in public, in that culture. There is a media aspect to consider in all similar cases nowadays. Words travel. Shamsi himself mentioned how the presence of journalists meant that there were some things he could not say. He had five children, three of them in Afghanistan, and was afraid of revenge against them. True, he spoke in a district court in a regional Norwegian town, but he had a far-ranging audience to consider. "World opinion"—to borrow Rahmi Sahindal's expression.

Neither the defense nor the prosecution mentioned honor killings. But some witnesses for the defense reported that Shamsi had said that in his home region a wife would be killed for doing what

Anooshe had done, and that if he didn't do it, someone in his family would have killed her. Also, he had pleaded with an elderly Afghan "white-bearded man" in Norway to help him to meet with Anooshe so that he, Shamsi, could initiate the divorce. It would help him save his honor. "How else can I go with my head held high among my relatives?" he had said. But the problem of custody of his sons remained.

None of Shamsi's relatives attended the trial. He appeared a lone figure in court; it may have been part of a collective strategy; or it might indicate his group's disapproval of him.

To this day, his sons are living at a secret address and have police protection. The risk of their being kidnapped by Shamsi's powerful clan is still real, according to the police.

We have seen that "honor" makes a poor defense in a Scandinavian court and that the defendant's cultural background can be used against him. In August 2002 the Norwegian media reported what they saw as a significant event in legal history. Black headlines announced, "Issue of Principle against Kurdish Culture Raised in Court."[14] A male Iranian Kurd, twenty-seven years old, was accused of threatening to kill his younger sister (age twenty-three) on two occasions, because she refused to marry their cousin. The young woman told the police but later withdrew her charge. The police took the initiative and carried on with the investigation. They were convinced that the man's code of honor had driven him both to the death threats and to one act of violence: he beat up his sister and inflicted blows to her face. Regardless of her wishes, the police decided to charge her brother. Police lawyer Per J. Zimmer said, "In the opinion of the public prosecutor, the brother's motive can be identified as part of the culture he brought with him from Iran." Zimmer added, "I am not familiar with other cases in which a motive originating in cultural issues has been given prominence."

The brother was convicted and sentenced to ten months in prison, twice as long as the normal sentence in such cases. The reasoning behind the long sentence was articulated thus by the judge: "This is an increasingly common social problem. In the view of the court, an exceptionally severe punishment is appropriate in this type of case."[15] The reason for the swift pretrial investigation—it took only ten weeks from the report of the threats to start of the trial—was the public debate about honor killings and forced marriages. The police wanted to alert immigrant communities to how such cases would be handled.

Let us return to the question of where honor killings take place. Have such things happened in Norway? As we have seen, the answer is yes, there are cases, but no if what we meant was that young women are proved to have been killed by members of their immediate family for the sake of honor.

But young Norwegian women may have been killed abroad by their immediate family. In 1999, the TV program *Rikets Tilstand* (The State of the Nation) ran a series of documentaries about forced marriage, which showed that there may have been instances when Norwegian girls were killed in Pakistan while their murderers went free in Norway. The uncertainty is due to lack of evidence and witnesses willing to testify. A recent case illustrates the problems.

In 2005, public attention was aroused by the much-publicized case of Rahila Iqbal, who died in a car accident in Pakistan. Rahila, age eighteen, had been born and raised in Norway. Her father, her grandfather, and the family chauffeur were all charged but acquitted. The publicity focused on the fact that Rahila had been the target of death threats because she had married "the wrong man." He was also a Norwegian Pakistani, but his caste and brand of Islam were unacceptable to her family. By the time Rahila died, the couple was separated, but her husband was convinced that the car accident was an honor killing. So too were other friends and acquaintances of Rahila who knew of the threats she had faced.

Currently in Pakistan there is no state prosecution of honor killings. It is up to the family of the deceased to decide whether they want to bring charges. Usually charges will not be brought because the family of the victim is in on the act.[17] The killer has been picked by the family of the victim. But in Rahila's case, her husband managed, with the help of Norwegian authorities, to be accepted as her

[margin annotation: Killings go un-charged]

next of kin, against protests by her family. He filed charges against the three men: Rahila's father, her grandfather, and the family chauffeur. Rahila had drowned in a pond as the car driven by the family driver went off the road. The two were alone in the car. The chauffeur escaped unharmed.

Rahila's case raises a number of crucial issues regarding the investigation and trial of transnational crimes. The Norwegian police were barred from investigating the case in Pakistan and could not dispatch the evidence obtained in Norway to the police in Pakistan because Pakistani law decrees the death penalty for honor killings. True, so far that law has not been enforced. Actually, only about 7 percent of honor killings in Pakistan are tried in court.[16]

Norway shares with other European countries a ban on deporting people to countries where they risk torture or execution. One effect of this was seen in the case of the man who had killed his brother-in-law and protested against deportation to Pakistan because he risked being the victim of a revenge killing there. For the same reason, if a Norwegian citizen commits a crime in Pakistan that would rate—at least in principle—the death penalty, the Norwegian police must not hand over any incriminating evidence.

In the Rahila case, a further, crucial problem was that the Pakistani police would not order an autopsy to establish the cause of her death. Neither did they respond to the Norwegian police's request to share some of their documentation from investigation of the case. Cooperation is lacking. Rahila's father is now back in Norway. Since he is a Norwegian citizen, his lawyers in Pakistan were paid for by the Norwegian government. The Norwegian police would have wanted to file charges, but since it could not be established that Rahila was murdered and not just drowned, it would seem useless.

A positive effect of this very problematic case is a demand on the part of politicians and human rights activists that Norway and Pakistan establish some sort of cooperation regarding the investigation of cases like Rahila's. It would require interventions at the highest diplomatic level, as the issues are sensitive in many ways. But a change is needed.

Let us now look at another trial in which transnational relations and a conflict of law complicated matters. It attracted a lot of attention, and honor was a crucial issue. The young woman who was "offended against" has fortunately not suffered any serious physical injury, although she has been a target of death threats. The case in fact offers a glimmer of hope.

It is time for us to examine the case of Nadia.

13 Nadia's Case: Another Question of Honor

On October 3, 1997, the case of Nadia hit the Norwegian public like a bomb blast. Nadia's parents had taken the eighteen-year-old girl to Morocco. Nadia herself managed to raise the alarm, but by then she had been confined for three weeks. She was desperate to be free.

Nadia and her parents were Norwegian citizens (her father has died). Nadia was born and brought up in Norway. Her parents had lived there for about twenty years.[1]

The case was difficult for a variety of reasons, not just because Nadia had been taken out of the country. In addition, she and her parents had dual citizenship. Nadia was still a child in Morocco, where twenty is the age of majority for girls. It was up to her father as her guardian to decide whether she could go free.

He would agree to her release only on condition of free passage. He wanted an assurance that he would not be subject to prosecution when he returned to Norway. The Norwegian ambassador to Morocco, who negotiated on behalf of Norway, could make no such promise. This set the stage for a clash of steely wills. Nadia's father promised several times to set her free; then nothing happened. When contact with Nadia ceased and she allegedly had been carried off to a small village in the mountains, many feared that Nadia's battle was lost.

And then she suddenly turned up in Oslo. It seemed that her father had sent her back voluntarily. However, she had been "set free" immediately after the authorities had taken two actions: Nadia's younger brother was taken into custody on suspicion of having helped to kidnap his sister, and her father's benefit payments were stopped. Probably both interventions contributed to the father's willingness to collaborate.

But now Nadia retracted her kidnapping story. The truth, she said, was that she had traveled willingly to visit her grandmother, who wasn't well. When her parents asked her to stay longer than she herself wanted, she had invented the tale of the kidnap. She regretted what had happened and asked to be left in peace.

A short time afterward, her parents returned to Norway. Through their lawyer, they announced that they intended to file a lawsuit for libel against two daily newspapers and the Norwegian ambassador to Morocco. Their demands for damages would be considerable.

Now the Norwegian state took action against Nadia's parents. They were charged with "depriving a person of liberty." The sentencing guidelines for this crime indicate a minimum of one year in prison and a maximum of eight years.

The case was heard in November 1998. Nadia was the main witness for the prosecution. Shortly after her return to Norway she had gone to the police and told them than she had been pressured into telling a fabricated story about the sick granny. It had been her parents' condition for setting her free.

A police investigation was already under way by then. Now Nadia became a leading witness for the Crown.

The Nadia case was a landmark in Norwegian legal history.[2] As far as I know, it was the first time the Norwegian authorities had charged parents with kidnapping their own child. For one parent to remove a child from the care of the other is a different matter—it happens quite often—but this time both parents were in on the act.

Their treatment of Nadia was a matter of honor as far as the parents were concerned, although the concept did not play a particularly large part in the court case. Most of the time it remained implicit, on the margins of the proceedings.

The parents argued that they had acted in good faith and were in no way to blame. They believed themselves to have been wholly within their rights when they made Nadia stay in Morocco. Legally, then, the two defendants were mistaken in law. They had had strong reasons for making Nadia stay away from Norway. In their view, her lifestyle had become depraved. Just as Rahmi Sahindal appealed to the Swedish court for understanding, so did Nadia's parents: surely, they argued, any Norwegian parent in their place would have wished to do what they did. They wanted to protect their child. It was unheard of that parents should be criminalized for doing their best.

Nadia's story was different: she had been threatened and pressured not to "become Norwegian" and instead "be Moroccan and Muslim." She was forbidden to dress as she liked, have a Pakistani boyfriend, go out in the evenings, work in a café. The family rows became so bad that at seventeen Nadia contacted the Child Protection Services and was given a protected place in a youth hostel. She moved back home after her eighteenth birthday, trusting her father's promise that she would be free to behave like an ordinary Norwegian girl. But instead she was sedated and carried off to Morocco. The court listened to a tape recording of a telephone conversation in which Nadia's mother confirms that she has threatened Nadia with being forced to stay in Morocco until she is a properly married Moroccan woman with children.

Nadia's maternal grandfather, a wealthy and powerful patriarch, was called as one of the witnesses for the defense. He rounded off his testimony by saying that on his return to Morocco he would take the Norwegian ambassador to court for having blackened the family's reputation. He would also let Moroccans know that Norway is not a democratic country: the authorities there prefer to believe a girl rather than her parents! Unheard of! Earlier he had drawn a picture of a warm, caring family who only wanted the best for Nadia. She had traveled to Morocco to visit his wife, who was ill.

I won't go into the details of the witness statements or the proceedings. Our spotlight is trained on "honor." Her parents were committed to the idea that Nadia was to be "made over" into a Moroccan Muslim woman. For them it was a matter of honor; their reputation and standing in public depended on it. Nadia's "free and easy" lifestyle shamed them. The drastic action of sedating and kidnapping her is an indication of how much was at stake. Nadia was convinced that her parents had strong support in Morocco; it came from her mother's family, which is very wealthy and influential. It is noteworthy that during the trial, Nadia's grandfather was up in arms because the Norwegian ambassador had suggested sending a car to pick up Nadia and take her to the airport—imagine, a car with an unknown chauffeur to take a young girl away from her family!

Most Muslims would share his outrage, or at least understand it. One must never expose a young girl on her own to the company of a strange man. To do so would mean dishonor—quite apart from what might happen to her.

Honor became an explicit concern at one point during the trial: the issue was Nadia's virginity. Her father raised it. During a part of the trial behind closed doors, Nadia told of how, on the way to Morocco, she had confided to her mother that she was no longer a virgin.[3] Her father grabbed hold of this piece of information and harangued the court about it the following day. Without being called up, he demanded to speak and stated that everything in Nadia's testimony was a lie. How could any parent do to their child what she had accused them of? Nadia had shamed the entire family. That was why she acted so desperately. Nadia was no longer a virgin, and in Morocco, a girl who has lost her virginity has no future; she will end up on the street.

"Here, in this court," Nadia's father said, shaking his head, "you believe that we have done wrong. But Nadia is crying because her honor is ruined. Everything she says is a lie, everything. But I know she doesn't want to lie. She has been made to do this. People have conspired with her." He turned to the journalists, who in his view were interested only in making money out of Nadia's story. This was a theme that turned up again and again in the parents' explanations. Nothing was really Nadia's fault; the guilty parties were people in the media and her bad friends.

Apart, of course, from the fact that Nadia wasn't a virgin and therefore had dishonored the family. The abyss that had opened up between Nadia's view of reality and her father's is obvious from his belief that Nadia was in despair because girls who have lost their virginity no longer have any future in Morocco. She, on the other hand, looked forward to a future in Norway. They regarded her as a Moroccan girl who must marry a Moroccan man. Nadia thought that she risked being forced into marriage when she was taken to Morocco. Her parents had shown her pictures of her intended husband. Because there was no evidence, however, forced marriage was not part of the charge. Nadia's parents were accused only of deprivation of liberty.

In Nadia's case, the defense again did not raise the matter of "culture." The lawyer, like his clients, painted a portrait of loving, responsible parents, ready to make sacrifices for their child—just like most parents. "Ordinariness" was the watchword; they weren't different, they wanted only the best for their child.

Wouldn't Norwegian parents have acted the way they did? Couldn't Norwegian fathers and mothers identify with their situation? There was an obvious intent to create a resonance in the minds of the judge and jury and others in the court.

But next, like Jack-in-the-box, up pops the fact that Nadia is not a virgin and the difference it makes. Now she's no longer "Norwegian" in the eyes of her parents—she is a Moroccan, but worth nothing in Moroccan society. Gone is the picture of a girl they would have allowed to marry anyone she cared for—even a Pakistani. The image of a fallen woman is back.

Is it not the case that the *father* shoves Nadia into the limelight? Is he not the one who shames the family by going public with what Nadia had admitted behind the closed doors of the courtroom? Dishonor, as we have shown, follows when shame is made public. Why announce Nadia's discreet testimony to all and sundry?

It could be that her father did not believe that Nadia's statements would remain behind closed doors. Or he may have felt so humiliated already that he might as well let everyone know how worthless she was. These are, however, "Norwegian" arguments—the world as seen by "outsiders." From the perspective of Nadia's parents and their kind of people, we should realize that the truth looks different: reputation is primary. Any girl who lives as Nadia did will be seen as shameless—it's inescapable. To distance himself in public from his daughter's admission can be understood as her father's gambit to keep his honor. He had every reason to confront a rumor that had already been in circulation for quite a while and do it emphatically: my honor leaves me no option other than to reject my child.

Nadia's mother and father were sentenced respectively to one year and one year and six months in prison, both conditionally. This was less than the minimum penalty for the type of crime they had been charged with. They immediately appealed both sentences. When Nadia's father died six months later, the charge was withdrawn. In effect, both parents were cleared. The court hoped that this would help to bring about reconciliation between Nadia and her family.

True to his honor, her brother, now eighteen, protested against the withdrawal of the charge. He wanted his family's honored restored publicly in court. But his request was refused.

In court Nadia had stated that her father had wanted to free her in response to the strong urging of the Norwegian ambassador to Morocco. Her mother's family had resisted; this established that her father was not the main agent. His wife's powerful family exerted a lot of influence over his choice of action. As a son-in-law in her family, he had a duty to respect his male in-laws, father and brothers; a younger man must also respect an elder. Also, his honor *collective honor*

was intertwined with theirs. Whatever he did with regard to his daughter would reflect back on them. Nadia's behavior was not just a matter for her parents; it concerned her mother's Moroccan family to the highest degree—especially as the Nadia case attracted much attention there as well as in Norway.

A court had chosen to believe a young girl instead of her parents! Naturally Nadia's grandfather was indignant and determined to tell everyone back home about the failing democracy in Norway. Fadime's family was just as offended to find that the court, as well as the media, trusted Söngül. When societies hold on to the belief that wisdom and knowledge come only with age, such pandering to the young is unacceptable.

Six years after the trial of her parents, Nadia was still living at a secret address. She did become reconciled with her family after the death of her father, but she was once more a target of death threats when she stepped forward after Fadime's death and spoke out about her own experiences. Until then she had refused to speak to the media. Now she wants to devote her life to working on behalf of girls with immigrant backgrounds to ensure that their human rights are protected. Like Fadime, she wants her own life experience to benefit others. But it was costing her dearly. Her Norwegian-born brother holds on to ideas of honor that are ripe for revision. It is very obvious that it is the girls who go into battle to this end. Where are the boys?

Nadia's mother and two other siblings would like to stay in touch with Nadia. They too were victims of honor.

Postscript: The story had a happy ending. Nadia has now become reconciled with all her family. She is studying and managing her own life well. But she had to withdraw from the public scene. It was perhaps a small price to pay for getting a family back.

14 The Zedini Case: Was Honor at Stake?

On May 8, 1999, Barbro Zedini, age twenty-six, was killed by her husband. Hassen Zedini was sentenced to fourteen years in prison for homicide with intent. He was of Tunisian origin.

The case attracted intense media attention, both because of the gruesomeness of the act and because of the circumstances around it. I discuss it here in order to cast some light on two aspects: how "culture" can be used or misused in trials and how careful one must be before concluding that a murder is an honor killing, even when there are good grounds for believing that the perpetrator felt disgraced. This might sound paradoxical, but the explanation will emerge.

Barbro Zedini worked in the travel business and was also an outstanding dancer. She had trained in both classical ballet and modern dance, but in the end she fell in love with Middle Eastern styles, especially belly dancing. Barbro Zedini performed in front of audiences, set up training courses, and became a leading personality in the belly dancing community, at home and internationally. She was highly respected for who she was, as well as for her dancing, and her death caused widespread shock and grief far outside Norway.

It was inevitable, given the state of her body when it was found, that questions would be raised about the relationship between the motive for the killing and the perpetrator's cultural background. We need not know the ugly details, though they were publicized in the media.

Barbro Zedini was killed in her own home one night after giving a performance in a restaurant. By then she had apparently started divorce proceedings. Authorities assumed that Hassen Zedini's younger brother, who had just arrived from Tunisia on a visit, helped the killer to clean up evidence and get rid of the corpse. It was found in a woodland waterway nine days later.

In court, Hassen denied that his wife's belly dancing had caused him any concern. Why should it, he asked, when belly dancing was part of his culture? All women do it. How could he possibly feel ashamed over the culture he grew up in? He took *pride* in her dancing and her interest in his native culture.

The trouble with this argument is that the local cultures do not approve of belly dancing in public, not in Tunisia nor in other Arab countries—not, that is, if you are a respectable woman. It is fine to dance at lively parties, but only in private and fully dressed. So to belly dance in public half undressed is to stain your family's honor.

Hassen Zedini could safely stand by what he had said. Belly dancing is part of his culture. What he failed to mention was that the dancing must take place according to special rules and in special circumstances. By limiting himself to generalities, he evades the fact that public dancing is considered shameful—very shameful indeed—in traditional Tunisian culture. Instead he suggests that he was proud of his wife!

So Hassen Zedini denies that honor is involved. To admit that something might affect a man's honor is to also admit to a possible motive for the act you are charged with. As we have seen, "honor" is seen as a compromised concept in Scandinavian courts. A reference to honor does the defendant no favor. It follows that to admit feeling ashamed is pointless. In everyday Scandinavian usage *shame* and *honor* are linked. Hassen Zedinin denied feeling ashamed. Nadia's parents never mentioned shame, and Rahmi Sahindal did so on only a few occasions.

In 2002, I wrote: "I foresee scenarios in Scandinavian courts based on greater awareness of honor; courts may even be on the lookout for 'honor'—and its counterpart, dishonor—as a motive for acts of violence. Meanwhile the accused will downplay honor and shame or even deny that such notions are relevant at all." This has indeed happened. In court people tend to make declarations about their culture that should be taken with a hearty pinch of salt. It was predictable that Fadime's father should say that there are no honor killings in his Turkish home region and that Hassen Zedini should say that belly dancing is a matter of pride in his culture.

Internationally, the murder of Barbro Zedini has been referred to as an honor killing. My expert witness statement to the District Court has been used to support this conclusion. But this is based on a mis-understanding. In belly dancing circles, both in Norway and inter-nationally, my testimony caused a major upset because it punc-tured the inflated romance around the dance and instead placed it in a cultural context where to dance half-naked in public means shame. Leading figures from the world of belly dancing have con-tacted me to say how good it was that I started off the debate—though I did it unwittingly. But it does no harm if Western prac-titioners become aware of the lack of authenticity of the aesthetic and romantic qualities that *they* see in belly dancing.

Barbro Zedini perfected the dance to a real art and reaped inter-national recognition for her excellence.

Interestingly enough, Hassen Zedini made no objections to my statement outlining the shame that goes with public belly dancing in his home territory, despite his earlier strong protests against my appearing in court as an expert witness. I felt that he knew that I knew. Thus far, we were on the same wavelength.

On the other hand, I have never said that the murder of Barbro Zedini was an honor killing. To dance with your arms, shoulders, and belly bared to public gaze is shaming in North Africa and the Middle East, but this does not imply that, by definition, Hassen Zedini felt dishonored by his wife's performances. People are dif-ferent, and that's true everywhere. Zedini had lived in Norway for nearly ten years. Just because he is Muslim and Arab we should not jump to the conclusion that he had remained unaffected by Norwegian ideas. But we can object to his claim that Barbro's dancing would be acceptable to people of his background. Her career was kept secret from her Tunisian in-laws, with whom she had a generally warm, close relationship.

There are communities and societies in which a man is shamed if his wife demands a divorce. People close to Barbro Zedini say that she was about to do just that. Her husband denies it. But it does not make killing her a matter of honor, even if it were true that she wanted a divorce and he knew it. Tunisian women can divorce without reprisals. And Hassen Zedini may well have felt humiliated, rejected, jealous, desperate—any number of possible emotions come to mind.

For a murder to be called an honor killing it must be demonstrated that the perpetrator was a member of an "honor group" with a shared code of honor. We cannot do that in this case—not on the basis of what was established in court. And my conclusion is not even affected by learning that Barbro Zedini's Tunisian relatives had not known of her second career as a dancer until the recent visit by her brother-in-law. Her murderer was a heroin addict, and some of Barbro's friends thought that it was losing the family wage earner that made the divorce such a threatening prospect. If Hassen had not been convicted, he would have inherited. The couple's flat was in her name.

In conclusion, then: honor may have been at stake for Hassen Zedini, but it would be going too far to declare that his murder of his wife *must* have been an honor killing. He may well have had mixed motives. To establish an honor killing, evidence must be at hand which was not presented in Zedini's trial. On the contrary, there is much to indicate that Barbro's in-laws in Tunisia loved and respected her and deeply mourned her death.

Let us instead examine another case, in which an honor killing was established and atoned for.

15 The Lørenskog Murder: Rethinking Honor

In the Nordic countries adult men only rarely admit to having carried out an honor killing. But N. S. did. He had killed his wife in the fall of 1998. His sentence was twelve years in prison. It is well worth listening to his reflections on the subject of honor killings. They also cast a helpful light on the fate of Rahmi Sahindal.

N. S. has given two interviews to the Norwegian daily *Verdens Gang*, one in 1998, the other just after Fadime's death. The following account is based on these.

When he was thirty years old, N. S. turned into a killer. His wife was only twenty-four when she died. Their mothers had taken the initiative for their arranged marriage. N. S. had a master's degree in journalism. He looked forward to a career in Pakistan and was not that keen to move to Norway. However, his family insisted that his economic prospects would improve in Norway. After one year's engagement, during which the two young people kept in touch by telephone, letter, and e-mail, they met at the wedding ceremony in Pakistan and then moved to Norway together. They had been married for only three months when the murder was committed.

N. S. explains the background to the murder as a collision of cultures. He was alarmed to find out how Westernized his wife was. He had married her on the understanding that she was a "girl of the

East" who respected the South Asian traditions. His own family was conservative and religious. He was very well educated and spoke fluent English, but all the same, his wife's behavior upset him. She wore clothes that were too tight, she befriended Norwegian men, and she even agreed to undress in front of a male doctor during a consultation. It was too much for him: she was liberated to a nightmarish extent. They argued endlessly, and after the visit to the doctor, he lost control.

"She was in the sitting room watching TV. I grabbed her collar and pulled her up, then dragged her along, first into the bedroom, then the kitchen. And there I got hold of a knife and screamed at her 'I'll kill you!'

"She was so terrified. She started crying and that was the moment when I lost everything. I can never restore that moment. She wept and I wept. I was so ashamed over what I had done."[1]

After that his wife went to live with her mother. Over the month that followed N. S. tried desperately everything he knew to persuade her to move back to be with him, but without effect. On the fatal evening his mother-in-law had come to see him. She told him that he didn't have a hope; all he could do was to move back to Pakistan. This was the moment when he decided to kill himself in front of his wife. Everything was hopeless. Suicide was the only thing left for him.

The journalist who interviewed him asked, "Why was it impossible for you to return to Pakistan?" The reply was that he loved his wife and that he saw no possible future for himself in Pakistan. Also, there was the matter of his family: "They would have got at me for coming back. It was simply not on. I would've lost my honor."

Instead he went to his wife's family home in the Oslo suburb of Lørenskog. "I was sitting in the kitchen, and then she came in. She was rude to me, I was crying and she said I had to get out, that our marriage was useless. . . . And she began to make fun of me, called me a coward, a man without honor. And then . . . you know, afterward . . . I don't know how it happened."

As he speaks, he is crying, his face buried in his hands.[2]

After Fadime's murder, we were allowed to share N. S.'s reflections on honor killings and his experiences, acquired at such great cost. Now he regrets deeply what he did, but he knows there are many others who will respond as he did.

"You are expected to kill. It doesn't matter how badly it affects you afterward. When you face something like that, it seems to be your only option."[3]

He goes into the details of his tragic story in order to make others in similar situations realize that murder is a bad way out.

He was looking forward to moving back to Pakistan in summer 2005, when he would have served his sentence. In Norway he would be marked for life as a man who has killed, but in Pakistan he can live normally.

"I think it will be all right. It helps that people understand, one way or another, what happened."

He has had problems getting his mind around how he was able to take his wife's life. He thinks it has to do with culture. "From one point of view, it's a matter of a sociological mechanism, of the social expectations on a man. When you come face to face with these expectations, you feel you have no choice. Your conscience tells you what you must do."

pressure causes action.

He spoke of his upbringing in Pakistan and of how the thought of killing another human being takes root inside you. "This kind of thing is discussed in the family circle. I remember when I was between fifteen and twenty years old, how I talked about it with cousins and brothers. We went on as if we were prepared to do it. I believe that's the beginning."

"What is honor?" the interviewer wants to know. N. S. explains that when a Pakistani woman is raped, she is shamed. This is how a man feels if a woman in his family has an improper relationship with a man. You feel raped somehow. Now in his case it didn't happen, his wife did not have an affair, but he felt it in the same way: his honor depended on his wife's behavior.

"Honor is your whole life. When you have it, you are respected. To be dishonored means that, for the rest of your life, you cannot meet the eyes of your friends, family, and acquaintances."

He is convinced that in his situation, many men would have acted the same way—they would have had no choice. He has one piece of advice for them. "They must try to find a better definition of honor. Honor means to care for someone and respect that person instead of . . ."[4]

Well-chosen words, spoken on the day after Fadime's murder had become known.

Fadime's message to us was: People who think in terms of killing for honor's sake are themselves victims of a culture, a system, a structure, that appears to offer them no alternatives. She used the word *integration*. A failure to integrate promotes such thoughts and escape routes, even among people who have lived in Sweden for a long time. She was thinking of her parents. Now it is time to return to them.

Pol should become integrated to avoid dishonor felt/associated when offspring integrate. Integration is inevitable.

V / *The Appeal*

16 · *The Man in the Woods*

We are in the Swedish High Court, where the appeal against the conviction of Fadime's father is being heard between May 21 and 23, 2002. The man in the woods turns up here.

It was the man in the woods, not Rahmi, who killed Fadime. There, you see, everything I've told you is wrong. Part of my project was to give the family a voice, but that's no good anymore. Whatever they said in the police interviews was false. Their consciences have been tormenting them. Time to speak the truth now. It is a dramatic story. To be truly involved, you must feel part of the situation as it develops:

You are at home one evening, watching television. The doorbell rings. The man outside the door is someone you know. "Hurry up," he says. "Put your shoes on and come along out with me!" He takes your hand: "Listen and do as I tell you! I've shot your daughter! Now, do exactly what I tell you!"

The two of you walk along to a nearby parking lot. A white car is parked there, its engine running. The man makes you get inside and tells you to phone your daughters. You're shocked, can't remember the phone numbers, but your cousin's number comes into your head. You say to your cousin, "I've shot my daughter." (Next, the cousin contacts the police.)

The man drives to a small wood and gets out of the car. He leads the way into the wood. You stand under a pine tree for two hours while he tells you about everything that happened. "You see, two of your daughters and your wife were together when they saw me!" (in Songül's flat).

You ask him: "But if my wife has seen you, how can she say that I killed that daughter?"

The man grabs you by the throat. You fight back. His nails are digging into your flesh. Together you fall to the ground. When you manage to get up again, he says that he has shot the girl twice in the head, but there's one bullet left. "I'll shoot you. Listen to me! If you don't do what I tell you I'll shoot you and your whole family, your grandchildren too!"

This is how it came about that Rahmi Sahindal agreed to plead guilty. It was for his family's sake. The man in the woods made the two of them swap coats and shoes. During the two hours in the woods he informed Rahmi about the whole incident, and when they went their separate ways, he put the gun into Rahmi's pocket and told him what to do next: "Go to the police and give yourself up, right away." Rahmi obeyed, first phoning another relative (he was ordered to do that too) to explain where he was and let the police know where to find him.

Rahmi swears that he is innocent: "I did not do this deed. Never in my life could I have done it! I took it on myself. He did it. But he threatened me."

Instead of immediately digging into Rahmi's narrative and taking it apart, the prosecutor asks the defendant to describe his family and his life in Sweden. Fadime's father has had a good life. "My family were very happy here. But then, that daughter, she caused us problems, problems about the wedding party . . ."

The prosecutor steers him back to his family and his life. Rahmi speaks of how he was sent to school for eighteen months to learn Swedish before looking for a job. He has worked all his life until he fell ill and started receiving benefits in 1998.

"What did you think about the way you and your family lived in Sweden?"

"Very good, but then there were the problems with that daughter."

The prosecutor wants to learn of any differences between the way children are brought up in Sweden and in Rahmi's native country.

"There are some," Rahmi admits. "The difference is because there are different cultures. But there isn't really any difference."

"How do you go about marrying someone? Are there any differences?"

"No, that's the same. No differences. A girl gets to marry whoever she loves."

But isn't it true that two of Rahmi's daughters have married his brothers' sons?

"Yes, they have chosen them themselves."

What was all that about death threats to Fadime? On January 15, 1998, she pressed charges against her father and her brother because they had threatened to kill her.

It wasn't true. At the time Fadime was studying in Sundsvall. One day she phoned and said she wanted to marry. Rahmi said, "First you must finish your studies." She wouldn't listen. "No, I'm getting married," she said. Afterward Rahmi spoke to the Swedish boy's father, who came with his mother to ask for Fadime's hand. Then there was a row about who should cover the cost of the wedding.

The prosecutor is not convinced and refers to the sentence of May 7, 1998, which ended the court case that Fadime had brought against her father and brother. At the time, Fadime stated that she had been told to marry a Kurd so that he would have a future in Sweden. Also, she had said, a girl like her with a relationship with a Swede would be regarded as a whore. Such girls had to pay with their blood. If her brother Mesut had managed to kill her, he would have become a hero. The risk of being punished doesn't matter by comparison. And if he were to be prevented somehow, her father would kill her instead.

According to the judge's statement, it had been the *united* opinion of the parties that "there was nothing Fadime could do in order to regain her good name and reputation in the Kurdish community."

"No, that's not right," Rahmi says. He hadn't objected to her marrying the Swede. The problem was Fadime's wish that her family should pay for the wedding.

It seems, after all, that there are differences between Kurdish and Swedish marriage customs, or so Rahmi Sahindal says, but he also says that there are none. When everything is said and done, the two cultures are the same in their views on bringing up children and marrying them off. What Fadime had said was untrue.

What about Rahmi's earlier statements about how Fadime harassed him?

"No, that's not right."

He was confronted with his previous statements in court and in police interviews. He insisted: "I never said that."

How had he reacted to her exposure in the media?

"I was angry with my daughter at the time, because she showed us up in the media, a little angry, but it passed . . . you know, if she goes around lying, you become angry, of course, but that was then. I was just a little angry anyway."

How did he feel when his relatives came to know about it?

"They haven't stuck their noses in what we do as a family. I didn't feel anything special."

The prosecutor reads extracts of Rahmi's statements, one after the other, to the court and the police. The constant refrains are "she did dreadful things to me" and "she showed us up, me and my family, in front of world opinion."

But—it is *the man in the woods* who's talking. He is the one who had told Rahmi what he was to say, to the last detail.

"He gave you extremely precise instructions, this man in the woods," the prosecutor comments.

"Yes, he did. He brainwashed me."

What was the man-in-the-woods's motive for killing Fadime?

"He didn't want to tell me."

"I don't understand the plan. Why should you take on the guilt for what he had done? Why didn't he just make himself scarce, disappear?"

Rahmi has no answer to that.

The prosecutor wants to know if Rahmi isn't still afraid to talk. Yes, he's still afraid of the man-in-the-woods. But he feels that he can tell now because he pleaded guilty in the lower court. Besides, he won't describe the man.

The prosecutor then asks if he feels his story is believable at all. Maybe his experience in the District Court in Uppsala influenced him and made him try this new version? Previously he had claimed, emphatically, that he was not a well man. How had he reacted to the psychiatric report, which concluded that he was not ill?

"*That man*, he told me: You must go to see a doctor, then he'll write you a sick note."

"Had you thought that perhaps you'd be taken into medical care and instead you were given a prison sentence?"

"The man said it. You go to the doctor, he'll say you're ill."

The prosecutor refers to his concern about his honor in the District Court hearings. He had said: "It's about one's honor, you know. I have my relatives to think of."

"Do you think it is honorable to sit here and tell lies to get around the fact that you've murdered your own daughter?"

"I didn't do it, I definitely didn't do it! The man had told me how I should put things to be believed."

And he was believed. The High Court sentenced Rahmi to life imprisonment for murdering his daughter Fadime.

Leif Ericksson, Songül's solicitor, is present during the appeal hearing. Songül herself has to miss it; she is too ill to attend. However, her taped testimony to the Uppsala District Court is played in its entirety. In this way she is, once more, very much present. When you are no longer able to see her, when you no longer can observe her bright eyes and steely body, her voice stands out all the more. And you notice how hard it is for her, how heavily the effort weighs on her as she formulates her thoughts and feelings and memories. She wants to get it right, whatever the cost. She takes no shortcuts, assesses her words before speaking, thinks carefully, and articulates slowly but emphatically. "I stood by her." "It was her life, her choice." "She would have done the same thing again." Her sentences spread light during the otherwise rather appalling proceedings.

For Songül too is said to be a liar now. The emergency call center's tape is run, and we hear again Songül's heartbreaking cry, rising from among the shrill voices of her shocked mother and little sister, a crescendo of women's screams: "My sister is dead! My father has murdered my sister!"—but even this unmistakably clear indictment is, according to her father, a lie. And her mother agrees. Elif Sahindal testifies in her husband's favor and supports his story. So Songül lied. She had been told to say that her father had shot Fadime. Seconds after her beloved sister had been attacked and killed in front of her eyes, she was able to play her role very well.

On the District Court tape, the High Court hears again what Songül had to say about her father's behavior that night. He had not sounded angry, only determined, when he shouted at the women that they were to let him in. And when he moved in for the kill, his face confirmed it: he looked determined, not angry.

"She had to be gotten rid of, out of the way." Songül repeats that she had heard the head of the family, her maternal uncle and a man whose presence was strongly felt during both trials, pronounce, "That one, we've got to kill her." And on another occasion her father had said, "She's a whore and we must get rid of her, one way or the other."

Songül is not well enough to testify again. But she does not retract anything. She still stands by Fadime—and does not back the story of the man-in-the-woods.

Father was desperate.

17 The Mother

Songül does not back the story of the man-in-the-woods, but her mother does.

Elif Sahindal does not have to testify in the High Court. Her close family relationship with the defendant is good enough reason to stand down, as she had done in the lower court. But now she chooses to step into the witness stand.

Does she really want to ambush her dead daughter? She did just that during the trial of her husband and son, when they were charged with threatening to kill Fadime. Later, Fadime spoke of how it had hurt her to be betrayed by her mother in open court. Now her mother has been given a new opportunity to show where her allegiances lie. This time Fadime is spared the experience.

The mother's tale:

There were never any serious problems in the family. That was why she felt rather cross with Fadime when she told her stories to the papers and on TV programs. "We didn't have any problems, nothing we could go on about to the TV people and the mass media, we didn't have any big problems—no really serious problems, that is, if there had been something serious happening in the family you might have defended what she did ..."

And this about Patrik: "He wasn't Swedish, his parents came from Iran, but they came to see us and we talked with them in our own language[1] and we had nothing against the marriage . . ."

Contrary to what both Fadime and Songül had testified, their mother denies being the person who told Fadime on January 11, 1998, that she must leave Uppsala for good. "No, that's not right," Elif Sahindal insists.

When asked about her contacts with Fadime during the four years since 1998, Elif confirms that for three years there were none. But over the last year or so, their relationship was good. They had met four times and spoken now and then on the telephone. Fadime had phoned to say she was sorry and asked to be forgiven, it was all her fault. She had said, "Please forgive me." That was how it came about that the two of them could meet again.

The mother's narrative is closely followed by her brother and her son, one of her daughters and one of her sons-in-law, as well as two younger female relatives, all of whom are seated in the public part of the courtroom. Admitting that she has had clandestine meetings with Fadime carries its own risks.

Why had she kept it secret?

"There was no reason to tell people" is what she replies to the prosecutor's question. Then she adds that because Rahmi and Fadime were on bad terms, she didn't want to remind him of her.

Would it have worried her if Rahmi had known?

"No."

Later on, did he learn that mother and daughter were in touch? She isn't sure but says she thinks so.

The prosecutor returns to what Elif Sahindal had stated in her interviews with the police with regard to her husband: he was in poor shape and suffered because of Fadime. What was the relationship between husband and wife like?

"Good, quite good. There were no problems."

"How did Rahmi feel inside himself?"

"What he saw on TV and in the papers was bad—it made him feel stressed."

"In a police interview you have said that your husband was ill. You said that he was run down, unemployed, a little depressed. He talked to himself."

"Yes. That's right."

"Fadime moved out of the family home in 1997. Did you miss her?"

"She is my child. You know what mothers are like."

"Did you blame her for anything?"

"I went to help her get her room in order [in her lodgings in Sundsvall]."

"You didn't feel that you had let her down?"

"She moved out before the problem with Patrik."

"Did you ask her to come and live at home again?"

"I didn't ask her to come home, but after the mass media . . . I mean, if I had said 'come back,' she wouldn't have come."

Elif is asked about her last meeting with her daughter. How did the meeting come about? Who was there and could listen in when Songül phoned to say that Fadime had arrived? And so on. No one was around at the time of either of the two calls, she says. But we know from Songül's and Nebile's statements that Mesut answered the phone on both occasions.

Then she says that between two and three months had passed since her previous meeting with Fadime. Any special reason they met at that time?

"She was going away for six months. She wanted to see me and say good-bye."

Why didn't they open the door when Rahmi was outside, shouting that he wanted to come in?

"I worried a little, I didn't want to open the door."

"Songül says that Fadime had suggested that she should hide under the bed. Then you could open the door."

"*Fadime pitied her father. Three times she said 'Poor Daddy' after he had gone.*" (It sounds as if Elif wanted her husband to take this in. She spoke emphatically. Fadime's words showed that she cared for her father and murderer.)

Why didn't they open the door? Were they afraid?

No. No, she can't tell why they didn't open it. If they had, maybe nothing bad would have happened. "No, you know, it was just that we didn't open the door."

She had turned the light off in the kitchen to make Rahmi think that no one was in. Had he worked out that they were there all the same? "I don't know. I don't think he did."

When Nebile arrived around nine o'clock, Fadime had hidden behind the door to surprise her little sister. "They hugged a lot afterward." Fadime had brought presents for Songül and Nebile. "They were both ever so pleased with their presents." They had sat around talking for a while. Then Nebile and Fadime wanted to leave. Fadime started to pack the pies her mother had baked for her. "I told her, 'You're welcome!'" Elif had been lying down on the sofa: "She hugged me and told me to stay where I was, my knee hurt, you see. She had phoned a friend who was coming to pick her up . . ."

Next, the tragedy takes place. The perpetrator is the man in the woods. The man had shouted to Elif; she was to say that Fadime's father had done it. He told Songül that if she didn't say so, he would kill her and the rest of her family.

But Elif refuses to describe the killer. "Can't you even tell us if he was old or young?" the prosecutor asks—she sounds resigned. "Why can't you?"

"I'm so scared, he threatened me, us—my children have been threatened."

Today, as I write up my courtroom notes, I suddenly realize that Elif Sahindal is speaking a kind of truth now. She has been threatened, her children have been threatened, and she is afraid. She will not say whom she fears. Behind this lack of words several alternatives open up.

To explain how her child was killed, Elif takes the interpreter's head in a firm grip. It is moving to watch her intensity as she shows how "the man I saw" grabbed hold of Fadime's long hair (it was 60 centimeters long, the prosecutor explains) and pointed the gun at the back of her head. The muzzle was inside her hair, Elif says, which fits the forensic report: it indicated a distance on the order of 50 centimeters.

The murderer fired twice. He was shouting at Songül to say that her father did it. The girls' mother grabbed his arm and said, "Don't shoot Songül! Shoot me instead!"

"That man, who had come to the door, was he someone you knew?"

"Yes. But I won't say who it was."

What did she do after the murder?

"I tried to run outside, I was afraid he'd kill all of us."

"Why run away when Fadime had just been killed by a man with a gun who was still in the flat and threatening Songül?"

"I was in shock . . . and on the way to the police car I said to my daughters that they were to say their father had done it. Or we'll all die."

"Apart from Rahmi and Mesut, who else has a motive for killing Fadime?"

"I know there's someone else."

"What could be the motive of that someone else?"

"I know what it was, but I can't tell you."

"If you are to make us trust what you say, you must be able to describe this man and give us an idea of why he wanted to kill your daughter."

"I was in shock. I can't describe what he was wearing."

Now the prosecutor fires off a series of questions: Why did she tell the police that Rahmi had fired the shots? Why not say that it had been an unknown gunman? Why did the killer want to put the guilt on Rahmi? Why didn't she speak up about him in the District Court?

She answered the last question: "I knew that I couldn't tell the truth there. I was afraid."

"Who could be so important to you that you point the finger at your own husband, mark him as a murderer, and send him to prison for life?"

"I was afraid. I had been threatened. It's for my children's and grandchildren's sakes."

"What about now—aren't you afraid?"

"As long as I don't say who he is, I'm not afraid . . . for my children's and grandchildren's sakes, and anyway, if Rahmi didn't do it, how can he get a life sentence?"

"How have you been feeling since this incident?" the prosecutor asks.

"I was unhappy when I said that he had done it. Now I'm relieved."

Elif Sahindal carries a heavy burden on her shoulders. She must have been assailed by fear and anguish. Now she has to play the leading role in the fateful drama that follows the death of her child. She is the main witness for the defense. And she was the cause of her daughter's fatal visit to Uppsala.

"You could have prevented Fadime's death—have you ever thought about that?"

"I had no idea that she would be killed."

When the prosecutor asks if Elif doesn't feel that she is betraying Fadime by her actions, her voice breaks. She bursts into tears: "I mustn't tell the truth about who did it. I'm frightened. I've lost one of my children."

Then she swears that it wasn't Rahmi.

Since the murder she has seen the killer twice. He threatened the entire family again. Now she feels she can tell the story.

"I want my children, grandchildren, neighbors, and the Swedish people to know that he didn't do it." And she points at her husband.

It is to no avail. Once more, Rahmi is sentenced to prison for life. No one was persuaded by the story about the man-in-the-woods.

A package containing a gun, two matching bullets, and a pair of bloodied gloves is delivered to the office of Rahmi's lawyer. The bullets are of the same brand but not the same caliber as those that killed Fadime. Just before the appeal hearing started, an anonymous letter was sent to the Stockholm newspaper *Dagens Nyheter*, saying that the killer is someone else. The sender claims to be Fadime's murderer. Is this the man-in-the-woods or a fourth man? The package is presumably intended as part of the same strategy (that is, meant to support the man-in-the-woods story). However, the attempt bombs. The Swedish authorities investigate the letter in the hope of finding out who sent it. The perjury issue—should the man who stated in court that he couldn't remember a thing be tried for perjury?—is still not settled at this point. (Later he was sentenced to four months in prison.)

"Was it worth it? Was it really worth it?" Fadime's little sister Nebile says that she kept asking her big sister this question after Fadime had presented her case to the media. Regrettably, the question is very relevant here: was it worth it, was it really worth making up the story about the man in the woods to appeal against the sentence of Fadime's father?

A mother has been put in the dock, shown off as someone who had betrayed her dead child—a child who had been betrayed by everyone close to her, except Songül. Now the undertow is dragging Songül down: her mother has sunk her as well. But Elif Sahindal has four more children; one of them, her son, had wanted to kill Fadime and had a conviction for inflicting grievous bodily harm. Her two sons-in-law are both sons of her husband's brothers. His sister married her brother. And her husband is a convicted murderer. She is deeply immersed. The mafia-style setting in which she lives does feature men who turn up at your door and order you about: "Put your shoes on and come along out with me!" Threats to exterminate whole families are part of, if not everyday life, dozens of familiar stories that everyone has heard. The stories are taken seriously. They must be taken seriously.

And so the narrative about the man in the woods is not as wild as it sounds. In another context it would have been plausible. This time it serves only to put the Sahindal family in the worst possible light—that is, in the view of the public with whom they are all so keen to reestablish their credibility: the Swedes. "This Sweden, it is such a good country," as Rahmi Sahindal put it. Elif must have been desperately concerned about what the Swedes would think about her once everyone learned from Fadime what her mother thought about them. Nebile too worries that the Swedes will feel that these foreigners are there only to chase welfare handouts. The head of the Sahindal family argues that the Fadime affair has ruined their standing, not only his family's but all Swedish Kurds'. The mass media are blamed.

What I heard when following the first trial and then the second one has not supported this view of the situation. On the contrary, the experience has cast new light on the world of fear that Fadime had to live in and revealed the webs that were spun—and still are—to encase a family from which no escape is tolerated. Elif Sahindal is doing her best to submit.

Mother
is a victim.

VI | *The Way Forward*

18   *Speaking in Parliament*

We have already learned that Fadime's talk in the Old Parliament Building preyed on her family's collective mind and also that she had refused the invitation at first. The occasion was kept secret even though her audience was about 350 people and the minister for integration, Mona Sahlin, had promised to be there. To Fadime, who was keen that her message should reach the minister, this had mattered a great deal. At the last moment, Sahlin found that she was unable to attend after all. Still, she read the text of the talk afterward and told Fadime how impressed she was.

Fadime's talk was arranged to form part of a seminar titled "Integration—on Whose Conditions?" organized by the community network Violence Against Women. The date was November 20, 2001; the text of Fadime's talk was published in the evening paper *Aftonbladet* on the day of her funeral, February 4, 2002.

This is what Fadime said when she spoke in public for the last time.

"Hi—my name is Fadime and I'm twenty-five years old. I've been invited here today to tell you about my experience of what it is like to live as a foreign girl in Sweden, with its laws, customs, and culture. How hard it is to balance between the demands and expectations of one's family and the Swedish society, with its quite different values and attitudes.

"I thought it would help you to understand how vulnerable immigrant girls often are if I told you about what has happened to me. It's not my intention to point the finger at anyone, only try to help you realize the whys and wherefores of conflicts like those I'm about to describe, both from my own point of view and from my family's.

"But I'd like to begin by stressing that it is not only girls from the Middle East who are oppressed; it happens in many families from different parts of the world.

"I was born in a small village near the town of Elbistan in the Kurdish region of Turkey. My parents owned land there and earned their living as farmers. We all worked on the land and looked after the animals, side by side. We were one large and happy family with clear roles and tasks. It was a warm atmosphere, even though it is true that we were not rich in material things.

"When I was seven years old, we moved to Sweden—for economic reasons. At first it seemed all fun and games, but as I grew older, my parents imposed more and more restrictions. I noticed it first when I was no longer allowed to play with my Swedish friends or join out-of-school activities. I had to come straight home after school and help my mother in the household and be a properly brought up girl [en fin flicka].

"My parents' view of my going to school was that it was good for me to learn to read and write so I could be their link out to the Swedish society, since they were both illiterate. On the other hand, there was no call for me to go on to higher education. You don't need a fine education to care for your husband and children.

"When I was in my teens, my parents wanted me to go down to Turkey and marry one of my cousins, just as my older sisters had done. I resisted doing as I was told. I felt far too young and immature for a big decision like that. Besides, I wanted to make up my own mind about the man I was to share my life with.

"The mindset my parents had was that family and kin matter more than anything else, which is why I must always put the family's best interests before my own well-being. It is better that one person suffers rather than an entire family or clan. The difference between my parents and me was that I lived in, and was a part of, the Swedish society. I went daily to a Swedish school, ate Swedish food, had Swedish friends, and watched Swedish TV.

"It goes without saying that I took on board Swedish values and points of view. I began to push the envelope more and more. I carried on seeing my Swedish friends, went with them to cafés, and came home later than the time I had been told.

"Naturally, I dreamed my own dreams and set myself goals in life. I wanted to create my own conditions for my life, make my own mistakes and learn from them. I wanted to stand on my own two feet and take responsibility for my actions. Not let anyone else determine what I felt or thought or did. Also, it was enormously important for me to be free to become educated and to develop myself as a person. To your ears, this won't sound very special, because it is part of the way Swedish people live, but for my family it was something terribly alarming.

"Their view of Swedes and the Swedish lifestyle was that they were promiscuous and that they had neither culture nor morals or ethical standards. All they did was get drunk, go clubbing, and have free and easy sex. They also believed that Swedes had no respect whatsoever for family life, because they divorced as and when they pleased.

"These opinions grew straight out of their own prejudices. They didn't know any Swedes and didn't want to socialize with them anyway. In the beginning I kept a balance between the Kurdish traditions and the demands that Swedish society made on me. I felt enormously split and enormously confused. I was forced to lead a double life, trying as best I could to meet the expectations that the two cultures had of me as a young woman.

"But then, one day, that happened which must not happen: I met a Swedish man. His name was Patrik, and Patrik and I fell in love. At first I was terrified of what this might lead to and kept explaining to him the conditions we must accept. My parents must not get to know anything about us, come what may.

"Despite the risks, we chose to begin a relationship, even though it meant that we could meet only within four walls and that we constantly lived with the fear of being discovered. After having been together for a year, we became tired of always meeting indoors and hiding our love. We began to be steadily less cautious.

"Gradually we began to go together to places where we could be reasonably sure we wouldn't meet anyone from my family or my relatives. One day, our carelessness led to our being discovered by my father, who naturally exploded with rage and started striking out at me and Patrik.

"To me, his reaction was entirely understandable. As my father and head of our family, he has the duty to guard the family honor. He has to protect and safeguard the sexual behavior of his female relatives and make sure that his daughters are still virgins when they marry. If the girl's husband finds out that his bride is not a virgin on her wedding night, he can demand an instant divorce.

"To this day, the bloodstained sheet is handed to the bride's mother-in-law so that she can show her people that they have got a chaste and pure woman. Once my family had realized that we, that Patrik and I were a couple, they could readily draw the conclusion that I had lost my virginity.

"To them, this meant that I could never . . . that they could never marry their daughter off in the customary way, to a Kurdish man—and in their view this was what my life should be. Now I had brought shame on the family and threatened their standing in the community. I had done something unforgivable, something that no one in my clan had done before.

"This shook their whole world and scared the life out of them. In their eyes, I had been transformed from a nice Kurdish girl into a stuck-up whore who thought she was special just because she lived in Sweden. In order to preserve their honor, they were compelled to prove to those around them that they could handle the problem. Behavior like mine must be punished, and my guilt washed off with blood.

"Alone and expelled from my family, I was forced to leave Uppsala at once, for I knew that if they got hold of me, they would kill me. I moved north to Sundsvall. It didn't take my parents long to trace me and find out where I lived.

"The men in my family [clan] started calling me and threatening me by phone. They warned me that I'd never get away with it. My little brother was given the task to kill me. It was a given that just he would be picked, because he hadn't reached his majority and so would not receive a heavy sentence. Besides, as the only son in our family, he had the duty to see to it that his sisters behaved as the culture demanded.

"Over time, the tone of the threats became fiercer. The more I stuck to my guns and refused to submit, the worse it got. In the end I couldn't stand it anymore and decided to go to the police for protection. I wanted to inform them about my situation so that they would be prepared if something happened to me.

"It was very frightening to realize that the police didn't take me seriously. To them, my story sounded like a fairytale. Their only advice to me was to approach my family and make it clear to them that they must cease all threatening behavior and show respect for Swedish laws and customs. In other words, the police failed to grasp the seriousness of my situation, and their disbelief struck me as disrespectful and even humiliating.

"'What do you expect?' they asked and added, 'We can't afford a round-the-clock guard service to look after you.' I left the police station with a heavy heart, not having received any help at all. I was simply forced to try to help myself as best I could.

"Turning to the mass media was my last chance. And this became my most effective protection. My idea was to create a public debate about the problems and, as part of it, have the spotlight directed on my own family. This way I hoped to make them back off. And my case did attract a lot of attention, because several other crimes motivated by honor were in the news.

"The most newsworthy one was the case of Sara in Umeå. She was, like me, a girl from the Middle East. She was strangled by her cousins because she wanted to lead her own life. A girl from Stockholm was stabbed by her relatives for the same reason. Quite deliberately, I spoke out about the conditions under which foreign girls were forced to live here in Sweden. I gave voice, and lent face, to girls who were kept very strictly and risked being rejected or killed if they did not submit to the way of life their families insisted on.

"When I made another attempt to alert the police, I was lucky enough to come into contact with a policeman experienced in casework with foreign women who had been threatened or abused by their men. He understood at once how serious my situation was and informed me about my rights as someone under threat. Unfortunately, because my relatives had confined themselves to verbal threats, the police could not offer me any more concrete help than a personal safety alarm kit and a promise that my personal data would be protected.

"I accepted the kit but turned down the option to change my name and go into hiding. What crime was I guilty of? Why should I hide? Later, the media circus grew explosively. I was positively bombarded with inquiries from journalists from lots and lots of Swedish papers and radio stations. Among other things, I collaborated in an educational documentary film made by the Institute for Public Health and appeared in the TV program *Striptease*.

"In the end, my complaint to the police led to my father and brother's being charged, tried, and convicted of threatening behavior. My brother was also convicted of having caused me serious physical harm. Immediately after the trial, I went back to Sundsvall, but with a heavy heart. It hurt me to think that I would never be with my family again. And I missed my mother dreadfully. I wished for nothing more than to be held in her arms, but I knew it was impossible. Because, as my mother, it had been her task to bring me up to be a good and obedient girl. She had obviously failed and they blamed her for it.

"She could never risk standing up for me. It would just make her situation even worse. She is accusing herself. Today, I live in Östersund, where I am a student. I study to become a social worker so I can carry on with my work to help girls who try to cope with problems similar to mine. Now I feel strong and stable, but it has taken a very long time for me to get to where I am today.

"I have had to give up my whole background and make a fresh start, rebuilding myself, my identity, from the beginning. I have succeeded in making myself a platform on which I stand with my own two feet. I have struggled so hard to get there, and I have paid such a high price. My sense of security I find with my new friends who have become my new family. But despite having had to pay such a high price, I don't regret my decision to pack my freedom and leave.

"Obviously, I'm awfully sad about what has happened and over what I've lost, but I'm not bitter about it, nor do I ever intend to be, for then it would feel as if the whole thing had been pointless. My family has lost its honor and a daughter, and I have lost all my nearest and dearest.

"Looking back now, I believe that things need not get as out of hand as they did in my case. If my parents had been supported and helped by a national organization, like for example the Kurdish Society, it should not have come to this.

"If society had accepted its responsibility and helped my parents to feel that they had a greater stake in Swedish society, then perhaps this might have been avoided. What happened to me cannot be undone, but I think it is important to learn something from it and do something in the future so that such cases are not repeated.

"I have chosen to tell my story for you today in the hope that it might help other immigrant girls, so that others won't have to go through what I've had to endure. If everyone carries their straw to the haystack, then this kind of thing need not happen again. Regardless of one's cultural background, it should be obvious that every young woman should be able to have both her family and the life she wants for herself.

"Sadly, to many girls this is not at all obvious. So I hope that you won't turn your backs on them—that you don't close your eyes to them.

"Thank you for listening."

Fadime took a big risk when she agreed to give this talk. She spoke to a close friend of how afraid she was of appearing in front of this audience and how much she'd have preferred not to go. But she felt obliged to do it, for several reasons.[1] The organizers had agreed to keep her talk secret. Even so, Fadime was fearful. She had good reason to be. Some of her relatives had almost certainly gotten wind of her engagement. Her brother later told the police that their father had been "in deep despair about Fadime's appearance in the Parliament in November 2001." Probably he was not the only one.

Fadime had kept a low profile ever since the autumn of 1998. "Never again the media! I've done my bit!" she said when her brother was convicted for the second time.[2]

In her talk in Parliament, she described the media circus around her as "growing explosively." Initially, she had hoped that being a celebrity would help her survive. But she had become more and more conscious of the stress and pain that the media coverage of her story was inflicting on her family. Her address in the Old Parliament Building in Stockholm was her last public engagement.

Her plan backfired.

19 | Integration

Do need to adopt customs to integrate successfully?

Was Fadime an example of successful integration? The Swedish minister for integration, Mona Sahlin, raised this question in a lecture she gave in Norway on May 14, 2002.[1] She also raised another question: Was Fadime's father an example of poor integration? Sahlin's answers were, respectively, "yes" and "yes, partly." Fadime was an example of successful integration, because she had embraced the value of freedom and fought for it vigorously. Her father was an example of partial integration, because he had spent much of his working life in Sweden and worked in a firm that employed Swedes almost exclusively. Also, he knew that it was wrong of him to kill Fadime. In other words, he had acquired at least some idea of Swedish laws and regulations, even if not Swedish values.

Are Sahlin's questions the right ones to ask? Is "successfully integrated" a meaningful way to characterize someone who was made to pay with her life for having learned to long for the freedom cherished by the Swedish system? My immediate reaction is to say no. It cannot be right to speak about *success* in this context. The phrase is inept—it seems to imply that Fadime existed independently of her social milieu and her kin. As if human beings were atoms, unconnected to others.

Also, to my mind, it cannot be right to speak of Rahmi Sahindal as partly integrated on the strength of his awareness that he ought not kill his daughter. We must assume that he would have known that even if he had stayed in Turkey. There as in Sweden, it is not acceptable to commit murder—though, admittedly, honor killings are carried out and approved of in some parts of Turkey, especially in the southeastern region where the Sahindals come from.

Besides, it was never established whether Rahmi Sahindal was truly aware that it was wrong of him to kill his daughter. On the basis of the facts that emerged in the High Court hearing, where he denied having anything to do with the murder, it is still not possible to draw the conclusion that he knew it was wrong. When he stopped insisting on how ill he was—that defense was dropped when the case reached the High Court—his argument, "you must be sick if you kill your own daughter," was negated as well. A statement made by the head of the Kurdish Association in Malmö, Kamaran Shwan, supports my interpretation: "That father thought he had done the right thing. That's why he killed Fadime."[2]

But Mona Sahlin has a point. She wanted to avoid people's using Fadime's case for their own ends. So she tried to highlight the positive aspect, which is there for all to see: Fadime is an example, indeed a shining example, of someone who has taken human rights to heart and is prepared to devote her life to putting these ideas into practice. That the outcome was so different from what one had hoped means that Fadime emerges as a martyr for her cause. No one can take that away from her—nor from Sweden. In that country, Fadime has come to represent all that is best in a human being. She is regarded as living proof that integration is possible. She was and will remain a pioneer.

Fadime's father is an ambiguous figure. He killed because he saw no other way out. Does it improve matters that he knew that murder was wrong, because it is against the law? How naive and primitive can we suppose him to be? Was he really unable to grasp the most elementary facts about living in Sweden after twenty years there?

Work is often used as a measure of integration, and it is a useful indicator. But the data suggest increasingly strongly that holding down a job does not necessarily imply participation in and belonging to the wider society. That integration at work promotes integration into society as a whole is an unproven assumption. It is perfectly possible to choose to sell your skills and capacity for work while leading a withdrawn and segregated life—many do just that.³ Fadime's father needed an interpreter in court, despite twenty years in Sweden and sixteen years at work there. His wife may not even speak Turkish, only a local variant of Kurdish. Her interpreter had to be summoned from Stockholm; there was no one in Uppsala with the right dialect.

Fadime's brother, who arrived in Sweden as a three-year-old, was unable to cope with coming across his sister in the streets of Uppsala, so she had to be exiled to another town.

There is something odd, even wrong, to talk about integration in this case, let alone calling it "successful." I suggest that the issue should be approached in other terms.

We need to consider to what extent a person sees herself as part of the larger society, rather than looking for external indicators of integration.

Fadime's father is an example of failed integration, despite his history of working and his partial knowledge of Swedish law. More must be in place before we call someone "partly integrated." It is probably a reflection of the overall failure of the integration process that the Scandinavian public debate has made "integration in the workplace" the most commonly used measure or indicator. For various reasons, many asylum seekers and immigrants have never entered the job market; far too many have been subject to "welfare colonization."⁴ Doling out social benefits is the way we Scandinavians buy ourselves peace of mind. Fadime's father earned his living, which is honorable both because it is quite a feat and because there was so little need to bother. The Scandinavian welfare state gives people an alternative, but he didn't choose it; in that respect, he was "one of us."

Of course he is like us. He responds to much of what life brings as "we" would, but he is also fundamentally different. Fadime

understood that he had failed to integrate in the ways that matter. It isn't enough to work and take home a regular pay-packet.
Many Scandinavians exist outside the labor market for a variety
of reasons but are nonetheless regarded as fully integrated. Rahmi
Sahindal's mental outlook was anchored elsewhere; his roots were
deeply sunk into a culture, or set of traditions, with core values
other than freedom and equality. The Scandinavian model of egalitarian welfare embodies values that are totally opposed to those
of traditional Kurdish culture: hierarchy and inequality, patriarchal rule, the extended family or clan as the basic social unit,
and the use of violence to resolve conflicts.[5]

These observations do not imply any estimate of how many of
the Kurds based in Scandinavia—or in Turkey, Syria, Iran, or Iraq—
believe in these traditional values. People are different wherever you
go, and in the case of the Kurds, there are big differences based on
region, religion, rank, and clan.[6] Still, much of what has emerged
in the public domain suggests that Fadime's father belonged in a
world radically different from the Scandinavian welfare state.

Within the family circle, Fadime's mother carried the blame for
her daughter's failings and ultimate betrayal. Why didn't the minister for integration wonder about the integration of Elif Sahindal?
Was she a success? Or was the answer a foregone conclusion from
the moment she sided with her husband in the High Court trial?
Elif, the mother who let her daughter down by supporting her
husband and son when they were charged, back in 1998, with
threatening to kill and beating up her daughter. Was Elif already
so deeply compromised that it goes without saying that she was
"not integrated"?

It is worth examining the situation of this mother in order to
bring the problems of integration into sharper focus. She was a mediator between two life worlds and worked at integration, although
it meant staking her daughter's life on it. Perhaps she hardly understood the risks. Anyway, she was willing to pay a high price in
order to give Fadime what she really wanted: a family, despite everything. She went all the way to reconnect to her daughter—and

did it despite the media excitement. Elmas, her second daughter, who couldn't forgive Fadime, is on record saying that her mother had agreed to the marriage between Fadime and Patrik. Not immediately, of course, but she had adjusted to the idea as time went by.[7] Elif has told of how she went to Sundsvall to help her daughter get her lodgings in order when, in opposition to her family's wishes, Fadime had decided to go on for higher education.

Elif Sahindal had gone out on a limb—far from the Turkish-Kurdish world where her roots were. Without a language to cope with her new surroundings, gagged and bound, she still struggled to create a future for her children—all of them, including Fadime, the black sheep of the family.

Elif wanted reconciliation and togetherness. She pushed her eldest daughter, Fidan, to meet with Fadime, and the two sisters often talked on the phone. In this way Fadime found her mother and two of her sisters (Fidan and Nebile) again; she had been in touch with Songül all along. The mother's balancing skills must not be underestimated, nor must her capacity for forgiving and comforting her children. *Tolerance* is a word that fits her: this woman who seemed to exist further away from Swedish society than the rest of her family—who had never worked outside the home and knew no Swedish—tolerated her daughter's change of allegiance. As a matter of fact, she did more than tolerate her daughter: she loved her. Some family members said that Fadime pressured her mother into meeting with her, but that makes no difference to the actuality. Elif reached out to Fadime.

In this way Fadime's mother became a mediator between two realities, two cultures. And she must have known the risk she ran that Fadime in the end would influence Elif's youngest daughter, so that Nebile too would look outside the family for greater independence and "Swedishness." It was in the cards. Although her mother may not have been aware of it, Fadime had said in public that she hoped Nebile would with time break free from the family.

These conciliatory moves within the family circle should not be seen as signs of integration into a *Swedish* reality or value system; Elif would probably have done the same in Kurdistan. You stand up for your child. This is what is expected of a mother in most Middle Eastern cultures and settings: she is a loving, tender being for whom *every single child* means everything. It is reflected in the division of labor, in emotional terms, between mother and father. The mother is the healing, soothing force in the family, while the father's role is more authoritarian and distant. This is why mothers are so important in a culturally diverse society: they have the possibility to tolerate and accept "deviations" in their children, which makes them well suited to serve as bridge-builders even when they remain rooted in their own culture. Of course, this is not the case of all mothers. Personality and life circumstances matter. Still, it is true of very many mothers.[8]

Integration is all about networks and relationships. It is meaningless to ask whether someone is integrated without a qualification— integrated *into something*. In her talk in Parliament, Fadime said, "If society had accepted its share of the responsibility and helped my parents to feel that they had a greater stake in Swedish society, then perhaps what happened might have been avoided."

Like the other Scandinavian countries today, Sweden is a conglomerate, a patchwork of different faiths and social ideas. One in every five inhabitants has at least one immigrant parent. It is perfectly possible to argue that Fadime herself was not well integrated in Swedish society, simply because she stood with one foot each in two groups separated by a deep cleft, living alongside each other, not together. In that situation, the art of balancing will not do. Until things change, something has to give; until the two camps become prepared to tolerate, if not respect, each other, you must decide which one to abandon.[9] Fadime did not want to make a break; she wanted continuity and had a right to do so. She should have been allowed it as a matter of course.

She mistook the degree of fervor in her old community. Its members saw breaking with them as the only possible option. It is easy to be wise after the fact and declare that was it. I would urge reflection: to characterize a certain community—in no way exceptional—that is part of Scandinavia today, part of the society that is "us," that is ours. This society, like many others in the new Europe, has failed to become integrated, and the failure afflicts people in various ways. None of us can rise above such facts. In our everyday life we are all affected a little, some deeply so. It is to *them* that the integration project is critically important. It is not above all about getting people jobs, although work matters. It is about instilling respect for the value and worth of the individual and the right of each one of us to lead our own life.

I have no recipe for how this can be brought about. In other books and essays I have gone on record with a few indications about the direction to follow. So have many others. Political authorities, as well as organizations and individuals, are all making important contributions, but there is still a long way to go. Integration must mean that people are given equal rights and opportunities but are also made to understand their social obligations. Arguably Fadime was not well integrated into Swedish society, because she did not have the chances in life that were open to most Swedish girls of her age. Also, she was not realistic about her life chances. She wanted more than the society of which she was a part could offer her. Her brother put it clearly in his interview with the police: "The family had consented to Fadime's breaking away, but on condition that they shouldn't have any contact with Fadime ever again . . . that was the bit she wouldn't buy."[10]

"That was the bit . . ." She did not buy it. She broke "the contract," probably without comprehending that it was an ultimatum, a condition for allowing her to live. Had she been better integrated into the Kurdish part of her world, she would perhaps have realized that in her parents' home region expulsion or exile is an alternative to killing when the family honor is at stake. That is how conflicts are resolved. That is how honor killings can be avoided.

But in contemporary Sweden, to apply this kind of mindset, is it not beyond the pale? In principle, no. In practice, yes. Such are the realities for some population groups in Scandinavia. "Fadime's murder shows that the honor culture is a problem for Sweden, and not a single event," Breen, Pela's sister, says. Kamaran Shwan, head of the Kurdish Association in Malmö, puts it a different way:

"Someone should've put a brake on her father's thoughts during those four years that the conflict carried on."[11]

There is no way one can guarantee not being murdered. It can happen in the best of families and at the most unexpected moments. Some people enjoy taking calculated risks and play with their lives at stake.

This was not what Fadime wanted. She wanted to live. And she came to regret having provoked her family as much as she did by talking to the media, according to three of her close friends. Nalin Pekgul, a Swedish Kurd and an MP, says that Fadime underestimated the Kurdish community in Uppsala. That is easy to understand. But should not some sensible males, some males in her family, for instance, have warned her?

Or warned Fadime's mother—this woman who cried out, "I did it. It was my fault!" within minutes of the killing. Had she allowed herself to be led, and led astray, by her well-educated daughter's courageous and dauntless actions? (Fadime was the only one of her five adult children who had gone on for higher education.) Elif Sahindal's husband, and probably others, had warned her: she must not stay in touch with Fadime. The warning was motivated by the possibility that Fadime might come to Uppsala and, if so, certain things might happen. Had Fadime's courage rubbed off on Elif? A close friend of Fadime has spoken of how Fadime became more and more confident about going to Uppsala and that she visited quite often (could it be that she saw her mother more frequently than Elif admits?). Once she even met her little sister Nebile in a café. Haydar, Rahmi's best friend, says that he believed that Fadime slept at home during the summer of 2001, when Elif was there but Rahmi was away on a trip to Turkey.[12] Regardless of whether this is true, there was a conspiracy afoot that would truly have challenged the males in the family if they had heard about it. We know that they suspected something early on and that they later became certain.

What will be the future consequences for Fadime's mother? Already she has to carry the guilt of having caused her daughter's death, and she has also failed to free her husband from the murder charge, despite her daring support for his defense. On the night of the murder, her second daughter, Elmas, said to the police that if Rahmi had done it, then it wasn't worth it: two lives for one. Also a father and a husband was "sacrificed" because his women wouldn't yield and carried on doing things their way.

Everything discussed here is based either on witness statements (to the police or in court) or on my interpretations of the material and my own observations. I have never talked with Fadime's mother, only observed her in the District and High Court hearings. Like many others, I thought that her refusal to testify in the District Court was a betrayal. And until the last moment, I hoped that she would not be a witness for her husband's defense; I couldn't believe the media when it was announced that she was going to back him in the High Court. But I came to feel sympathy for her. I think Fadime would have said "Poor Mummy."

It is when such women are integrated—when people like Elif Sahindal have been offered the possibility to reflect on their social setting and respond more actively and independently to their surroundings—that society will be able to consolidate its many segregated communities into a greater whole. Language learning is essential. The Swedish minister for integration, in her speech on May 14, 2002, made a point of saying that Sweden was not considering requiring language learning of asylum seekers, unlike Denmark and Norway, where that decision had been made recently. This might be understood as a sign that Sweden is the more liberal state, but it could also signify that the challenge of integration was not taken seriously enough. In fact, the Swedish government did introduce compulsory language teaching to political asylum seekers and refugees two years later, in line with decisions made in several other European countries.

Elif Sahindal has not been able to respond independently to Fadime's statements to the media or in court. Other people had to translate the texts and interpret statements for her. What distortions may have resulted from this process? This question applies also to Elif's husband, whose knowledge of Swedish was minimal. In 1998, Fadime declared, "All this stems from my parents' fear of Swedish society. My parents are illiterate and find it difficult to understand the Swedes. They live surrounded by their own people and the satellite dish which makes it possible for them to only watch Turkish TV."[13] In her talk in Parliament in 2001, she said her parents thought that the Swedes were promiscuous and "had no culture, no morals or ethical standards." Nonetheless, it was Fadime's mother, like Sara's and Pela's mother before her, who was prepared to support, for as long as she could, her daughter and her project: to be set free.

This commands respect, especially when one understands what limitations are imposed on mothers. That is not true of them all, but of many. It is important to in turn support *their* chances of independence.

This is true for men too—men, who are easily forgotten and passed over as attention focuses on women. Riyadh al-Baldawi, a psychiatrist and Swedish-Iraqi who has worked a great deal with immigrant families from the Middle East, has warned us: "It is important for social workers to realize that they must not takes sides uncritically. The entire family must be considered, including the husband or father, who is often condemned out of hand."[14] Fadime tried to do that. Her talk in Parliament is a clear example of balanced judgment. She condemns neither her father nor her brother but gives an account of their situation and the rules that govern their lives. She speaks of how her little brother has had to cope with the expectation that, as the next head of the family, he will rein in his five sisters, four of whom are older than he. And of how her father has to do what is required of him when his daughter ruins his life and the standing of the whole family. "Fadime wanted to understand even her father and her brother," say some of those who knew her best. The fact of a traditionally strong patriarchy means that, in many families, the men wield power and the women's duty is to submit. This makes it all the more important to enter into dialogues with men. This is a crucial task for immigrant organizations to take on.[15]

"We did try," says Sores Bladhede, a Kurdish politician in Uppsala; he claims that offers of help were made but that Fadime's father replied, "It isn't me who makes the decisions, other people decide over me."[16] This may be all too true. The honor or chastity culture, as it is called in Sweden, works precisely this way: it demands individual submission to more powerful social forces. Gossip and coffeehouse talk form part of the picture.

"The sense of being forced is false. Everyone believes that people talk, and yes, everyone can go on about customs and traditions, but we must define our traditions, we must find a solution," says Keya Izol, head of the national Swedish-Kurdish Association. "People who know the family must talk with them."[17] Fadime agreed with him but was given no help. Fadime's friend Malin Ström says, "She wanted to be, like, here I am, this is my family, we have a problem, we need help. But no one helped her."[18]

"We have to find a solution that suits us Kurds, even though we live in Sweden," Izol says. "We have to show understanding to all involved, not just to one person while making scapegoats of everyone else. The authorities are wrong. It could well be that not everything Fadime said was true. We must understand both sides. . . . Young people must understand their parents, and parents must understand their children but not limit their freedom. Understanding must be mutual. Those in the Kurdish community who recognize this [the problems] must try to solve them in a Kurdish way."

I have talked to many Norwegian Kurds who agree: problems must be solved through dialogue with the family, not by crossing the family.

All the men I've listened to insist that society failed Fadime's family. However, a family is many things, including a mother and a little sister—not least a mother—who saw powers outside of their control play fast and loose with their interests. "We must define our traditions and find a solution in a Kurdish way, even though we live in Sweden," says the leader of the Swedish-Kurdish National Association.

Such reflections offer hope: what Fadime wished for was a redefinition of tradition so that it preserves respect for both the individual and the family. Her life was one long testimony to how much she cherished her family.

We need a way of measuring integration that reflects normative practice. To what extent have people come to accept the individual worth of others? It means showing respect for law and order. It means tolerating, if not respecting, each other's values and lifestyle, insofar as these are not in conflict with existing laws and regulations. It means, above all, protecting the idea of the intrinsic worth of the individual.

Fadime was the victim of a crime. She has become an icon and, on the strength of that, will continue to affect posterity. Her testimony about the failing integration of immigrants like her parents into the larger society is relevant in many countries. Let this sink in: Fadime's father had been at work almost all his adult life—twenty years—in Sweden. Then recall "the man in the woods" and her mother's despair as she testified against her daughter. Recall the statement by Rahmi's nephew: "If Fadime had stayed in Östersund, all this wouldn't have happened."

This is Sweden in the early twenty-first century. Other Western countries may be in the same place soon.

20 *At Stake: A Perception of Humanity*

The debate in the wake of the murder of Fadime took different turns in the neighboring Scandinavian countries of Sweden and Norway. In both countries there was public outrage and massive engagement by many people, organizations, and politicians voicing their views of how to proceed to prevent similar tragedies in the future. At stake was also an explanation, or understanding, of what went wrong. Why was Fadime murdered? Who was to blame? What part, if any, did religion or ethnic identity play? This is where the debate in the two countries came to diverge: in the salience accorded to either religion or ethnicity. Let us ponder the contrast for the light it sheds on the intricacies of the "immigration debate" even in countries as similar as Sweden and Norway. The composition of the immigrant population makes a difference, as does the country's stand on multiculturalism. All the Scandinavian countries are culturally diverse, but only in Sweden is multiculturalism a national ideology: Sweden accords special value to the preservation of the collective culture of ethnic groups.[1]

In Norway, the debate focused on the question, Was Fadime a Muslim? Or, rather, she was said not to be a Muslim, an opinion defended in so many contexts with such energy that there was obviously a subtext at stake. Crucially, everyone had to know that

Fadime is not "one of us (Muslims)"—that is, honor killing has nothing to do with Islam. More than in Sweden, this was a major issue in Norway.[2]

In Sweden, people argued about ethnicity. It mattered that everyone should be told that Kurds don't approve of honor killings, that in fact no specific ethnic minorities practice, or would defend, such horrors.

The Norwegian concern that a particular religious group not be stigmatized is matched by a Swedish concern that any one ethnic group—particularly the Kurds—not be stigmatized. Why the difference? Where does it originate?

First, a fact must be established: Fadime *was* a Muslim. Her sister Songül told the police that the entire family was nonpracticing but Muslim. The head of the family in Sweden, Cemal Sahindal, told the media the same: "Religion means little for the family, but both Fadime and the family are Muslims."[3]

I asked one of Fadime's cousins, who replied, "We're just ordinary people, we don't have any special religion."

"Ordinary people" in Sweden and Norway are not actively religious. I assume that this is what he was implying. He wanted to make it clear that the Sahindal family consisted of ordinary people—there was nothing unusual about them. Since Fadime's murder, this has always been important for them. Important in order to avoid both being seen as "exotic" figures and causing others to be dragged down with them. The Sahindals were all keen to prevent other Kurds from having to suffer for the deed committed by one of their own. They knew the danger only too well: Sara and Pela were Kurds too. Three murders, all attracting huge media attention, have contributed to making Kurds suspect. And Kurds are Muslims, by and large.

Muslims are so many things. Nonpracticing Muslims are much more common than people in Scandinavia seem to think. You are born a Muslim and you remain one, unless you explicitly declare that you want to leave Islam. This is extremely rare, because Islam does not allow religious freedom. Islam is linked to the father's bloodline. A child with a Muslim father is a Muslim too. Such was the case with Fadime. What her innermost thoughts and feelings were I do not know.

But neither do those who deny, or argue against, that she belonged to the Muslim community. They make their case in good faith, I imagine. The problem is not Fadime. The problem is whether Muslims will be pilloried because it was a Muslim who shot Fadime.

Which goes to show how far we still have to travel before Norwegian Muslims feel confident that they are respected. The terrorist attack on September 11, 2001, intensified the image of a hostile Islam, an image that—in many people's opinion—grew stronger still after Fadime's murder.

But as I said before, this is more true in Norway than in Sweden, judging by the directions taken by the public debate. One difference is that Norway does not have a specific ethnic minority—Kurds, in this instance—under scrutiny. Another is, as one Swedish Muslim put it to me, that "the Swedes are aware that Christians commit honor killings too" (the first known honor killing in Sweden involved a Christian Palestinian). In addition, in Norway there are some particularly well-known public figures whose pronouncements against religion and imams have been extremely critical. Others have in turn felt obliged to stand up for Islam. And so the debate about Islam and honor killings gathers steam.

Yet another difference between the integration debates in these two countries is that in Sweden the emphasis on the *different* ethnic minorities is stronger. For instance, Chileans, Iranians, and Indians are carefully distinguished, also with regard to religion. In Norway—where the religious spectrum is equally diverse—the prototypical immigrant is always assumed to be a Muslim. The media do their bit by pretty consistently consulting "immigrant representatives" who are Muslims. Muslim organizations also come on strongly. This adds up to a distorted image of cultural diversity in Norway, since in reality Muslims make up only about a third of the non-Western immigrant population. In my view, the intense focus on Islam in Norway, relative to the *ethnic* diversity, may well have shifted the debate that followed Fadime's murder, making Muslims feel under suspicion, and so led many of them to insist that Fadime was not one of them.

That she was not seems to have become an accepted piece of mythology. I come across this assertion often and in different contexts.[4] But it means that finding people prepared to admit that they were wrong—and to reflect on the fact—is a positive experience. A young woman, herself a Muslim, told me, "Fadime didn't wear a headscarf, you know that, and people think you have to wear the scarf if you're a Muslim. But being a Muslim is between the person and God. God is the only judge."

So it is important to repeat this: Honor killing is not an Islamic practice. Islam does not justify it. Honor killing is unknown, and would have been unheard of, in many Muslim societies. It has been practiced among Christians, Hindus, Buddhists, Confucians, and others, as documentary evidence shows. Honor killing of women is a device that serves to control female sexuality and to assert the power of the collective over the individual. But that's not enough. A code of honor must exist to legitimate murder and reward it with honor.

Islam can be used to this end, and in certain population groups it is. But the agents are the people who make up the group. Religious doctrine cannot be blamed. True, religion can be used in many ways, including to justify or to condemn murder. But religion as such has no independent capacity to act—people use faith-based systems of thought to justify their actions. You need awareness and motivation; then religion can be turned into anything you want. This also is true of Islam.[5]

Islamic law, sharia, can make it relatively easier for those looking for an Islamic sanction of violence against women.[6] But liberal Muslims insist that this is a misinterpretation and a misuse of sharia, a literal reading of texts written down more than a thousand years ago.[7] They claim that the spirit of Islam is humane. And they are right. Historically, Islam improved the status of women in many respects.

When a social group justifies violence against women in terms of Islam, the practice is based on ancient texts (the Qur'an and traditional Sunni teaching from the time of the Prophet Muhammad) being applied to today's reality. If Bible texts were to be used in the same way, the outcome might well likewise be abuse of women—as we have seen historically and still do now in some Christian fundamentalist communities.

The tragedies of Fadime, Sara, and Pela teach us that "culture" must never take precedence over the individual's basic human rights, that respect for a culture must always be secondary to respect for every human being's integrity and welfare, and that culture is a product of human inventiveness. As a prescription, a set of rules, cultural standards and ideas are in flux. However, people can "take over" culture, inscribe it on tablets of stone, and back its pronouncements with power. Fadime claimed that her parents, having arrived in a foreign place, had invented rules and called them "culture" in order to control the girls. Others make the same point. Sükrü Bilgiç refers to the research done by Esma Ocak in several villages in Turkish Kurdistan: Girls of twelve or thirteen had boyfriends and their mothers knew. It was seen as natural. But among Turkish Kurds in Norway this is unheard of, Bilgiç says. He also presents a series of other examples of how "culture" is made much stricter for Kurdish and Turkish girls living in Scandinavia than it is in Turkey.[8]

Nasim Karim—a Norwegian-Pakistani young woman who first drew Norway's attention to forced marriage, after she barely managed to escape alive from such a plight in 1992—has criticized the Norwegian authorities for backing away from their responsibility when it comes to "culture." Young people with an immigrant background do not receive the support they should, apparently because of "their culture" and the ongoing "cultural conflict."[9] In this way the authorities renege on the human rights of a sizable part of the population. "When a man is subjected to violence, it is called torture, but when a women is subjected to violence, it is called culture," Karim said in a lecture to a group of members of the Norwegian parliament, voicing a pain that Fadime had also experienced.

Culture and power go hand in hand. This is how the Indian anthropologist Veena Das puts it: "Culture is a means of distributing pain unequally within a population."[10] Someone has the power to define what the rules are. Had it been up to the mothers of Fadime, Sara, and Pela to decide, the girls would all have lived. Mothers have their role in Kurdish culture but no power to set the agenda.

Culture per se cannot claim respect; respect is due only when it promotes the welfare of all, and especially the weak.[11] The French Lebanese writer Amin Maalouf has said, "Traditions deserve respect only insofar as they are themselves respectable, that is to say that they embody respect for the fundamental rights of all men and women."[12] Bhikhu Parekh, a British Indian professor, agrees: "Respect for human beings does not necessarily entail respect for their cultures, for the latter might show no respect for human beings."[13]

At this point, a few words about religion are in order. Can culture and religion be kept apart? The Nordic countries have freedom of religion, but what should be done when a religion dictates rules and regulations that are in conflict with human rights?

Religion is part of culture. In practice, the two cannot be separated. One can always try, but when all is said and done, religion is a matter of interpretation and understanding. Which is why we observe an enormous variation in practice within all religions and systems of faith. In order to promote humanism and counteract fundamentalism, many attempt to "free" religion from narrow-mindedness and traditions that justify or even glorify violence. Such projects are important. When a distinction is made between religion and culture, violence and oppression can be explained away as culture, independent of religion. But in the end, religion is a matter of culture, of what the eyes see and the mind understands.

Freedom of religion can be in conflict with human rights, but it is not inevitable. Human beings have options and abilities to shape their religious practice in ways that are in harmony with ideas about human rights. The Universal Declaration of Human Rights was hammered out and signed by representatives of all the great world religions. It is based on universal ideas, as many outside the Western sphere have pointed out.

"Respect for culture" has been a central tenet of the integration policy of most Western societies—so central that you risk being branded "racist" if you do not show respect for the culture of others.[14] The intention is good: to support equality among groups and avoid stigmatization. Ethnic minorities should not be assimilated and feel pressured to "become" Swedes or Norwegians. Everyone should be allowed to keep their identity, their culture, within certain limits. There must be respect for law and order. Respect for a culture is secondary to respect for the law.

In theory, this is straightforward. In practice, it causes problems. Remember the case of Sara: Then the debate focused on whether culture had a role in directing violence toward women. That time victory went to the party that denied any connection. The politicians listened to them. In Norway too, many try, with the best of intentions, to avoid recognition of many of the problems that people of immigrant background feel are part of their basic experience. Shabana Rehman and Kadra Yusef have made a remarkable effort to open the eyes of politicians, journalists, and others. So have Walid al-Kubaisi, Nasim Karim, and others. When Mona Sahlin, the Swedish minister of integration, says that she has "betrayed immigrant girls," what she refers to is her previous denial that certain types of violence can be culturally driven.[15] When Fadime says to her audience in Parliament, "I hope you won't turn your back on them," she is speaking from her own hard-won experience. As one of her friends put it: "The honor culture is an ideology, and that's what Fadime wanted to speak about." But how to talk about it in a Sweden unwilling to hear about "culture" in terms of a problem?

Now, after the death of Fadime, a new understanding is finally emerging—better late than never. But the reason it took so long is that there is a dilemma that is neither Swedish nor Norwegian; it exists in all multicultural democracies, in India, South Africa,

Australia, and elsewhere. The rights of ethnic minorities to sustain their identity and preserve their culture may come into head-on conflict with the individual's right to self-determination. The Universal Declaration of Human Rights emphasizes the individual's right to leave a group—the right to *exit*.[16] Respect for culture is on the other hand often based on an opposing principle: that people have a duty to belong, that they have been given to the group to own. Fadime rebelled against this principle, as did Sara, Pela, Breen, and others in Sweden, as did Nadia, Nasim, and others in Norway. The work to further human rights in Scandinavia is on the right track now: we have them to thank.

Ethnic identity forms an important part of human life. People have a need to feel part of a group and display it. Some are able to cope perfectly well with a multiethnic identity. Others find it problematic. "We were outsiders, in both the Kurdish and the Swedish communities," Breen says of Fadime, her sister Pela, and herself. This means a sense of homelessness, of belonging nowhere—of not being allowed to belong because society is divided into fundamentally opposing camps. When this is the case, many are lost, however well they seem to cope with the situation. We must remember that identity is always a question of wholeness. Or, as Amin Maalouf says: "My identity is that which means that I am not identical with any other human being."[17]

Our democracy and our welfare state are both based on the principle of freedom and equality. The individual is central. The idea of "human rights" has grown out of the perception that each individual is unique; hence the individual both needs and has a right to have protection from oppression by those in power, be it in the family, the church or religious groups, the clan, or the state.

Belonging to a fellowship of some kind is essential for happiness and, indeed, survival. Ethnic affinity can be an important part of people's sense of identity. But a person is always more than that: our whole self is the sum of relationships that reflect different aspects of who we are, depending on context. To elevate ethnicity to a super-identity with unrestricted influence is to diminish human beings, to limit their potential and capacity for development. In culturally diverse societies it is destructive, since tolerance and respect for the integrity and worth of each individual *must* be maintained.

Fadime wanted to marry her Patrik. Her family said no. If Fadime had it her way, all the girls in the family might decide to marry Swedes. What was at stake? The identity and continuity of the ethnic group. Girls, as we know, bear children. Were the Sahindals to allow the community's girls to give birth to Swedish babies? Besides, through marriage, girls like Fadime can serve to obtain permits for more Kurdish relatives to stay in Sweden and, as a consequence, increase the community's strength and the family's income. Size means strength. The stakes were high. It was not even likely that Fadime would be allowed to marry a Kurd of her own choice. In many communities, a girl is too valuable to be allowed to pick her own mate. This can be true of boys as well.[18] But here we are considering Fadime, and Patrik Lindesjö was actually Swedish.

Or was he? "But he was Iranian!" little sister Nebile exclaims. The media won't listen. They've tried to make it clear, she complains hopelessly, but all the media only want more stuff to blacken the Sahindals. Look, Patrik wasn't Swedish at all, he was Iranian.

In her testimony in the High Court, Fadime's mother says the same thing: Patrik was an Iranian, not a Swede. Meanwhile Fadime's father insists that Patrik was a Swede. In the police interviews and in both trials, he emphasizes that he had no objection to Fadime's marrying a Swede. Songül, their daughter, confirms that in the eyes of the family Patrik was a Swede. Fadime spoke of what a nightmare it was for her father to have a daughter with a Swedish boyfriend. And Songül knows that that their relatives vetoed the marriage. The head of the whole family is quoted as having said at a family conclave: "If Fadime gets away with marrying Patrik, all the girls in our family will want to marry Swedes."

Also, Fadime has said that Patrik's relatives were Iranian and against his marrying into a Kurdish family like hers.[19]

In court, Fadime's mother said that they could speak with Patrik's family in their own language. (She meant Turkish. It is a language many Iranians know.)

In such ways as these does ethnic identity become a matter of what eyes are seeing, of what kind of flags are being flown. I understand why Elif Sahindal wanted the court to know that Patrik was of course an Iranian and also why her youngest daughter Nebile protested against the media presentation of Patrik as a Swede: these are strategic moves. Elif wanted to remove the suspicion that her husband had killed their daughter because she had a Swedish boyfriend; Nebile wanted to stop people from regarding the Sahindals as hostile to Swedes.

But everything went wrong for Fadime and Patrik, regardless of what he was: Swedish or Iranian or Swedish-Iranian. To each other, they were just human. And the right of human beings to be themselves, in their own right, should matter more in a modern democracy than any ethnic identity.

"Kurdish Woman Murdered" was the message broadcast and printed in the days and weeks following Fadime's death. She was laid in her grave after a ceremony in a Swedish church: her last resting place is the Old Cemetery in Uppsala. She became the very incarnation of the Swedish desire for freedom. But in history she goes down as a Kurd. Another reason for reflection.

One might as well have said "Swedish woman murdered in an honor killing." Somehow this is uncomfortable, though. It makes honor killing a part of Sweden.

VII / Reflections

21 / Longing for the Family

"One only ever has one mother and one father," Fadime said and talked about the sadness and longing she felt having lost them both. "I'll never get them back. Of course I feel the sorrow."

At the time, she still had her Patrik. "If she loses Patrik—what's left for her?" asked her lawyer, Leif Ericksson.

"Fadime lost everything worth living for, her entire identity, when she became alone, without either Patrik or her family," her friends say.

"Now there's no chance of reconciliation," Fadime said after Patrik's death. She was certain that her family had rejected her for all time.

"Fadime was as brittle as glass," Ericksson says. "Where her strength to carry on came from is beyond understanding."

Fadime devotes herself to studying social work. She wants to use her experiences and knowledge to specialize in working with vulnerable young people from immigrant backgrounds. Her friends are her new family, but she misses her real family intensely. In the summer of 1998, she says: "Once my anger has cooled, I miss them so much, my mother, my sisters and brother, all the family." After a breach of three years, she phones her mother and asks, "How are you?" Her mother responds. They're in touch now.

"She was over the moon when she got to speak to her mother!" says Fadime's close friend Olcay Karatas.[1] Olcay warns Fadime that visiting her mother in Uppsala means taking a risk. But Fadime is simply happy. "Look what time can do!" she said. "Just three years! In six or seven years—imagine!"

"She didn't really believe that she would be killed," Olcay comments about Fadime's last year.

When asked if she ever had any more death threats after her brother had gone to prison in the autumn of 1998, Leif Ericksson says, Fadime always answered, "No. Everything is fine." Which is a Swedish way of expressing the Kurdish phrase "My whole family is sheltered." Perhaps that was how she felt, or perhaps it was what Fadime wanted to convey to others. She had a project: to take charge of her own life and put the bad times behind her. Also, she profoundly hoped to be reconciled with her family. Her sister Songül says that Fadime even missed her father and her brother.

A Kurdish teacher at the college in Östersund had warned Fadime against going to Uppsala before leaving for Kenya. However, Fadime was used to evaluating risks on her own. The teacher speculates: "I think she wanted some kind of restitution, she wanted to show that she had succeeded." Fadime had gone all out to get an education against her family's wishes. Now she had almost reached the end of that road: she was off to Kenya to complete her course of study. She was proud and happy—she felt on top of things.

"We kept giggling that last night together," Songül has said. There was a party atmosphere. Their mother had baked pies especially to please Fadime and they all enjoyed them. Everyone was delighted with the gifts Fadime had brought. They admired her new coat. They hugged each other and Fadime promised to phone her mother as soon as she arrived in Kenya.

Friends confirm that Fadime felt safer and safer on her trips to Uppsala, despite her brother's threat: "Your days are numbered, I'll get you when you least expect it."

Olcay muses that in her heart of hearts, Fadime was scared of being alone and lonely. She missed everyone in her family, even her father and brother. She was always on her guard. She said to Olcay, "'Don't let me down when you talk to my family." For her, studying was a way to get her own back. She wanted recognition and to get away from being labeled a whore. She wanted to show how strong and wise she'd become through education, by acquiring knowledge.

"She wanted to be not just a human being, but a wise one."

"Until last night, this was a story with a happy ending," said Fadime's lawyer and friend on the morning of January 22, 2002.

"She was a happy person at heart, she was happy about her life," says the journalist Marianne Spanner, speaking about her last talk with Fadime: "She was determined not to let what had happened dominate her life. She was so incredibly strong. She wanted so strongly to lead a normal life."

"She was the most courageous client I ever had," Leif Ericksson says.

"Fadime was just a bit too brave. It won't do to be that brave," says a woman whose family had rejected her.

But courage was Fadime's badge of rank—courage and the strength to stand by the path she had chosen. Yet she was vulnerable too. As Olcay has said, "Fadime's love for her mother was her weak spot, the one feeling she could not control."

Fadime is at peace. Her mother lives on. Only when her story is told can we hope fully to understand Fadime's life—and her destiny.

Pressuring mother to speak out ='s of others like her.

AFTERWORD

On January 21, 2007, Fadime was commemorated in Sweden with a memorial seminar in her honor. Five years had passed since her life was cut short, and every year, on the fateful date, her legacy had been commemorated in both official and less formal ways. I had been invited to take part yearly since the publication of my book in Swedish on January 21, 2004. (It had been first published in Norwegian a year before, to the day.) Twice the memorial seminar had taken place in the old parliament building where Fadime gave her celebrated "speech in Parliament," and it was a special experience to stand there, in the same spot where she had addressed her audience, thinking of the momentum of her message.

Ministers of integration, equality, and justice and other politicians have all marked their respect for Fadime by participating in seminars and debates in her honor. So too have leading public figures and human rights activists of various ethnic backgrounds. The abiding challenge remains: how Sweden can lead the way in combining respect for human rights with social welfare and dignity for all inhabitants, regardless of culture, creed, race, or gender.

What can be done on the home front? And how can one help and sustain work on the international arena?

On January 21, 2007, an organization named Fadime's Memorial Fund was in charge of events in Stockholm. I had been invited to give the main talk on the theme "Why has Europe betrayed its immigrants?" Then there would be a discussion between Nalin Pekgul and me. Pekgul is a Kurdish-Swedish parliamentarian who spoke out against honor killing early, at the time of Sara's death. She had been a friend of Fadime and one of the pallbearers at her funeral.

We all felt honored when Mona Sahlin, though she was in an exceedingly hectic political process, called to say she wanted to join us. It would have mattered so much to Fadime, who had decided to give her speech in Parliament, despite her fears for her life, precisely because she wanted to reach Mona Sahlin with her message. (Sahlin was then minister of integration and equality; she has been a leading politician in Sweden for more than two decades.)

I was sitting with Mona Sahlin and Nalin Pekgul, and the proceedings were about to begin, when I noticed three young women entering the hall. I leaped up and ran over to embrace Songül, whom I recognized. Then my eyes fell on the girl next to her. She was tall and poised and strikingly beautiful, with Fadime's features. It must be Nebile. I was overcome. I hadn't seen her since the court case in Stockholm in May 2002. From age thirteen to nearly nineteen, she had metamorphosed into a real beauty, with a radiance that seemed to come from within.

The third girl in the group was Malin Ström, Fadime's and Songül's good friend, whom I also had not met before. She had helped Fadime write her "speech in Parliament."

With Nebile present, my plan collapsed. I simply could not deliver what I had prepared: a devastating critique of European integration policies (in line with the title I had been given), using as a critical case an honor killing in Denmark that I had just followed in court, where nine persons were found guilty of complicity to kill eighteen-year-old Ghazala Khan and her husband Emal Khan. Ghazala died, Emal barely survived. Her father had ordered the murder, her brother had carried it out, and six family members, including an aunt, and three family acquaintances were involved.

The father had lived in Denmark for thirty years and was a well-respected, dignified man who was seemingly perfectly integrated in Danish society. He spoke Danish fluently.

I had meant to use the Ghazala case, among others, to highlight how tricky the concept of integration is; integration in the labor market and language integration may not serve as any indication of integration at the level of values. On the contrary, integration on the more public levels can be misleading, bewildering, deceiving. I had also planned to talk about the failure of the police: Ghazala and Emal sought help from the police three times, in vain. Three times in the course of Ghazala's last eighteen days. Just as with Fadime the first time she sought help, the police to whom Ghazala and Emal appealed were disbelieving, naive. But in 2005, how could that be?

Ghazala too had chosen her own love in life and had "gone public" by eloping with him. It was her only hope: after confiding in her mother in the hope of gaining some support, she had been beaten by her brother (a different brother from the one who killed her) and made to understand where she stood. She knew full well the risk she took by eloping. She was convinced that her father would have her killed.

But her case was in some ways even worse than Fadime's in that there is evidence of a plot whereby scores of people knew she was going to be killed and several dozen helped to hunt the couple down. A sizable part of the taxicab community in Copenhagen was involved; Ghazala's father was a major cab company owner.[1]

The case had shaken Denmark; it had shaken me. A memorial for Fadime was an occasion to reflect on where we stand in Europe today and what needs doing to prevent atrocities of this kind.

But I could not deliver that speech as planned, not with Nebile there. She had come for the very first time to attend the memorial for Fadime on a date that for Nebile had been catastrophic: her sister was murdered before her very eyes; her family fell apart; her father, kind and loving, became a killer. It was a big step forward for Nebile to come; no doubt she had been encouraged, perhaps even prodded, by Songül, who was herself coming for the first time since 2003, the first anniversary of Fadime's death. She was sitting right in front of me, in the second row, and all I could think of was how to deliver my message with caution so as not to strew salt into open wounds.

On the fifth anniversary of Fadime's death it was time to think not only of the tragedy but also of the joy and happiness she had had, not least thanks to her family. I restrung my lines, so to speak, and gave a different talk from the one I had planned: I used Fadime's life to reflect upon the support of a mother, the love of sisters, female resistance and defiance, courage, hope. After all, and this is important to remember, Fadime died a happy young woman. She was so determined to put the bad times behind her, and she seems to have managed, according to the testimony of those who knew her best.

Robin Grönstedt, chair of Fadime's Memorial Fund and a fellow student of hers, reflected to me that she wasn't at all like the serious, grave, burdened girl that the media depict. She was full of laughter, fun loving, rode a snow scooter. She lived a full life, went on holiday to the United States, and but for the coincidence of 9/11 might have had a marvelous time there. Robin's image of her is not like the one I have depicted, which shows only the grave and responsible side.

She took risks, says her friend Malin Ström—too many risks. She was so eager to lead a normal life and was full of so much fun, so much laughter.

What about Patrik, I ask Malin: does she think that he died in an ordinary traffic accident or not? An ordinary accident, Malin replies. Both Fadime and she were convinced of that. Patrik had a BMW, and he liked to drive fast. Fadime was always afraid he might have an accident. He was such a big, strong, handsome man. Malin had thought to herself: someone strong enough to take care of Fadime. It was not to be.

Deliberately, Patrik's death was not mentioned in Fadime's speech in Parliament, which otherwise traces the contours and main events of her life. His untimely death was absent from the story. Why? Malin says it was because the bare mention of it would have led the audience to be filled with empathy for Fadime's grief. That was not what she wanted. She had a message to convey.

The 2007 memorial seminar for Fadime in Stockholm also featured a Kurdish-Swedish singer performing a song whose lyrics I wish I could have understood. It led Nebile, Songül, and many others to burst into tears. Evidently the song was about the kind of tragedy Fadime faced: where you are destined to meet death for choosing your love in life. It was a Kurdish folk song. Hearing the translated lyrics made me once more aware of the limits of my own understanding—I who grew up in a place where you naturally chose your own love.

After the memorial, we go together—Malin, Songül, Nebile, and I—to a café where we can sit and talk before Songül and Nebile must return to Uppsala that evening. Malin leads the way. It is freezing cold and rainy, and we pass one coffe shop after the other in our search for a better place. Malin suggests we head for a hotel lobby she knows; we will be more comfortable there, it will be quiet. And it is. We sit together for a couple of hours or so, precious hours. Songül I already knew; she is a survivor, and I always thought she would manage. But I naturally feared for "the little one," whose presence now comforted me; I couldn't help but feel that she had a guardian angel.

After seeing Songül and Nebile off on the train to Uppsala, Malin and I go out for dinner. It is then that she tells me something I had not noticed: how she places herself when she is out with the two girls.

Always so that she can see the entrance doors. Always facing the doors, alert.

The hotel lobby had been convenient not only because it was quiet and cozy but because we were seated far inside, with a good view, for Malin, of the entrance.

What's she afraid of? I ask. Not of the girls' close family, they wouldn't harm them. But there are many cousins; the kin group is large. You never know.

Malin should know better than most what is at stake. She had been Fadime's and Songül's close friend since the autumn of 1997, when Songül appealed to her for help on Fadime's behalf. Malin was then working with an organization helping girls of immigrant background. She had come to Songül's school to talk about the project. Songül knew of someone desperately in need of help. It was the beginning of a friendship that has outlived Fadime. Nebile has joined in. Songül was always in on it.

What then was Fadime's legacy? What has been achieved in the battle against honor killings and other forms of honor-based violence? What developments can we trace, in Sweden and internationally?

To begin with Sweden: In May 2005, the country changed a law that had permitted girls as young as fifteen to be married if the law in the children's parental homeland permitted it. The law applied even if a girl was Swedish born and a Swedish citizen.[2] In force since the early 1970s, the law had evidently been formulated with the intent of showing respect for the culture of ethnic minorities. It was part of Sweden's multicultural agenda. None of the other Scandinavian countries had a similar law. In Norway, Denmark, and Iceland, eighteen years was the legal minimum marital age for all, regardless of parents' background.

The law had been a sore point for human rights activists in Sweden for a long time. But it took Fadime's death to have it changed— so I and many others think. Among the authorities, some say that the legal reform had been planned before. Perhaps so. But Fadime's death, and legacy, certainly accelerated the pace.

"When the girls are about sixteen," Fadime had said, "they are taken to their families' homelands." They say it is only a visit to the old country and that they won't agree to any marriage proposal. But in fact, the pressure is too much for them.

Forced marriage is a form of honor-based violence (or honor-related violence, as the Swedes call it). A refusal to marry according to the family's wish is a common trigger of honor killing, perhaps *the* most common. With the new law in Sweden, the pressure on the very young will diminish, one hopes. Now a girl cannot enter into marriage before she is eighteen, whatever the law in her parents' homeland. Or rather, a marriage before that age will not be accepted in Sweden. "Culture" has lost out to equal human rights.

Sweden has taken further steps to protect persons who face threats from their families or communities. Since 2004, the government has set aside 200 million Swedish kronor (ca. US$35 million) for the purpose of sheltered housing for persons at risk.[3] In some cases this program has also come to the aid of Norwegian girls, who have been able to find secure lodgings in Sweden after the failure of Norwegian authorities to grant the same. Internationally, Sweden emerges as exemplary in its commitment to protect the lives of persons threatened with honor-related violence (in the broad sense of the term). Again, this came about "after Fadime." Her legacy has helped to save the lives of others.

At the ground level, numerous organizations and individuals are participating in efforts to combat honor-related violence in Sweden. Social workers, child welfare workers, teachers, police, prosecutors, and others are being trained regarding the issues and ways to deal with them. I have been invited yearly to partake in many such workshops, seminars, and courses. I am impressed with the engagement of so many dedicated persons and organizations. Sweden is clearly at the forefront in this regard.

The Swedish police, too, have been a forerunner in Europe. "After Pela," they formed a special investigation unit to investigate and deal with honor crimes. The police in some other European countries have drawn on the expertise of Swedish police.[4]

Mentioned too must be Sharaf Heroes (Sharaf Hjälter). *Sharaf* is the Arabic, and also Turkish, Kurdish, and Persian, word for "honor." This is a group of young men of immigrant background who have been widely recognized, in Sweden and elsewhere in Europe, for their commitment to change the ways youngsters think about honor. They visit schools, communities, and youth clubs and try to teach the boys, and their fathers too, that honor is about protecting life and health, not about control and supervision. These boys, Sharaf Heroes, are saying no to being the guardians of their own sisters' chastity. They want to be free of the obligation to control and subjugate. Honor, they say, is about liberty and freedom. They are creative in the ways they convey their message, using theater, songs, sports, games. A female counterpart, Elxia, has been formed and is now working to reach girls and women.

In Norway too, Fadime's tragedy had a major effect. Organizations working to help girls and women of immigrant background report a vast increase in appeals for help from girls and also boys. In Norway, in fact, one-third of all requests for help to avoid or escape forced marriage now come from boys, though the threshold for them to seek help is higher. Fadime's murder was a signal to many others of what might be in store should they opt for their freedom as she did.

In April 2004 Norway became the first country in Europe to criminalize forced marriage. Belgium and Denmark have followed suit, and several other countries are considering doing the same. The Norwegian legislative change came after extensive public and political debates in the wake of Fadime's murder. Her death did not effect the change by itself, obviously. But it generated awareness and intensified commitment among politicians to outlaw forced marriage. Until then, forced marriage had been a civil offense. By criminalizing forced marriage, the state is undertaking the obligation to prosecute offenses, relieving victims of that burden.

As of this writing, only one case has come up for trial: a father and brother were convicted of attempting to force a seventeen-year-old girl to marry in Kurdish Iraq. The case went all the way to the Supreme Court, and the sentence was increased at every level of the trials. (The father got two and a half years in jail, the brother got one year and eight months.) I was an expert witness, called by the prosecutor at both the district and the high court and followed it closely. When Bakan Honer, the girl in question, was in danger of her life in Norway, she was temporarily placed in sheltered housing in Sweden. The Norwegian police were thus able to draw on the help of Swedish authorities.

Bakan's father had declared, before five Norwegian officials, "I take you and you and you and you and you as witnesses that I will

[handwritten margin note: Duty of law to step in when violates human rights.]

kill my daughter because she has ruined my honor." He had just then been informed that she sought help from child welfare agencies. Bakan testified against her father and brother in the District Court, but she withdrew her testimony in the High Court and insisted that all she had said at the lower court was a lie. She loved the man in question and wanted nothing more than to be with him in Iraq. Above all, she did not want her mother and younger siblings to be bereft of a husband and father. She wanted her father out of jail. Like Fadime, she also wanted the best for the family, and she felt guilty about her part in the drama.

Younger than Fadime, more vulnerable than her, Bakan—as the first girl to testify in a case of forced marriage before a criminal court in Europe—reminds us of what is at stake for girls like her. Nothing less than their families. In a choice between your family and liberty, which way do you go? And why should anyone have to make the choice?

Said Fadime in her speech in Parliament, "It should be obvious for any young girl to be able to have both her family and the life she wishes for herself. Sadly, this is not at all obvious." Fadime's words pertain even today.

In Europe it is estimated that thousands of youngsters live with the risk of forced marriage. Not arranged marriage, which many willingly enter into, but a marriage forced on them. In London in 2005, the metropolitan police dealt with some four hundred reported cases. The picture is similar all over Europe, where material stakes intertwine with "honor" to perpetuate, or even increase, the incidence of forced marriages. In the part of Pakistan where most Norwegian Pakistanis come from, *visuni* is a common label for Norwegian Pakistani girls.[5] It means visa. Marriage to such a girl means a "green card." Boys, too, are often obliged to marry by force. Families build and perpetuate alliances through marriages that often leave young people little ground for self-decision.

It remains to be seen, though, whether penalizing forced marriage will have the desired effect of protecting young persons. The difficulty of getting anyone to testify is a major obstacle to bringing cases through the courts.

On the international scene, significant steps to stamp out honor killings and honor-based violence have been taken over the past few years.

In October 2004, the United Nations General Assembly passed a historic resolution on the elimination of crimes against women and girls committed in the name of honor. Known as "Crimes of Honor," the resolution stresses the need to treat all forms of violence against women and girls, including crimes committed in the name of honor, as criminal offenses punishable by law. It emphasizes that such crimes are incompatible with all religious and cultural values and calls upon all states to intensify efforts to prevent and eliminate crimes against women and girls committed in the name of honor. It also underscores that such crimes take many different forms and require many different measures for their prevention.

In October 2003, the Council of Europe had passed a similar resolution on "So Called Honour Crimes."

What is significant about these resolutions is the use of a term, *honor crimes*, or *crimes of honor*, which could hardly have been spoken, and would certainly not have been acceptable, just a few years before. Asma Jahangir, the UN special rapporteur on freedom of religion or belief, noted at a conference in Stockholm in December 2004 that it was only since about the turn of the millennium that in her country, Pakistan, one could speak of honor killings at all. The prevailing official climate had been one of denial. Nazand Begikhani, a human rights activist and leader of the British-based KWAHK, Kurdish Women Association Against Honour Killing, agrees. She said that honor killings were "shrouded in silence and denial." Even now, speaking out against them can lead to the person being labeled a traitor by her or his group.

Asma Jahangir and Nazand Begikhani were among one hundred experts gathered at an international conference convened by the Swedish government in Stockholm on December 7–8, 2004. The conference was called "Combating Patriarchal Violence Against Women: Focusing on Violence in the Name of Honour." Participation was by special invitation and included experts and top-level officials from many different countries. The Swedish minister for integration and gender equality gave the opening address, and the minister for foreign affairs gave the closing remarks—emblematic of the fact that both national and international action is needed to combat violence in the name of honor.[6]

One of the speakers was Philip Alston, the UN special rapporteur on extrajudicial, summary, or arbitrary executions. He labeled honor killings executions (just as the verdict against Rahmi Sahindal had done). The reason, Alston said, is that honor killing involves a group of people who in actual fact passes a death sentence onto the victim. This pattern to honor killings sets them apart from domestic murders. That is why the UN engages with this issue. Domestic violence does not come under the aegis of the UN, but honor killing does because it is extradomestic.

Alston also spoke of the resistance he had faced, as special rapporteur, from a number of male ambassadors who had contacted him and implored him not to categorize honor killings as human rights violations but to regard them as matters of the state—internal affairs. This was how it used to be, this was how it should remain.[7] In other words, they wanted no interference. However, honor killings are now included in the mandate of the UN special rapporteur on extrajudicial, summary, or arbitrary executions, who reports yearly to the UN Commission on Human Rights and to the General Assembly.

Speaking of a pattern: Nilofar Bakhtiar, adviser to the prime minister on women's development in Pakistan, has said, "I'm ashamed to admit that in my country, there are special graveyards for the victims of honor killings."

Fadime's death was one of the tragedies that helped raise awareness and trigger action to bring about the resolutions noted above. Her death made headlines far beyond Sweden. It was publicized internationally, as were a few other cases in Pakistan, Great Britain, and Sweden (Pela). Thousands had gone before her without leaving much trace. Their names were erased, their bodies thrown away. A remark made by Runak Faraj Rehim, a Kurdish Iraqi journalist and human rights activist, at the Stockholm conference in 2004 is telling: if Pela and Fadime had not been Swedish, the world still would not have cared about honor killings.

It may be all too true. For years in places like Iraq, Pakistan, and Jordan, courageous organizations and individuals have tried to marshal international support in their battles against honor crimes but have often been met with a cold shoulder or sheer denial. The legacy of Pela and Fadime was to have brought home to the international community that East and West are one world as regards honor-based violence. The battle against it requires international cooperation.

As we have seen, the crimes are often—probably increasingly— transnational: decisions are made by parties located on different continents. Modern telecommunications facilitate such decision making. Diasporic communities have vested interests in family affairs across borders and boundaries. Lenient laws in some countries lead citizens of other countries, or citizens with double citizenship, to seek to commit the crimes where the punishment will be less severe.

The European Council's decision to require Turkey to amend its laws regarding honor killing, so that "honor" is no longer an extenuating circumstance in murder, was a significant step.

So was Sweden's high-level maneuvering to influence the Kurdish Regional Government in Iraq to change its laws. True, the most effective campaign for legal reform was organized in the Kurdish diaspora by a network of women who were able to access and help shape international public opinion and to raise awareness among representatives of Western governments. However, as Nazand Begikhani notes, "The focus sharpened when a number of high-profile honor killings reached the courts and resulted in media attention in Western Europe. It is understood that in January 2002 [after Fadime died], a Swedish government minister intervened personally to exert pressure on the Kurdish authorities in Iraq to take action against honor crimes."[8]

But in the final analysis, it is people, not the law, that can really make a difference. In Denmark, "after Ghazala," a brother refused to kill his sister. He was beaten by his relatives, long-term Denmark residents from Pakistan. He and his sister testified against the family at the trial in November 2006. In England, another brother also refused to do the deed. His sister Banaz Mahmod (twenty years old) was killed anyway in January 2007; her father and uncle and two hired murderers were in on the act. But Banaz's sister testified in court that their brother had refused to kill her. Such resistance gives hope.

Police forces are learning belatedly to take cries for help in earnest. Fadime was lucky in that she received help after asking only twice. In Denmark in 2005, Ghazala and Emal were turned down three times, as was Banaz in Britain that same year. Now the Danish police and the British police have formed special competence units to ensure that such requests will be taken seriously. This gives reason for hope.

A critical silence has been broken. In one place after the other we see resistance, courageous people speaking out against these crimes against humanity. In Syria, in Israel, in Turkey, in Sweden there has been a shattering of the silence that shrouded these crimes in denial. In Syria, religious leaders have declared a fatwa against honor killings. In Turkey, imams are speaking out. In Kurdish Iraq, where a horrid case recently took place with policemen watching as a girl was stoned to death, international media coverage and protests have led to investigations to ensure that the perpetrators, and the silent bystanders, will be brought to court. These are small steps in the right direction—significant steps along the road Fadime pointed out.

I opened this book with a question: what drives a man to murder his child for honor's sake? I close with the same question. It remains with me till the end.

In his book *Shame*, Salman Rushdie writes of an event that had a major impact on him. I only discovered it recently, but it resonates with me. Rushdie writes of a case, in Britain, where a father had killed his one and only daughter, a beloved child. She had brought dishonor upon her family. "The tragedy was intensified by the father's enormous and obvious love for his butchered child, and by the beleaguered reluctance of his friends and relatives (all 'Asians,' to use the confusing terms of these trying days) to condemn his actions." What troubles the writer is that he feels he can understand the action, however abhorrent it is to him. "I too found myself understanding the killer."[9] Even the fact that Rushdie had just become a father himself and was overcome with love for his child did not set him apart sufficiently that he could just condemn and not empathize. This was profoundly unsettling to him, as it was to me to come to feel that I could understand Rahmi Sahindal to some degree.

But my feeling of comprehension fell apart when I attended the court case in the murder of Ghazala Khan in Copenhagen in 2006 and 2007. I came to realize the pertinence of the Tolstoyian saying "Happy families are all alike; every unhappy family is unhappy in its own way." This certainly applies to families caught up in honor killings.

Rahmi Sahindal was relatively easy for me to sympathize with in court. I followed Fadime's lead. She had said "Poor Daddy" three times on the evening when she was killed. She had wanted to be reunited with her father. She felt pity for him. In the accounts of many people he appears as a loving figure. He cut a tragic figure in court, but not evil, not unaffected.

Ghazala's father appeared emotionless, cut in stone. Not exactly a hard figure—he was dignified—but frightening nevertheless. In this trial there was none of the emotional drama that Rahmi Sahindal had got himself entangled in. The nine defendants behaved with stoic calm. For an observer like me, it was disheartening. I longed for signs of a human face, some crack in the facade, some gesture that betrayed regret. It was not there, or I could not detect it.

Later I came to know that Ghazala had been the apple of her father's eye, his most beloved child. Like him, she was the one who loved learning; she excelled at school. Her father gave in to her every wish; she was a spoiled child, a child adored by everyone, not only by her father but especially by him.

She used to be called Baby, a term of endearment.

How could he bring himself to order her to be killed? I asked a man who should be in the know. He answered, "The more you love someone, the greater your sense of betrayal when she lets you down. The more you love her, the deeper your sense of humiliation. Supreme love makes you attribute to her the purest and noblest qualities. Your hatred will be bottomless when she betrays you. But Ghazala's father should have just cast her out, not had her killed."

Why do I struggle so hard to understand this father? Why my deep dissatisfaction because I cannot understand?

Rahmi Sahindal had come to be for me a man who was somewhat, though barely, comprehensible. It was comforting. But in the end it is the community, the collectivity that perpetuates the structures, that must change if individuals are to feel relieved of the duty of human sacrifice. It doesn't matter that much what a father feels. He is not an independent actor. As Asma Jahangir, UN special rapporteur and a leading advocate of human rights, said at the Stockholm conference in 2004: structures must change, but responsibility must be placed somewhere. Therefore we cannot absolve a father, like Fadime's or Ghazala's, of the deeds he has done.

They were both given life sentences.

Yet we can see them as victims too, victims of inhuman traditions.

These traditions are now being changed thanks to the work and engagement of numerous organizations and individuals in many parts of the world.

Labeling honor killings and honor crimes as a human rights violation is the way to go. It enables people to take pride in their culture without compromising values of freedom and liberty. Reforming culture to encompass human rights works to make it all the more precious.

Today Nebile lives with her mother, the two of them alone. She is given much more freedom than her sisters ever had. Even her traveling from Uppsala to Stockholm, an hour's journey by train, to take part in the memorial for Fadime on January 21, 2007, and staying out late afterward—is evidence of that. Songül has taken her under her wing and helped her get a summer job. Nebile has chosen courses at school that will enable her to work with immigrant youths. So far the story has a happy ending.

Of the mother, all I know is that whenever I ask, I am told *hon mår vel*—she's doing fine.

ACKNOWLEDGMENTS

I am grateful to many people who, in various ways, have helped me to understand more than I could ever have hoped to understand on my own, and to the many who have encouraged and sustained me along the way. I can name only a few. My gratitude and indebtedness extends much further.

To Arne Ruth, a very special thanks. As editor-in-chief of *Dagens Nyheter*, he invited me in 1997 to a day-long debate with the Swedish minister of integration and some Swedish scholars. The occasion was Sara's murder. This event shaped my path. Arne is a model to me of a public intellectual who works for freedom of expression and human rights. His encouragement and support have been inestimable.

In Sweden, many others have also helped and inspired me. I want to thank especially Leif Ericksson, Marianne Spänner, Johan Åsard Niklas Kelemen, Sara Mohammed, Rasool Awla, Rigmor Mjörnell, Astrid Schlytter, and Kickis Åhré Âlgamo.

I am also indebted to Mona Sahlin for interesting talks and debates and for her enduring commitment to bring Fadime's legacy forward.

To Mona Ström, my warm thanks for her sharing her memories

of Fadime with me. We did not meet until this book was almost finished, but it meant the world to me to meet her and to be able to share in some of her recollections.

To Breen Atroshi, Pela's sister, whom I have never met, my thanks for her example and for her telling her story through books and media. It allowed me to understand things I might not have understood otherwise.

I am grateful to the staff of Uppsala District Court, Uppsala Police, and the High Court in Stockholm for their help and courtesy.

Svein Skarheim was my editor for the original Norwegian edition of this book. I am forever grateful for the way he helped and encouraged me.

In Norway, the names of all those I am indebted to could fill pages. Special thanks to Sukrü Bilgic, Nasim Karim, Nadia Latiaoui, Farid Bouras, and Walid al-Kubaisi.

In 2004, the Freedom of Expression Foundation honored me with its award. It meant more than words can tell. It helped me to persist in work that was not entirely free of risk and that had earned me many enemies. My speaking out against violence in the name of honor was part of this work. I owe an immense debt of thanks to the Foundation, chaired by Francis Sejersted, former chair of the Nobel Peace Price committee.

In Denmark, I want to thank Elisabeth Arnsdorf Haslund, Johanne Tuxen, Arne Schmidt Møller, and Klaus Buhr, journalists who attended the trials in the Ghazala case. It helped, both spiritually and intellectually, to be in their company. Special thanks to Jeanette Vincent-Andersen, prosecutor, for sharing many reflections with me.

In the United States, I have been invited to give lectures on the themes in this book to the departments of anthropology at Emory University, Harvard University, and the University of California at Los Angeles. I want to thank the participants for their feedback and reflections.

A special thanks to students at the Mellon Seminar, Heyman Center for Humanities at Columbia University, New York, and to the seminar leaders, Akil Bilgrami, Jon Elster, and Jeremy Waldron for their invitation and very incisive discussion.

Thanks also to the participants in my lecture at L'Institut d'Etudes de l'Islam et des Sociétés du Monde Musulman, Paris, for their constructive responses. I am also grateful to Marcelo Suárez-Orozco and to Elliot Turiel for inviting me to present my work at conferences they organized, and for their very important encouragement and feedback.

In Oslo, to my students who have attended my courses on honor, warm thanks—in particular to Eva Schreiber, my seminar leader.

My debt to Frank Henderson Stewart will be evident to all. I also want to thank Asma Jahangir, Nazand Begihani, and Rana Husseini.

My translator, Anna Paterson, has managed the challenging task of rendering my text into English. I thank her for her dedication and effort. To NORLA, my thanks for financing the translation.

Ruth Goring, my copy editor, has seen this book through the lengthy process of the final stages. She has been superb. Thanks for the fine work and the good spirit.

For David Brent, my editor over many years, it is hard to find words to say. I cannot imagine this, or any other of my books, without him. I rely on David, I take courage from him, and his marvelous good humor is a lifesaver. Deeply felt, warmest thanks.

My husband, Fredrik Barth, has been my companion in life and work. Crucially for this work, I have been able to draw on his experience of living as a man among men with Kurds in Iraq, Pashtuns in the North-West Frontier Province, Pakistan, Persians in southern Iran, and Marri Baluch in Afghanistan. and on his knowledge of Pashto and Farsi (Persian). As a woman, I am limited in what I can come to understand of the male world in strictly sex-segregated societies, though my knowledge of Arabic helps. Fredrik has been tireless in his support of my work and has provided my most inspiring critique. This work is also his.

My son and daughter-in-law give me hope for the future. I cannot but reflect on their love relationship, which began when they were seventeen and continues fifteen years later: how lucky they have been to live in a society where it is a human right to choose one's own love.

My two grandsons, still so young—will they live in a world where boundaries matter less, individual freedom more? I pin my hopes on them.

Songül Sahindal is to me a model of courage, compassion, and wisdom. To her, my greatest debt and gratitude.

I dedicate this book to Songül and Nebile.

NOTES

CHAPTER ONE

1. Dr. Nazand Begikhani is a Kurdish-Iraqi researcher and writer, resident in Britain, who is an active advocate of women's human rights with particular focus on Kurdish women. She states that in her country of origin most girl victims of honor killings are proven innocent (autopsy evidence). In other words, they were killed on the basis of unfounded rumors (statement in the Swedish TV program *Hederns Pris* [The Price of Honor; see SVT4 2002]).
2. I discuss this perspective on communication and cross-cultural understanding in my article "Beyond the Words: The Power of Resonance" (Wikan 1992).
3. Quoted in Jehl 1999.
4. According to Kurdo Baksi, the region of Malatya is one of the most conservative in the whole of Turkey. *Expressen*, January 25, 2002.
5. Over the last few years, twenty-odd young women from Malatya have been killed by close relatives *annually*. "Killing for the sake of honor is a familiar idea in that part of the world,' says a language teacher from Elbistan. *Expressen*, January 25, 2002.
6. *Expressen*, February 26, 2002.
7. *Aftonbladet*, January 23, 2002.
8. Police Authority, Uppsala County, 2002, Police Investigation Report, C 10-369-02, p. 63.

9. Yazdanism is an unorthodox sect with particularly many followers among Kurds. They are often spoken of as devil worshipers, but Yazadis think that Muslims' habit of referring to one of their gods as "Satan" is due to poor transcription or translation.

CHAPTER TWO

1. *Dagens Nyheter*, February 7, 1997.
2. In Arabic *th* is pronounced as in English; it makes the names sound very similar.
3. Fadime used "Sara" as her alias when she phoned her mother and did not want to be easily identified.
4. Umeå Regional Police Authority, Police Investigation Report, December 17, 1997.
5. *Svenska Dagbladet*, February 8, 1997. Subsequently Baksi was married and took the marital name Pekgul; thus later in my book she will appear as Nalin Pekgul.
6. Ibid.
7. Alcalá 1997b.
8. *Dagens Nyheter*, June 8, 2002.
9. Alcalá 1997b.
10. *Sydsvenska Dagbladet*, February 12, 1997.
11. That Sara's mother had herself rebelled against violence and oppression had probably impressed itself on Sara. She may have felt that she had her mother on her side. For that reason, Sara was in a special situation compared to many other girls with an immigrant background.
12. *Tidningarnas Telegrambyrå*, January 23, 2002.
13. Alcalá 1997a.
14. *Dagens Nyheter*, April 4, 2002.
15. *Svenska Dagbladet*, January 22, 1997.
16. *Dagens Nyheter*, February 12, 1997.
17. *Hufvudstadsbladet* (Finland), March 8, 1997.
18. *Sydsvenska Dagbladet*, February 11, 1997.
19. *Göteborgs-Posten*, February 16, 1997.
20. Alcalá 1997a.
21. It was also said that it would be in the boys' best interest to send them to a corrective institution rather than to prison, but the court would have had no jurisdiction over the length of stay. Umeå District Court, Judge's Summary, case B 2121-96, 1997.

22. *Samhällsmagasin* (Striptease), aired May 6, 1998, with reporter Marianne Spanner (SVT1 1998). *Samhällsmagasin* is a Swedish TV program of investigative journalism.

CHAPTER THREE

1. According to the Swedish TV documentary *Hederns pris* (The Price of Honor), first shown on SVT4 on October 16, 2002, "Pela's murder introduced a new concept into Sweden: honor killing." I am grateful to reporter Johan Åsard for a copy of the program (SVT4 2002).

2. Breen's story is told in the book *Hedersmordet på Pela: Lillasystern berättar* by Lena Katarina Swanberg (2002).

3. With two exceptions (see below), the direct quotes in this chapter, including the statements by Pela's sister Breen, have been transcribed from Swedish TV documentaries. They are *Fadime: Frihetens pris* (first shown on SVT1 on October 17, 2002) and *Hederns pris* (see note 1).

4. Swanberg, 2002, 32.

5. I have previously noted the observation by Veena Das that women in the regions of India and Pakistan (Punjab) that she has studied are not allowed to be present at honor killings (Das 1995). This prohibition seems less important in the Middle East, although women are normally protected from the sight. In the Pela case, the mother and sister were actually not present when the first shot was fired, but she didn't die after that first shot and her mother and sister ran to her rescue; thus they arrived in time to witness the murder.

6. The criminal court in Dihok, October 9, 1999. The law concerning honor killings was changed by the provincial parliament in Erbil (northern Iraq) in April 2002. Honor is no longer a mitigating circumstance.

7. Swanberg, 2002, 17.

8. This statement was made during an interview with Lise Borchgrevink on the Norwegian radio program *Sånn er livet* (That's Life). Sahlin has said similar things in interviews in the Swedish media, e.g., in the newspaper *Dagens Nyheter* (June 8, 2001): "For a long time now, society has shown itself to be more permissive than ever before, but also fearful and ignorant when it comes to what is going on behind the door of many homes. I too have been scared to be accused of racism and preferred to close my eyes. I betrayed these girls. But now my eyes are wide open."

9. *Expressen*, March 13, 2002.

CHAPTER FOUR

1. Kertzer 1993.
2. In 1997 in Peru a woman who had been subjected to gang rape had to marry one of the rapists—and he had to marry her to free the rest of the gang.
3. In Iran, the first law that made a distinction between rape of and adultery by a woman was introduced in 1995. Until then, the punishment for being a victim of rape had been death. Now, in accordance with the new law, the death penalty applies only to a woman who can be proved to have willingly entered into a sexual relationshship outside her marriage (Afshar 1998).
4. Barber 1957:275–76, quoted in Stewart 1994:108.
5. Albania and parts of the Balkans may be exceptions, but the evidence is lacking.
6. Gehl 1937:34, 42.
7. Dickermann 1997.
8. Begikhani 2002.
9. Stewart 1994:46. Many of my arguments in this chapter are based on Stewart's book.
10. The Kurdish word actually means "forehead" rather than "face." I am grateful to Sükrü Bilgiç for this information.
11. Hu 1944; Selstad 2002.
12. In some communities, the concepts "to save face" and "to lose face" are very important and associate with a whole array of polite and respectful expressions, which make it possible to save face despite having done silly or offensive things. Such informal norms also serve to protect others: to cause a person to lose face can provoke reprisals and revenge. Still, it is perfectly possible to lose face without losing your honor. Honor exists in another dimension. However, the concept of honor common in gangs of youths in many European countries can be tough about losing face: you've got to respond and get your revenge in order to regain respect.
13. Patterson 1982:80.
14. Stewart 1994:140.
15. Ibid., 54.
16. In my book Tomorrow, God Willing (1996) I describe and analyze the "people's talk," as it is called, among people in a poor area of Cairo. For studies in Europe, see Khader 2002 and de Vries 1995.

17. Khader 2002.
18. Wikan 1984. This article, "Shame and Honor: A Contestable Pair," includes a thorough discussion of "shame" in relation to "honor." See also Kressel 1981 and 1988 for an incisive analysis.
19. Afshar 1998:178. Iranian writer and feminist Haleh Afshar observes: "As yet, no woman has the right to kill her husband for dishonouring her, either by raping or seducing another woman. Honour remains very much a male matter, felt by and dealt with by men alone."
20. To quote a Kurdish friend, "Everyone knows—and no one knows."
21. Stewart 1994:116ff.
22. Anthropologists did not take up the notion of honor until in the 1960s, when they focused mainly on the Mediterranean region. Most of the studies were carried out by men, observing men. It is widely believed in the social science community that the Mediterranean honor concept was unique, distinct from its counterparts both in northern Europe and in landlocked Arab society. However, without results of empirical studies in northern Europe—so far, practically nonexistent—we cannot draw firm conclusions. However, legal research, notably by German lawyers in the nineteenth and twentieth centuries, has created a body of illuminating insights into honor (cf. Stewart 1994).
23. Dagens Nyheter, January 23, 2002.
24. Stewart 1994:80.
25. Pitt-Rivers 1977:9.
26. Stewart 1994:81.
27. Pitt-Rivers 1965:21.
28. Khader 2002:143, emphasis mine.
29. Lien 2002.
30. Stewart 1994; see also Bay 2002.
31. In Shakespeare's Hamlet, the line is part of Polonius's advice to his son Laërtes.
32. Wikan 1991a.
33. The conflict between India and Pakistan in the context of "partition"—the creation of Pakistan—provides the setting for the most moving and searching analysis I have seen of how women are used as puppets in the service of the purity and reproductive future of the nation. Both factions, Hindus and Muslims alike, carried off large numbers of women, only to later agree that the newly formed nations should get their own women back again. Meanwhile, the abducted women had given birth to children and formed part of new families. Regardless of

what individuals wanted, women—the still fertile ones, that is—were forcibly separated from their children and "repatriated." The motive was to maintain the purity and identity of each nation; Das 1995 contains a thoughtful analysis.

34. *Aftonbladet*, March 12, 2002.
35. *Dagens Nyheter*, March 11, 2002.
36. Kamali made this statement in the documentary *Fadime: Frihetens pris*, part of the series *Dokument inifrån* (Internal Documents; SVT1 2002). Someone else has expressed it like this: "There is truth in Fadime's experience, but some errors too. For the Kurds, maintaining their identity must come first. Kurds feel pressured from the outside; they must act and do something to keep their dignity."
37. Mater 2002. Mater has found that in almost every honor-killing incident in one of the larger Turkish towns, the victim and the perpetrator belong to a family that had moved into town from the countryside.

CHAPTER FIVE

1. Tsering 2001:57.
2. For an example from South Korea, see Kim 2000. Kim's moving story is told from the point of view of a little girl who witnessed the honor killing of her mother. The family followed the teachings of Confucius.
3. Tsering 2001:57. Here Tsering writes: "Adultery was not tolerated in our area [Amdo], *as it was in other parts of Tibet*" (my italics). It is obviously important not to generalize. My own fieldwork in Bhutan, a Buddhist society adjacent to Tibet, also throws Tsering's observations into relief: in Bhutan too, Buddhist women have a great deal of freedom, including sexual freedom. Realities here do not at all match the harsh subjugation of women that Tsering reports from the place where she grew up (Wikan 1991).
4. Pope 2004:101–10.
5. Hoyek, Sidawi, and Mrad 2006:129–30.
6. Kardam et al. 2006:16.
7. *Aftenposten*, January 24, 2002.
8. Hoyek, Sidawi, and Mrad 2005:132.
9. The Kurdish-Iraqi woman, Bakan, who made this statement had herself barely escaped death at the hands of her brother. She was critically wounded but was saved by her brother-in-law, who took her to the hospital, and then helped by KWAKH, Kurdish Women Against Honor Killing, to escape to Europe. She is now living with a new identity in Germany. She participated at the First International Conference on Vio-

lence Against Women, "Focusing on Violence in the Name of Honor" in Sweden, December 7–8, 2004. Bakan's offense in her family's eyes lay in seeking divorce from her very violent husband.

10. *New York Times*, April 9, 1999.

11. Khan (2006:37) observes that in India, the three states of Haryana, Punjab, and Uttar Pradesh have a particularly bad record for honor-related murders of women and young couples. In Haryana, honor killings constitute 10 percent of all killings.

12. *Guardian Weekly*, June 6, 1999.

13. Pimentel, Pandjiarjian, and Belloque 2005.

14. Cohen-Almagor 1996:178.

15. Mojab 2004:16.

16. Shalhoub-Kevorkian 2005:170–71.

17. *Telegraph*, April 7, 2007.

18. For a case study, see Ginat 1987:117.

19. Abdo 2004; Touma-Sliman 2005.

20. Warraich 2005.

21. Khan 2006:35–36.

22. *Aftenposten*, August 14, 2001.

23. Kardam 2006:17.

24. *Aftenposten*, August 14, 2001.

25. Human Rights Watch n.d.; Abu Hassan and Welchman 2005.

26. Jehl 1999.

27. *Dagen Nyheter*, April 1, 2000.

28. Jehl 1999.

29. *Dagens Nyheter*, April 1, 2000.

30. Haeri 1995:169.

31. Ibid.

32. *New York Times*, March 11, 1997.

33. Centre for Egyptian Women's Legal Assistance 2005:157.

34. Personal observations in Yemen, 1980.

35. Strauss and Quinn 1994.

36. Wikan 1991a.

CHAPTER SIX

1. See Barth 1984; Wikan 1991a.

2. Awla 2002.

3. *Expressen*, January 10, 1997. For a fuller account of Anna's story, see Wikan 2002:98–106.

4. Shabaan 1991:10.
5. Ibid., 3, 4–5.
6. Ibid., 4–5.
7. Bearak 1999.
8. Wikan 1980.
9. Wikan 1996.
10. Jehl 1999.

CHAPTER SEVEN

1. He is actually brother-in-law of the accused twice over: he is the brother of Rahmi's wife and also the husband of Rahmi's sister. Also, the two sets of siblings are cousins; however, in a Swedish court only in-law relationships are valid reasons for being allowed not to testify.
2. Songül is supported by a solicitor called Leif Ericksson, who had also defended Fadime in the trials of her father and brother in 1998.
3. This fits in with Fadime's statement to the police, when she was interviewed in connection with the trial of her father and brother: "My father phoned our relatives in Turkey and asked if I should be allowed to be given in marriage to Patrik. But the marriage was not accepted." She said that some two hundred relatives had been consulted and discussed the matter.

   This did not surprise a language teacher in Elbistan, the Sahindal home territory, who commented, "In this part of the world, contact with members of your family is more important than anything else. It doesn't matter if they don't live in Turkey anymore. All take part in important decisions affecting a family member" (interview, *Expressen*, January 25, 2002).

   His opinion is confirmed by the Swedish Kurd Kurdo Baksi, who grew up in Turkey and was interviewed in the same issue of *Expressen*. "Everything concerns the family. Large families get together every second year in Turkey and have big family meetings. Weddings often take place in connection with these."
4. In my view, all this is so much wishful thinking. Songül said later that the TV had been on with the volume turned up. Besides, in her statement to the police, Elif said that Rahmi had seen her through the window when she went into the kitchen to switch the light off; the flat was on the first floor.
5. This is part of Rahmi's presentation in court. It is, in my view, an attempt to make Kurdish culture seem less unusual and more in tune

with Swedish customs. In reality, Turkish-Kurdish practice usually is that the groom's family pays for the wedding. In the case of siblings or cousins who marry, normal practice is different: because the two families are already related, they share the costs.

6. Police Authority, Uppsala County, 2002, interview 020313, K 193-02, p. 5.
7. *Expressen*, March 14, 2002.
8. It is the *Striptease* footage from 1998.
9. In Sweden a life sentence is twenty years, but after a set period, the prisoner can appeal to have the sentence reduced.

CHAPTER EIGHT

1. Police Authority, Uppsala County, 2002, record of investigation C 10-369-02, pp. 84–85. All the quotes from the transcript of the interview with Nebile are drawn from this document. In some cases they have been somewhat adjusted for written language, to facilitate comprehension.
2. Ibid., p. 106.
3. Ibid., p. 85.
4. Ibid., p. 108.
5. Ibid., pp. 86–87.
6. Fadime's brother was convicted on a charge of causing Fadime grievous bodily harm after meeting her on Central Square in Uppsala on June 11, 1998.
7. According to witnesses, Fadime was attacked by her brother while she was checking the bus timetable. She did not provoke him but was beaten nearly senseless.
8. SVT1 1998.
9. The recording was made on February 4, 1998; Fadime's brother phoned her after she had been to the police and charged him with threats to her life. On the same day, she spoke up for her cause, as reported in the evening paper *Aftonbladet*. This infuriated her brother, who phoned her and once again threatened to kill her. Fadime switched on the tape recorder that the police had given her.
10. Police Authority, Uppsala County, 2002, investigation document C 10-369-02, p. 93.
11. Ibid., p. 97.
12. Ibid., p. 105.
13. Ibid., p. 102.

14. Ibid., p. 104.
15. Ibid., p. 91.

CHAPTER NINE

1. Police Authority, Uppsala County, 2002, investigation document C 10-369-02, pp. 197–98.
2. Ibid., 79.
3. Ibid., 52–53.
4. Ibid., 82.
5. Ibid., 153.
6. Ibid., 160.
7. Ibid., 119.
8. Ibid., 54–55.
9. Ibid., 107.
10. Ibid., 145.

CHAPTER TEN

1. Police Authority, Uppsala County, 2002, Record of Police Investigation C 10-369-02, p. 245.
2. Ibid., 250–51.
3. Ibid., 253.
4. In Sweden, criminal law distinguishes between murder and manslaughter. The more severe category is murder. Whoever is proved to have deprived another human being of life should be sentenced for murder. However, on the basis of an overall evaluation of all relevant factors, the crime "may instead be judged to be manslaughter, with regard to the circumstances which had led to the act or otherwise caused it to be considered as less grave. Court precedents indicate that the question as to whether a case of killing should be regarded as murder or as manslaughter should be decided after taking into account all the circumstances of the case" (Uppsala District Court 2002, sentence 2002-04-03. case B 237-02, pp. 15–16).
5. Police Authority, Uppsala County, 2002, Record of Police Investigation C 10-369-02, pp. 253–54. The quotes in this section come from pp. 172, 168, 117, and 155.
6. Ibid., 257–58.

7. On the other hand, Rahmi's daughter Fidan says that her father would not contribute to the wedding. "You're living together and that is against my principles," he is alleged to have said to Fadime. Ibid., 118.

8. Ibid., 276.

CHAPTER ELEVEN

1. *Verdens Gang* (Norway's largest newspaper), July 25, 1998.

2. SVT1 1998.

3. Swedish law permitted girls with an immigrant family background to marry at fifteen, while "Swedish" girls must wait until they are eighteen. The law was only changed in 2004.

4. Statement in SVT1 1998.

5. *Verdens Gang*, July 25, 1998.

6. Sentence, Uppsala District Court, case K 15714-98.

7. *Dagens Nyheter*, January 24, 2002.

8. *Verdens Gang*, July 24, 2002.

9. See, e.g., Mørck 1996; Sandrup 1997.

10. Statement in SVT1 1998.

11. Bilgiç 2000.

12. For an extensive discussion, see Wikan 2002.

13. Fadime described her father as a small, harmless person and believed that he could never truly hurt her, her friend Moa Roshanfar states in her police interview. Police Authority, Uppsala County, 2002, Record of Investigation C 10-369-02, p. 22.

14. *Verdens Gang*, July 25, 2002.

CHAPTER TWELVE

1. A comparison is afforded by the cases of Fadime and Anooshe (see below). In both cases the murderer had confessed to the killing, and there were several witnesses to the act. The Fadime case took only six days in total in the Swedish system (district court and high court), whereas the Anooshe case used twenty-three days. A comparison conducted by jurists concludes that the Norwegian system tends to overinvestigate cases.

2. Göta High Court, sentence 2006-04-26, case B 1339-06. There was dissent among the judges: two out of five voted for convicting the parents.

3. Torry 1999: A cultural defense is not officially recognized or legally validated on the same basis as other forms of defense pleas, such as necessary force (necessity) and self-defense, but it is practiced and is a subject of extensive research and debate within the study of law and judicial process. See also Renteln 2004.

4. Woo 1989.

5. Sheybani 1987:769.

6. Guillou 2002.

7. *Dagens Nyheter*, February 11, 1997.

8. Uppsala District Court, sentence 1998-05-07, case B 350-98.

9. Swedish law states: "If a person has committed a crime before that person has reached twenty-one years of age, the court will pay special regard in the setting of the sentence to his or her youth" (Uppsala District Court, 1998, sentence 1998-08-05).

10. Cf. Grønhaug 1997 and Borchgrevink 1997 for a very interesting debate about the use of "culture" in a Norwegian court. The starting point for the discussion was an honor killing carried out in 1983. A Turkish father and son killed a close friend of the family because he had forced himself on the fifteen-year-old daughter of the family and had sex with her. Apparently she was not subjected to any reprisals. Reidar Grønhaug was an expert witness in the case, which went all the way to the Supreme Court. He argues strongly and well for the necessity of always considering a crime within its cultural framework—not to in any way defend the deed but to improve its basis for legal consideration.

11. Wikan 1999.

12. Letter from Ghulam Azarakhsh, May 12, 2005.

13. Romsdal District Court, sentence 2003-05-21, case 03-00226. The verdict was later confirmed by the High Court.

14. *Dagbladet*, August 19, 2002.

15. *Dagbladet*, August 22, 2002.

16. See Khan 2006; Warraich 2005.

CHAPTER THIRTEEN

1. For a more thorough inquiry and analysis of this case, see Wikan 2000; 2002.

2. I was an expert witness in the Nadia case and was therefore able to follow it closely. I was called at the request of the defense.

3. Whether Nadia was actually a virgin is irrelevant. She may have said this to her mother in order to prevent her being married off in Morocco. For our discussion, the crucial point is how this issue was handled in court.

CHAPTER FIFTEEN

1. *Verdens Gang*, October 12, 1998.
2. Ibid.
3. *Verdens Gang*, January 24, 2002.
4. Ibid.

CHAPTER SEVENTEEN

1. She means Turkish. Patrik's father and grandmother came from a part of Iran where Turkish is the main language.

CHAPTER EIGHTEEN

1. Statement made by Moa Roshanfar, report of police investigation, p. 222.
2. From a conversation with Leif Ericksson, November 12, 2002.

CHAPTER NINETEEN

1. The lecture was arranged by the Annette Thommessen Foundation.
2. *Dagens Nyheter*, January 24, 2002.
3. Anna, a Swedish Syrian living in hiding for fear of her family, has said, "My parents have been at work during all their time in Sweden, but as soon as they come home they shut out everything that has to do with Swedishness. They never watch Swedish TV, only cable channels in Arabic. I was never allowed to visit a Swedish family, and I had no Swedish girlfriends" (*Expressen*, January 10, 1997). There are many similar testimonials. See also Wikan 2002:98–106.
4. The concept comes from the American human rights activist Joseph Cortes Jr. (Lavelle 1995). I use the concept and discuss its relevance to integration policy in Norway in my book *Mot en ny norsk underklasse* (Toward a New Norwegian Underclass; Wikan 1995a).
5. Akman 2002.
6. Barth 1953.

7. From the police investigation report, p. 123. This is contrary to what Songül stated in court, but it is also possible that Elmas had access to more family information than did the younger Songül.

8. It is not uncommon for women in Turkish Kurdistan to be used as mediators in conflicts, both inside the family and between families (Akman 2002). This is especially true of older women, who enjoy a status and authority that make them well suited for this role. This is also true in some other Middle Eastern communities (see Wikan 1983; 1995a; 1996).

9. Some claim that tolerance is not enough. Here I follow the political philosopher Michael Walzer, who argues in his book *On Toleration* (1997) that tolerance and toleration have their own risks, which must not be underestimated.

10. Police Authority, Uppsala County, 2002, record of investigation C 10-369-02, p. 128.

11. *Dagens Nyheter*, January 24, 2002.

12. Record of police investigation, p. 149.

13. *Aftonbladet*, February 4, 1998.

14. *Dagens Nyheter*, December 19, 1997.

15. However, Rasool Awla, a Kurd himself, suggests that the authorities have too great a belief in what immigrant organizations can do; he presents a thought-provoking series of arguments to support his point of view (Awla 2002).

16. *Fadime: Frihetens pris* (Fadime: The Price of Freedom; SVT1 2002).

17. Ibid.

18. Ibid.

CHAPTER TWENTY

1. Carlbom 2003; Friedman 1999.

2. The president of the Islamic Council in Norway, Lena Larsen, said to the media, "This has nothing to do with Islam. They were not Muslims" (*VG*, January 27, 2002).

3. *Expressen*, January 27, 2002.

4. Sultan 2003.

5. I have studied Islam for more than thirty years, including fieldwork in several Middle Eastern locations. I speak on the basis of that experience. My studies have been conducted in local languages—Arabic and Indonesian.

6. Taking Turkey as her starting point, Nadire Mater writes: "It cannot be denied that the Islamic faith held by the people has a major role to play in the context of violence against women—with regard to both domestic abuse of women and honor killings. By prescribing [forordne] stoning of unfaithful women, and by giving men the right to beat disobedient women, Islamic sharia law has legitimized oppression of women and abuse of women in the home." She also refers to the high incidence of honor killings in some Turkish regions—in the south- and northeastern provinces—which are strongholds for Islamic parties, and to the likely connection between the two phenomena. On the other hand, "honor killings are very rare in societies which favor a more liberal interpretation of Islam" (Mater 2002).

7. Cf. for instance Al-Azm 1995; Mernissi 1991; 1995.

8. Bilgiç 2000:49.

9. Karim 1996.

10. Das 1990.

11. Wikan 1999.

12. Maalouf 1998:92.

13. Parekh 1999:70.

14. I will not analyze the problem more closely here. It has been extensively discussed in Wikan 1995 and 2002, and also by several others, for instance Walid al-Kubaisi (1996), Jonathan Friedman (1999), and Inger-Lise Lien (1997).

15. As late as December 8, 2000, the Swedish ministers Mona Sahlin (Integration) and Margareta Winberg (Equality) published an article in *Dagens Nyheter* that said, "To claim that a murder is motivated in any way by culture is to push the problems away. . . . This is why we must never accept talk of 'honor killings'" (Sahlin and Winberg 2000).

16. Ignatieff 1999; Mayer 1999.

17. Maalouf 1998:14.

18. At the Red Cross International Center in Oslo, one-third of all calls asking for help to escape a forced marriage are made by boys.

19. Interview, *Verdens Gang*, July 25, 1998.

CHAPTER TWENTY-ONE

1. This and other statements by Karatas are from the program *Fadime— Frihetens Pris* (Fadime—the Price of Freedom; SVT1, October 2002).

AFTERWORD

1. For book accounts of the Ghazala case (also referred to as the Slagelse case, after the train station where the murder took place), see Buhr and Sønderby 2006; Møller 2006.
2. Bergh 2004.
3. Ibid.
4. Âlgamo 2004.
5. Storhaug and Human Rights Service 2003.
6. Swedish Ministry of Justice and Swedish Ministry for Foreign Affairs 2004.
7. Ibid., 19.
8. Begikhani 2005:216.
9. Rushdie 1983.

REFERENCES

Aase, Tor. 2002. "The Prototypical Blood Feud: Tangir in the Hindu Kush Mountains." In *Tournaments of Power: Honor and Revenge in the Contemporary World*, edited by Tor Aase, 79–100. Burlington, VT: Ashgate.

Abdo, Nahla. 2004. "Honour Killing, Patriarchy, and the State." In *Violence in the Name of Honour: Theoretical and Political Challenges*, edited by Shahrzad Mojab and Nahla Abdo, 57–90. Istanbul: Istanbul Bilgi University Press.

Abu Hassan, Reem, and Lynn Welchman. 2005. "Changing the Rules? Developments on 'Crimes of Honour' in Jordan." In *"Honour": Crimes, Paradigms, and Violence against Women*, edited by Lynn Welchman and Sara Hossein, 199–208. London: Zed.

Abu-Odeh, Lama. 1996. "Crimes of Honour and the Construction of Gender in Arab Societies." In *Feminism and Islam: Legal and Literary Perspectives*, edited by Mai Yamani, 141–93. London: Ithaca.

Afshar, Haleh. 1998. *Islam and Feminisms: An Iranian Case-Study*. London: Macmillan.

Akman, Haci. 2002. "Honor, Feuding, and National Fragmentation in Kurdistan." In *Tournaments of Power: Honor and Revenge in the Contemporary World*, edited by Tor Aase, 101–14. Burlington, VT: Ashgate.

Al-Azm, Sadik. 1995. *Mot hevdvunne sannheter*. Oslo: Cappelen.

Alcalá, Jesús. 1997a. "Männen i familjen borde åtalas." *Dagens Nyheter*, February 7.

———. 1997b. "Inte ett mord, en avrättning." *Dagens Nyheter*, February 8.

Älgamo, Kickis Åhré. 2004. "Confronting Honour Violence: The Swedish Police at Work." In *Violence in the Name of Honour: Theoretical and Political Challenges*, edited by Shahrzad Mojab and Nahla Abdo, 203–10. Istanbul: Istanbul Bilgi University Press.

Ali, Ayan Hirsi. 2007. *Infidel*. London: Free Press.

al-Kubaisi, Walid. 1996. *Min tro, din myte*. Oslo: Aventura.

Alston, Philip. 2004. "Address by Prof. Philip Alston, UN Special Rapporteur on Extrajudicial, Summary, or Arbitrary Executions." In *Report from the International Conference: Combating Patriarchal Violence Against Women—Focusing on Violence in the Name of Honour*," 19–20. Stockholm: Government Offices.

Awla, Rasool. 2002. "Övertro på invandrarföreningar." *Göteborgs-Posten*, February 5.

Barber, Charles Laurence. 1957. *The Idea of Honour in the English Drama, 1591–1700*. Gothenburg Studies in English 6. Gothenburg: n.p.

Barth, Fredrik. 1953. *Principles of Social Organization in Southern Kurdistan*. Universitetets Etnografiske Museum Bulletin 7. Oslo.

———. 1959. *Political Leadership among Swat Pathans*. Monographs on Social Anthropology 19. London: Aldine.

———. 1983. *Sohar: Culture and Society in an Omani Town*. Baltimore: Johns Hopkins University Press.

Bay, Joi. 2002. "Honor and Revenge in the Culture of Danish Outlaw Bikers." In *Tournaments of Power: Honor and Revenge in the Contemporary World*, edited by Tor Aase, 49–60. Burlington, VT: Ashgate.

Bearak, Barry. 1999. "A Tale of Two Lovers, and a Taboo Recklessly Flouted." *New York Times International*, April 9.

Begikhani, Nazand. 2002. "Alla som tiger er medskyldiga till mord." *Aftonbladet*, March 12.

———. 2005. "Honor-Based Violence among the Kurds: The Case of Iraqi Kurdistan." In *"Honour": Crimes, Paradigms, and Violence against Women*, edited by Lynn Welchman and Sara Hossein, 209–29. London: Zed.

Bergh, Lise. 2004. "Swedish Government Initiatives to Help Young People at Risk of Honour-Related Violence." In *Violence in the Name of Honour: Theoretical and Political Challenges*, edited by Shahrzad Mojab and Nahla Abdo, 193–202. Istanbul: Istanbul Bilgi University Press.

Bilgiç, Sükrü. 2000. *Integrering: Fra teori til praksis*. Oslo: Kulturbro forlag.

Black-Michaud, J. 1975. *Cohesive Force: Feud in the Mediterranean and the Middle East*. Oxford: Blackwell.

Borchgrevink, Tordis. 1997. "Et ubehag i antropologien." *Norsk antropologisk tidsskrift* 8:26–36.

Buhr, Claus, and Helle Sønderby. 2006. *Bror, hvad er det du gør? Historien om æresdrabet på Ghazala Khan.* Copenhagen: DR Multimedie.

Carlbom, Aje. 2003. *The Imagined versus the Real Other: Multiculturalism and the Representation of Muslims in Sweden.* Lund: Lund Monographs in Social Anthropology.

Centre for Egyptian Women's Legal Assistance. 2005. "'Crimes of Honor' as Violence against Women in Egypt." In *"Honour": Crimes, Paradigms, and Violence against Women,* edited by Lynn Welchman and Sara Hossein, 137–59. London: Zed.

Chakravarti, Uma. 2005. "From Fathers to Husbands: Of Love, Death and Marriage in North India." In *"Honour": Crimes, Paradigms, and Violence against Women,* edited by Lynn Welchman and Sara Hossein, 160–80. London: Zed.

Cohen-Almagor, Raphael. 1996. "Female Circumcision and Murder for Family Honour among Minorities in Israel." In *Nationalism, Minorities, and Diaspora: Identities and Rights in the Middle East,* edited by Kirsten Schulze, Martin Stokes and Colin Campbell, 171–87. London: I. B. Tauris.

Das, Veena. 1990. "What Do We Mean by Health?" In *The Health Transitions: Social, Cultural, and Behavioral Developments,* edited by J. Caldwell et al. Canberra: Australian National University Press.

———. 1995. *Critical Events: An Anthropological Perspective on Contemporary India.* New Delhi: Oxford University Press.

de Vries, Marlene 1995. "The Changing Role of Gossip: Turkish Girls in the Netherlands." In *Post-migration Ethnicity,* edited by Gerd Baumann and Thijl Sunier, 36–56. Amsterdam: Het Spinhuis.

Dickermann, Mildred. 1997. "The Balkan Sworn Virgin: A Cross-Gendered Female Role." In *Islamic Homosexualities: Culture, History, and Literature,* edited by Stephen O. Murray and Will Roscoe, 197–203. New York: New York University Press.

Eldén, Åsa. 2004. "Life-and-Death Honour: Young Women's Violent Stories about Reputation, Virginity and Honour—in a Swedish Context." In *Violence in the Name of Honour: Theoretical and Political Challenges,* edited by Shahrzad Mojab and Nahla Abdo, 91–100. Istanbul: Istanbul Bilgi University Press.

Elster, Jon. 1999. *Alchemies of the Mind: Rationality and Emotions.* Cambridge: Cambridge University Press.

Friedman, Jonathan. 1999. "Rhinoceros II." *Current Anthropology* 40, no. 5: 679–94.

Gehl, Walther. 1937. *Ruhm und Ehre bei den Nordgermanen: Studien zum Lebensgefühl der Islandischen Saga.* Neue Deutsche Forschungen 121. Berlin: Junder und Dunnhaupt.

Ginat, Joseph. 1982. *Women in Muslim Rural Society: Status and Role in Family and Community.* New Brunswick, NJ: Transaction.

———. 1997 [1987]. *Blood Revenge: Family Honor, Mediation, and Outcasting.* Brighton, UK: Sussex Academic Press.

Göta Hovrätt. Dom 2006-06-26. Mål B 1339-06.

Grønhaug, Reidar. 1997. "Rettsstaten, det flerkulturelle, og antropologien." *Norsk antropologisk tidsskrift* 8:256–72.

Guillou, Jan. 2002. "Hedersmord har inget att göra med religion." *Aftonbladet,* January 23.

Haeri, Shahla. 1995. "The Politics of Dishonor: Rape and Power in Pakistan." In *Faith and Freedom: Women's Human Rights in the Muslim World,* edited by M. Afkhami, 161–73. London: Tauris.

Hjärpe, Jan. 1997. "Kan kultur och religion orsaka mord?" *Göteborgs-Posten,* February 16.

Hoyek, Danielle, Rafif Rida Sidawi, and Amira Abou Mrad. 2005. "Murders of Women in Lebanon: 'Crimes of Honour' between Reality and the Law." In *"Honour": Crimes, Paradigms, and Violence against Women,* edited by Lynn Welchman and Sara Hossein, 111–36. London: Zed.

Htun, Mala. 2000. "Culture, Institutions, and Gender Inequality in Latin America." In *Culture Matters,* edited by Lawrence E. Harrison and Samuel P. Huntington, 189–201. New York: Bantam.

Hu, Hsien Chin. 1944. "The Chinese Concept of Face." *American Anthropologist* 46:45–64.

Human Rights Watch. 2004. *Honoring the Killers: Justice Denied for "Honor" Crimes in Jordan.* Vol. 16, no. 1, April.

Ignatieff, Michael. 1999. *Whose Universal Values? The Crisis in Human Rights.* Praemium Erasmianum Essay. The Hague: Foundation Horizon.

Jehl, Douglas. 1999. "Arab Honor's Price: A Woman's Blood." *New York Times International,* July 26.

Johansson, Kenneth. ed. 2005. *Hedersmord: Tusen år av hederskulturer.* Lund: Historiska Media.

Kardam, Filiz, et al. 2006. *The Dynamics of Honor Killings in Turkey.* Ankara: Population Association.

Karim, Nasim. 1996. *Izzat—For Ærens Skyld*. Oslo: Cappelen.

Kertzer, David I. 1993. *Sacrificed for Honor: Italian Infant Abandonment and the Politics of Reproductive Control*. Boston: Beacon.

Khader, Naser. 2002. *Ære og skam: Det islamiske familie- og livsmønster i Danmark og Mellemøsten*. Copenhagen: Borgen.

Khan, Tahira S. *Beyond Honour: A Historical Materialist Explanation of Honour Related Violence*. Karachi: Oxford University Press.

Kim, Elizabeth. 2000. *Ten Thousand Sorrows: The Extraordinary Journey of a Korean War Orphan*. London: Bantam.

Kressel, Gideon M. 1981. "Sorocide-Filiacide: Homicide for Family Honor." *Current Anthropology* 22:141–58.

———. 1988. "More on Honour and Shame." *Man* 23:167–70.

Kurkiala, Mikael. 2005. *I varje trumslag jordens puls*. Stockholm: Ordfront.

Lavelle, Robert, ed. 1995. *America's New War on Poverty: A Reader for Action*. San Francisco: KOED Books.

Lien, Inger-Lise. 1997. *Ordet som stempler djevlene: holdninger blant pakistanere og nordmenn*. Oslo: Aventura.

———. 2002. "The Dynamics of Honor in Violence and Cultural Change." In *Tournaments of Power: Honor and Revenge in the Contemporary World*, edited by Tor Aase, 19–48. Burlington, VT: Ashgate.

Lundgren, Eva, and Åsa Eldén. 1997. "Våldsbrott mot kvinnor er inte något eksotiskt." *Svenska Dagbladet*, January 21.

Maalouf, Amin 1998. *Identitet som dreper*. Oslo: Pax.

Mater, Nadire. 2002. "Lagen har ändrats, men hedersmorden finns kvar." *Aftonbladet* 12. mars.

Mayer, Ann Elizabeth. 1999. *Islam and Human Rights: Tradition and Politics*. Boulder, CO: Westview.

Mernissi, Fatima. 1991. *The Veil and the Male Elite*. Reading, MA: Addison-Wesley.

———. 1995. "Arab Women's Rights and the Muslim State in the Twenty-first Century: Reflections on Islam as Religion and State." In *Faith and Freedom: Women's Human Rights in the Muslim World*, edited by M. Afkhami, 161–73. London: Tauris.

Mojab, Shahrzad. 2004. "The Particularity of 'Honour' and the Universality of 'Killing.'" In *Violence in the Name of Honour: Theoretical and Political Challenges*, edited by Shahrzad Mojab and Nahla Abdo, 15–38. Istanbul: Istanbul Bilgi University Press.

Møller, Arne Schmidt. 2006. *Ghazala—et æresdrab i Danmark*. Århus, Denmark: Siesta.

Mørck, Yvonne. 1996. "Køn, kulturel loyalitet, og multikulturalisme: Perspektiver på etnisk minoritetsungdom." PhD diss., Institutt for Kulturantropologi, Copenhagen.

Parekh, Bhikhu. 1999. "A Varied Moral World." In *Is Multiculturalism Bad for Women?* edited by Joshua Cohen, Matthew Howard and Martha C. Nussbaum, 69–75. Princeton, NJ: Princeton University Press.

Patterson, Orlando. 1982. *Slavery and Social Death.* Cambridge, MA: Harvard University Press.

Peristiany, J. G., ed. 1965. *Honour and Shame: The Values of Mediterranean Society.* London: Weidenfeld and Nicholson.

Pervizat, Leyla. 2004. "In the Name of Honour." In *Violence in the Name of Honour: Theoretical and Political Challenges*, edited by Shahrzad Mojab and Nahla Abdo, 137–42. Istanbul: Istanbul Bilgi University Press.

Pimentel, Silvia, Valéria Pandjiarjian, and Juliana Belloque. 2005. "The 'Legitimate Defence of Honour,' or Murder with Impunity? A Critical Study of Legislation and Case Law in Latin America." In *"Honour": Crimes, Paradigms, and Violence against Women*, edited by Lynn Welchman and Sara Hossein, 245–62. London: Zed.

Pitt-Rivers, Julian. 1966. "Honour and Social Status." In *Honour and Shame: The Values of Mediterranean Society*, edited by J. G. Peristiany, 19–77. Chicago: Chicago University Press.

———. 1977. *The Fate of Shechem.* Cambridge: Cambridge University Press.

Polismyndigheten i Umeå län. 1996. Förundersökningsprotokoll 17. December.

Polismyndigheten i Uppsala län. 2002a. Forhör av Murat Sahindal. 020313. K 1931-02.

———. 2002b. Förundersökningsprotokoll C 10-369-02. Datum February 28, 2002.

———. 2002c. "Om Fadime Sahindal i SVTs *Striptease*—98." Kopia Knr. 1931-02. March 5, 2002.

Pope, Nicole. 2004. "Honour Killings: Instruments of Patriarchal Control." In *Violence in the Name of Honour: Theoretical and Political Challenges*, edited by Shahrzad Mojab and Nahla Abdo, 101–10. Istanbul: Istanbul Bilgi University Press.

Renteln, Alison Dundes. 2004. *The Cultural Defense.* Oxford: Oxford University Press.

Rizvi, Javieria. 2004. "Violence in the Name of Honour in Swedish Society: What Lessons Can Be Learnt from the Swedish Experience?" In *Violence in the Name of Honour: Theoretical and Political Challenges*, edited by

Shahrzad Mojab and Nahla Abdo, 211–24. Istanbul: Istanbul Bilgi University Press.

Rushdie, Salman. 1983. *Shame*. London: Jonathan Cape.

Sahlin, Mona, and Margareta Winberg. 2000. "Kulturen ingen Ursäkt." *Dagens Nyheter*, December 8.

Sandmo, Erling. 2005a. "Æreskulturens fall og vekst." In *Hedersmord: Tusen år av hederskulturer*, edited by Kenneth Johansson, 207–24. Lund: Historiska Media.

———. 2005b. "Hvorfor ikke?" In *Hedersmord: Tusen år av hederskulturer*, edited by Kenneth Johansson, 7–10. Lund: Historiska Media.

Sandrup, Therese. 1998. "Sin mors datter: En studie av tyrkiske og pakistanske jenter og kvinner i en norsk drabantby." MA thesis, Institutt og Museum for Antropologi, Oslo.

Selstad, Leif. 2002. "The Attraction of Power: Honor and Politics in a Japanese Village." In *Tournaments of Power: Honor and Revenge in the Contemporary World*, edited by Tor Aase, 151–64. Burlington, VT: Ashgate.

Shaaban, Bouthaina. 1991. *Both Right and Left Handed: Arab Women Talk about Their Lives*. Bloomington: Indiana University Press.

Shalhoub-Kevorkian, Nadera. 2005. "Researching Women's Victimisation in Palestine: A Socio-legal Analysis." In *"Honour": Crimes, Paradigms, and Violence against Women*, edited by Lynn Welchman and Sara Hossein, 160–80. London: Zed.

Sheybani, M.-M. 1987. "Cultural Defense: One Person's Culture Is Another's Crime." *Loyola of Los Angeles International and Comparative Law Journal* 9:751–83.

Stewart, Frank Henderson. 1994. *Honor*. Chicago: University of Chicago Press.

Storhaug, Hege, and Human Rights Service. 2003. *Human Visas: A Report from the Front Lines of Europe's Integration Crisis*. Oslo: Human Rights Service.

Strauss, Claudia, and Naomi Quinn. 1994. "A Cognitive/Cultural Anthropology." In *Assessing Cultural Anthropology*, edited by Robert Borofsky, 284–98. New York: McGraw-Hill.

Sultan, Shoaib. 2003. "Fadime, muslim eller ikke?" *Ung Muslim* 4, no. 1.

Svea Hovrätt. Dom 2002-06-01. Mål no. B 4651-02:48.

SVT1. 1998. May 6 episode of *Samhällsmagasin* (Striptease), with reporter Marianne Spanner.

———. 2002. *Fadime: Frihetens pris* (Fadime: The Price of Freedom). Documentary. First aired October 17.

SVT4. 2002. *Hederns Pris* (The Price of Honor), with reporter Johan Åsard. First aired October 16.

Torry, William I. 1999. "Multicultural Jurisprudence and the Cultural Defense." *Journal of Legal Pluralism*, no. 44.

Touma-Sliman, Aida. 2005. "Culture, National Minority, and the State: Working against the 'Crime of Family Honor' within the Palestinian Community in Israel." In *"Honour": Crimes, Paradigms, and Violence against Women*, edited by Lynn Welchman and Sara Hossein, 181–98. London: Zed.

Tsering, Diki. 2001. *Dalai Lama, My Son: A Mother's Story*. London: Virgin.

TV2. 1999. "Rikets tilstand," with reporter Gerhard Helskog. Episode of *Tvangsekteskap*. First aired October 27.

Umeå tingsrätt. 1997. Dom 1997-03-25. Mål nr. B 2121-96, 25.

Uppsala tingsrätt 1998a. Dom 1998-08-05. Mål nr. B 1510-98.

———. 1998b. Dom 1998-05-07. Mål nr. B 350-98.

———. 2002. Dom 2002-04-03. Mål nr. B 237-02.

Walzer, Michael. 1997. *On Toleration*. New Haven, CT: Yale University Press.

Warraich, Sohail Akbar. 2005. "'Honour Killings' and the Law in Pakistan." In *"Honour": Crimes, Paradigms, and Violence against Women*, edited by Lynn Welchman and Sara Hossein, 78–110. London: Zed.

Wikan, Unni. 1980. *Life among the Poor in Cairo*. Translated by Ann Henning. London: Tavistock.

———. 1984. "Shame and Honour: A Contestable Pair." *Man* (n.s.) 19: 635–52.

———. 1991a. *Behind the Veil in Arabia: Women in Oman*. Chicago: University of Chicago Press. (First published by Johns Hopkins University Press, 1982.)

———. 1991b. *The Girl Child in Bhutan*. Thimphu, Bhutan: UNICEF.

———. 1992. "Beyond the Words: The Power of Resonance." *American Ethnologist* 19, no. 3: 460–82.

———. 1995. *Mot en ny norsk underklasse: Innvandrere, kultur, og integrasjon*. Oslo: Gyldendal.

———. 1996. *Tomorrow, God Willing: Self-Made Destinies in Cairo*. Chicago: University of Chicago Press.

———. 1999. "Culture: A New Concept of Race." *Social Anthropology* 7, no. 1: 57–64.

———. 2000. "Citizenship on Trial: Nadia's Case." *Dædalus* (Journal of the American Academy of Arts and Sciences) 129, no. 4: 55–76.

———. 2002. *Generous Betrayal: Politics of Culture in the New Europe.* Chicago: University of Chicago Press.

Woo, Deborah. 1989. "The People v. Fumiko Kimura: But Which People?" *International Journal of the Sociology of Law* 17:403–28.